TARGETED VIOLENCE

A Statistical and Tactical Analysis of Assassinations, Contract Killings, and Kidnappings

TARGETED VIOLENCE

A Statistical and Tactical Analysis of Assassinations, Contract Killings, and Kidnappings

GLENN P. McGOVERN

CRC Press
Taylor & Francis Group
Boca Raton London New York

CRC Press is an imprint of the
Taylor & Francis Group, an **informa** business

CRC Press
Taylor & Francis Group
6000 Broken Sound Parkway NW, Suite 300
Boca Raton, FL 33487-2742

First issued in paperback 2017

© 2010 by Taylor and Francis Group, LLC
CRC Press is an imprint of Taylor & Francis Group, an Informa business

No claim to original U.S. Government works

ISBN 13: 978-1-138-11615-3 (pbk)
ISBN 13: 978-1-4398-2512-9 (hbk)

Library of Congress Cataloging-in-Publication Data

McGovern, Glenn.
    Targeted violence : a statistical and tactical analysis of assassinations, contract killings, and kidnappings / Glenn McGovern.
        p. cm.
    Includes bibliographical references and index.
    ISBN 978-1-4398-2512-9
    1. Assassination. 2. Murder for hire. 3. Kidnapping. 4. Victimology. I. Title.

HV6278.M39 2010
364.15--dc22   2009043219

Visit the Taylor & Francis Web site at
http://www.taylorandfrancis.com

and the CRC Press Web site at
http://www.crcpress.com

CONTENTS

CONTENTS

INTRODUCTION

Sun Tzu wrote in his sixth-century B.C. masterwork *The Art of War*, "If you know your enemy and know yourself, you need not fear the result of a hundred battles. If you know yourself but not your enemy, for every victory gained you will also suffer a defeat. If you know neither the enemy nor yourself, you will succumb in every battle." This work has been studied over the centuries, continuing into today by military academies around the world, as well as heads of corporate entities and even professional football coaches. Tzu's theories on tactics and strategy work well in those fields in which the adversary is known or can be anticipated, but what of the small targeted attacks that are conducted by a wide spectrum of groups or individuals, with an equally diverse set of objectives and potential targets?

Approximately seven years ago, shortly after being assigned the primary responsibility for the training of my office's protective team, I realized that while the team trained regularly, we were practicing our responses in only the most basic of methods. Many of the team members had previously attended some sort of dignitary protection course or had prior SWAT experience. Several had even been involved in past presidential protective operations. But of all of this, the knowledge focused on the various pedestrian protective rings, the importance of avoiding choke points and routes, etc. It was also focused predominantly from the perspective of the large signature operations, similar to those provided to a head of state. The problem was there was little beyond that.

After conducting some initial research it became apparent that when it came to protective operations there wasn't—and still isn't—much out there that was beyond a basic level. While the Secret Service and State Department offered courses, they were difficult at best to obtain and, more importantly, were logically focused upon the large overt protective operations. As far as literature on the topic, what little had been written was focused on a few of the higher-profile terrorist organizations, but from the perspective of all of their operations, not focused on targeted killings/kidnappings. Further, there was nothing available on targeted attacks carried out by organized criminal organizations, or other adversaries. While I had no doubt there were some in-house studies conducted by government agencies, that information was either classified or simply not available.

Out of this grew a twofold goal: First, I needed to be able to train the team to deal with realistic attacks in the most effective manner. Second, with the responsibility for conducting threat assessments for victims, witnesses, and district attorney office staff, I needed more insight into how targeted attacks were carried out. I decided to put my tactical and analytical training to use and began to research past assassinations, contract killings, and kidnappings that had occurred in an urban environment not experiencing a war. I chose to begin this research somewhat arbitrarily with January 1950. I also decided to focus on those attacks against individuals who were targeted as a result of their position, or because they had become a perceived problem in someone or some group's activities, or for a group to make a political statement, or a ransom (such as with corporate executives), etc.

I excluded the attacks by the mentally disturbed in the world, unless it was upon a high-ranking official such as a world leader. The main reason for this was that their attacks are generally unpredictable and, in my opinion, fall into the category of protective details being aware of what is going on around them. I wanted to focus on the targeted attacks where a person(s) planned out, researched, prepared, and at least attempted to carry it out. It was this planning process by the adversary that I hoped to be able to exploit to my team's benefit. I also believed that by keeping the research to open-source material, I was more likely to obtain the same information that any new groups on the horizon might use to develop their own tactics and techniques, but more importantly, I would also be able to share it with others in the protective field.

With my tactical background, I reasoned that just as all of us fall into routines and tend to be creatures of habit, so too do our adversaries. I also believe that we tend to stay with what works, even tactically. Just as I preferred to go out on nights with a new moon and inclement weather when I was to attach a global positioning satellite (GPS) tracking device onto a suspect's car, I wondered if a similar method of operation would be used by those who had installed a booby trap to a target's car. Those involved in field operations, be they police, military, or terrorists, tend to develop a set of tactics that work for them. Occasionally they may develop or try some new technique or tactic, but generally they stay with what they know, with slight modifications due to given circumstances. I reasoned that assassins and kidnappers tended to follow the same philosophy.

Later in the research, I began to examine attacks that were known or strongly believed to have been carried out by government forces. This was not an attempt to pass judgment on the right or wrong of such operations, but rather to further document attacks that have worked, regardless of what side perpetrated them. This was also partly due to the abundance of crossover that tends to exist in the field of combat arts. Terror organizations are known to have trained with one another as well as received advanced training from such groups as the East German Stasi and the Russian KGB. Intelligence and special forces personnel have provided training to foreign countries, as well as military and law enforcement organizations. It is this training that has the potential to be used against us.

Early in the research process I discovered that while there had been a great deal written about organized crime, very little focused upon their tactics. With the number of targeted killings carried out by such groups as the Sicilian Cosa Nostra, the Colombian drug cartels, and most recently, the Mexican drug cartels, I felt it was critical to understand the tactics used by them. Part of the study of these groups examined attacks they carried out against their own people or rivals. Just as military and police stayed with what worked, it seemed logical that cartel and mafia hitmen would use the same methods they employed to eliminate their own as when they targeted a judge, prosecutor, police officer, etc.

While there are many terms for the different types of targeted violence, be it an assassination, a kidnapping, or a contract killing, in the end they are all an ambush, one of the oldest and potentially most lethal tactics in all of warfare. For those in the position of providing protection for another individual(s), you must have a solid understanding of what you could be dealing with. The ambush is practiced by a wide spectrum, from the world's military forces to predators within the animal kingdom, even serial killers.

Ambush Basics: It is critical that you have, at the very least, a basic understanding of the principles of the ambush. The ambush is often a close-quarter battle tactic (which ironically is considered an advanced technique taught to military and law enforcement special forces) that relies upon good preoperational intelligence, surprise, and speed and violence of action for effectiveness. The fact that it's such a flexible tactic is one of the reasons for its popularity. It can be used upon stationary as well as mobile targets with equal effectiveness.

The goal or mission of the attacking force is to inflict maximum damage upon its target in the shortest amount of time and quickly withdrawal into the surroundings. This is primarily due to the generally smaller size of the attacking force. This small unit needs to quickly overwhelm what may be a numerically superior force, and then leave the area before reinforcements can arrive. As a result, these attacks are often extremely short in duration, but with massive amounts of damage inflicted.

For terrorist and criminal organizations, the ambush is an effective tool against law enforcement, military, and executive protection units in that it doesn't require a large amount of resources to conduct (although for many of these groups, a lack of resources isn't a problem). However, the first requirement for any successful ambush is good intelligence. Some of the intelligence information includes:

- Locations of residence, office, and frequented locations
- Routes and times taken by the target
- The composition of the protective detail (number of vehicles, if armored; number of bodyguards, if armed; etc.), if any
- The weapons and level of training of the protective detail
- Identification of possible ambush sites
- Escape routes once the ambush has been conducted

If the protectee and protective detail can make this information difficult to obtain, they may successfully force the attackers to shift their focus onto some other target (which has occurred on at least one occasion and is detailed in the case summaries).

There are several types of ambush formations; however, generally those used upon civilians fall into two types: the linear and the L shape. The linear attack is by far the most common and, as its name implies, comes from the flank or side. From positions of cover, the attacking force delivers a vast amount of firepower into the target. In the case of a motorcade, in order to prevent it from merely driving through the ambush site, explosives or heavy automatic fire could be used to disable the vehicles. The L shape ambush comes from two directions, most often from the front and side, and is seen more often in attacks on pedestrian targets.

Site selection for an urban ambush is one of the most important factors for the attacker (and also the defender) to consider. Ideally, the site should naturally funnel or "bottleneck" the target, thereby constricting escape routes, as well as forcing the target to slow down. This is especially important in attacks targeting a vehicle-borne victim. If the vehicle is moving at speed, the chances of successfully triggering the explosive device or getting shots on target are drastically decreased. This site also needs to provide an effective escape route after the attack has been conducted, unless of course the attacker is to be a suicide bomber.

Fire superiority, a term that is foreign to most without military service, is perhaps the single most critical factor in an ambush, from the perspectives of both the attacker and the defender. The adversary will seek to overwhelm its target, if protected, with firepower to prevent any sort of counterresponse being conducted. Whoever is able to obtain and maintain fire superiority in an ambush will most likely come out the victor. To successfully counter the assault requires immediate action on the part of the defenders, as most of the damage will occur within the first few seconds of the attack. There will be no time for the defenders to think and plan—they must act. To do this requires training and preplanning.

The goal in most ambushes is to kill everyone, but some have the goal of kidnapping an individual. This requires more skill on the part of the attackers and is more difficult to execute; they will need to eliminate the members of the protective detail quickly. However, kidnapping ambushes can be an easier attack to counter. The attackers will most likely not employ the use of explosives or the level of automatic gunfire in an effort not to harm their kidnap victim. By their need to be more precise in their shot placement, they will be forced to slow down the pace of the attack (although it may be almost unperceivable), thereby allowing the defenders the slim chance to respond with overwhelming firepower (if they are even armed).

Using explosives in an ambush often comes from a linear or flanking attack (when used in the urban environment), generally through the concealment of the explosive in a vehicle, bike, etc. While there have been some devices placed under the ground that detonate when driven over, these are rare in the urban areas. One of the biggest hurdles in using explosives in an urban ambush is in the placement itself. Unlike operating in a jungle or forest area, the planting of explosives in a civilian environment means more chances of detection by what is referred to as third-party awareness, meaning neighbors and citizens in and about the area. As the placement will require more time at the site of ambush, there are more chances of there being witnesses. Terrorists often overcome this hurdle by building the device into a vehicle and then moving it to and parking it at the attack site at the last possible moment.

Unlike the typical ambush employed by military forces worldwide, an urban ambush involves issues not typically encountered by those conducted in a rural setting. First and foremost is the problem of the areas generally being heavily populated. This obviously dramatically increases the risk of detection not only by the target, but also more probably by general citizens in the area. The problem continues with an adversary's need to rapidly exfiltrate out of the attack zone safely, if it is not a suicide attack. Factors such as traffic and street layout, which affect the victim, also affect the adversary in the way they conduct the ambush and how they make their escape successfully.

While we may never be in a position to "know our enemy" as suggested by Sun Tzu, we can "know the tactics" commonly employed. By having this knowledge of what has occurred in the past, those assigned to providing protection or those most likely to be targeted are more apt to identify early a possible attack. If you conduct protective operations or find yourself in one of the occupations often targeted by hostiles, you need to be aware. It is hoped that this book will provide the initial information needed for you to survive, but you should never stop learning.

ABOUT THE AUTHOR

Glenn McGovern, district attorney investigator, Special Deputy U.S. Marshal, police officer, deputy sheriff, law enforcement specialist, began his law enforcement career in 1986 as an eighteen-year-old member of the U.S. Air Force Security Police. It was here that he first began his studies of terrorism, tactical operations, and protective details. Europe, at the time, was on fire as groups such as the Sicilian mafia, November 17, Red Army Faction, Hizbollah, and many others were conducting their terrorist attacks. As a newly minted law enforcement member who was also assigned to a police unit that had a combat mission and was deployable worldwide, the study of the tactics used by these groups was mandatory. It was also during this time that he had his first introduction to close personal protection operations, first with Soviet diplomats visiting under the INF Treaty, then later in Panama with the commanding general of all U.S. forces in South America. He was also involved in an unusual protective operation in that he was locked in with the protectee, which in this case was more than $16 million in cash en route to the U.S. military installations in the Pacific.

Upon completion of his military service, he went to work for the Orange County Marshal's Department, assigned to courthouse security as well as bailiff functions. Upon completing the sheriff's academy, he was assigned as a deputy sheriff working in the jails. Approximately two years later he obtained a position with the Pacific Grove Police Department in Monterey County. While there, he worked as a patrolman, detective, and corporal. He also held a collateral assignment as a member of the SWAT team. Although the Pacific Grove Police Department was small, as were many of the departments on the coast, being on one of only three SWAT teams in the entire county, he had the opportunity to participate in a variety of operations, from hostage situations to barricaded gunmen to many high-risk search/arrest warrant services. This assignment also led to his next major experience in providing protection, this time to President Clinton and Vice President Al Gore, along with their wives, during a visit to the Stanford University: Hopkins Marine Station.

He later took a job with the Bureau of Investigation of one of the largest district attorney's offices in California, where he remains to this day. Here he quickly became a member of the Special Operations Group tasked with protective operations for district attorney staff, primarily prosecutors, as well as victims and witnesses. It was as a member of this group that he became more involved in the nuances of protective work as well as the training of a protective team. In particular, providing protection to victims and witnesses involved an issue that most protective teams don't generally have to deal with. At times, the witness being protected was a member of an organized prison gang. As a member of the gang, even on the "outs," that person was in a position to see the methods of operation, equipment, members of the team, and how they operate. As anyone who has worked organized crime, and gangs in particular, can attest, it doesn't take much for a gang member to get back in the good graces of his or her gang, and as a result, bringing with him or her the inside knowledge of the protective operations of the DA's office.

While with the district attorney's office, he was assigned full-time to the FBI's Joint Terrorism Task Force as a Special Deputy U.S. Marshal conducting international terrorism investigations for a period of three years. In this assignment he conducted counterterrorism investigations into a variety of groups, including some that have carried out targeted killings. He also was able to attend training that included the construction and detonation of a 500-pound vehicle car bomb, as well as dealing with suicide bombers, which provided him unique insight into how these operations could be carried out.

He holds a bachelor's degree in criminal justice from the Union Institute in Ohio as well as a certificate in crime and intelligence analysis from the California State University, Sacramento. He is the author of several articles dealing with intelligence and SWAT-related subjects, as well as a bimonthly online publication of urban ambush case studies. He also speaks on the issue of protective operations, specifically the tactics employed in these types of attacks.

1

Chronology of Attacks

The nine hundred attacks researched for this work have been provided in chronological order, including the name of the target and the country in which the attack occurred.

    December 31, 2008—Kazbek Pagiyev (Russia)
    December 15, 2008—Nicolas Sarkozy (France)
    December 13, 2008—Alois Mannichl (Germany)
    December 10, 2008—Felix Batista (Mexico)
    December 9, 2008—Urasul "Islam" Janibekov (Turkey)
    December 8, 2008—Victor Hugo Moneda (Mexico)
    December 3, 2008—Jesus Huerta Yedra (Mexico)
    December 3, 2008—Ignacio Uria Mendizabal (Spain)
    November 26, 2008—Vitaly Karayev (Russia)
    November 25, 2008—Lyubov Drozdova (Russia)
    November 22, 2008—Mario Fernando Hernandez and Marcos Collier (Honduras)
    November 19, 2008—Amir Faisal Alvi (Pakistan)
    November 18, 2008—Yasuko Yoshihara (Japan)
    November 18, 2008—Takehiko Yamaguchi and Michiko Yamaguchi (Japan)
    November 17, 2008—Yaakov Alperon (Israel)
    November 5, 2008—Fateh Bouchibane (Algeria)
    November 3, 2008—Nestor Sanchez (Mexico)
    November 2, 2008—Juan Felix (Mexico)
    October 20, 2008—Ivo Pukanic (Croatia)
    October 20, 2008—Huang Zhaoluan (China)
    October 9, 2008—Maithripala Sirisena (Sri Lanka)
    October 7, 2008—Rodolfo Barragan (Mexico)
    October 6, 2008—Rashid Akbar Nowani (Pakistan)
    October 1, 2008—Julio Soto (Venezuela)
    September 24, 2008—Ruslan Yamadayev and Sergei Kizyun (Russia)
    September 22, 2008—Luis Conde de la Cruz (Spain)
    September 10, 2008—Saleh Aridi (Lebanon)
    September 4, 2008—Yuri Melini (Guatemala)

August 26, 2008—Lynne Tracy (Pakistan)
August 2, 2008—David Feldheim (United States)
August 1, 2008—Mohammed Suleiman (Syria)
July 30, 2008—Francisco Ventura (Mexico)
July 22, 2008—Khalid Shahanshah (Pakistan)
June 26, 2008—Igor Labistida Calderon (Mexico)
June 9, 2008—Giorgos Mylonas (Greece)
May 23, 2008—Tariq Khan (Pakistan)
May 10, 2008—Juan Antonio Roman Garcia (Mexico)
May 9, 2008—Estaban Robles Espinoza (Mexico)
May 8, 2008—Edgar Millan Gomez (Mexico)
May 6, 2008—Saul Pena Lopez (Mexico)
May 5, 2008—Berenice Garcia (Mexico)
May 2, 2008—Jose Gomez Martinez (Mexico)
May 1, 2008—Roberto Velasco Bravo (Mexico)
April 22, 2008—Manuel Diaz Lerma (Mexico)
March 28, 2008—Fazal-ur-Rehman and Mohammad Ibrahim
March 21, 2008—Dragisa Cvejic (Serbia)
March 14, 2008—Armando Villareal Martha (Mexico)
March 14, 2008—Mark Achilli (United States)
March 7, 2008—Isaias Carrasco (Spain)
February 28, 2008—Giovanni Piscitelli (Italy)
February 15, 2008—Julio Sanchez (Mexico)
February 13, 2008—Yevgeny Grigoryev (Russia)
February 12, 2008—Imad Mughniyeh (Syria)
January 25, 2008—Wissam Eid (Lebanon)
January 21, 2008—Fernando Lozano Sandoval (Mexico)
January 15, 2008—Margarito Perez Saldana (Mexico)
January 15, 2008—Jose de Arias Rico and Elbert Marquez (Mexico)
January 15, 2008—Rey Roda (Philippines)
December 27, 2007—Benazir Bhutto (Pakistan)
December 21, 2007—Aftab Sherpao (Pakistan)
December 12, 2007—Francois El-Hajj (Lebanon)
December 11, 2007—Kurban Pashaev (Dagestan)
October 31, 2007—David Figueroa (Mexico)
October 18, 2007—Benazir Bhutto (Pakistan)
September 19, 2007—Mario Lobato (United States)
September 19, 2007—Antoine Ghanim (Lebanon)
September 6, 2007—Abdelaziz Bouteflika (Algeria)
August 29, 2007—Clara Luz Lopez (Guatemala)
August 13, 2007—Werner Velasquez (Guatemala)
July 16, 2007—Tuncay Seyranlioglu (Turkey)
July 3, 2007—Khavazh Daurbekov (Russia)
June 13, 2007—Walid Eido (Lebanon)
April 17, 2007—Itcho Ito (Japan)

March 31, 2007—Vicente Diestro Rabaya (Philppines)
March 27, 2007—Maksim Kurochkin (Ukraine)
March 6, 2007—Fernández Solis (Mexico)
March 4, 2007—Sunil Mahato (India)
March 2, 2007—Mian Bhatti (Pakistan)
March 1, 2007—Cielo Gonzalez (Colombia)
February 26, 2007—Ramón Verdugo (Mexico)
December 16, 2006—Luis Bersamin, Jr. (Philippines)
November 27, 2006—David Figueroa and Maria Corral (Mexico)
November 21, 2006—Pierre Gemayel (Lebanon)
November 1, 2006—Alexander Litvinenko (United Kingdom)
October 19, 2006—Dmitry Fotyanov (Russia)
September 13, 2006—Andrei Kozlov (Russia)
September 5, 2006—Samir Shehade (Lebanon)
August 8, 2006—Bitar Bitarov (Dagestan)
August 8, 2006—Adilgerei Magomedtagirov (Dagestan)
July 19, 2006—Hernando Saturno (Peru)
July 14, 2006—Bala Bestauty (South Ossetia)
July 9, 2006—Oleg Alborov (South Ossetia)
June 26, 2006—Parami Kulatunga (Sri Lanka)
May 30, 2006—Georgios Voulgarakis (Greece)
April 17, 2006—Ali Mohammad Naik (India)
April 6, 2006—Mario Pivaral (Guatemala)
March 31, 2006—Viktor Dorkin (Russia)
March 10, 2006—Robert Feliciaggi (Corsica)
March 3, 2006—Luis Biel (Philippines)
December 20, 2005—Julio Enrique Acosta Bernal (Colombia)
December 12, 2005—Gebran Tueni (Lebanon)
October 26, 2005—Emil Kyulev (Bulgaria)
October 18, 2005—Biplab Goshwamy (Bangladesh)
October 16, 2005—Francesco Fortugno (Italy)
September 26, 2005—Miguel Angel Esquivel (Mexico)
August 12, 2005—Lakshman Kadirgamar (Sri Lanka)
August 2, 2005—Hassan Moghaddas (Iran)
July 12, 2005—Elias Murr (Lebanon)
May 16, 2005—Saul Ayala (Mexico)
May 16, 2005—Erick Galvez (Guatemala)
April 10, 2005—Anatoly Trofimov (Russia)
March 17, 2005—Anatoly Chubais (Russia)
March 15, 2005—Ibrahim Rugova (Kosovo)
March 13, 2005—Rowland Barnes (United States)
February 26, 2005—Michael Lefkow (United States)
February 14, 2005—Rafik Hariri (Lebanon)
February 2, 2005—Magomed Omarov (Dagestan)
January 27, 2005—Shah AMS Kibria (Bangladesh)

December 16, 2004—Deidra Hydara, Ida Jagne-Joof, and Nyang Jobe (Gambia)
November 19, 2004—Sarath Ambepitiya (Sri Lanka)
November 18, 2004—Danilo Anderson (Venezuela)
November 2, 2004—Theo van Gogh (Netherlands)
September 18, 2004—Vladimir Putin (Russia)
September 6, 2004—Munir Said Thalib (Indonesia)
July 30, 2004—Shaukat Aziz (Pakistan)
July 29, 2004—Arsen Khaidakov (Dagestan)
July 19, 2004—Adi Azar (Israel)
June 10, 2004—Ahsan Saleem (Pakistan)
June 4, 2004—D. Hristov, K. Savov, and Z. Mitev (Bulgaria)
May 26, 2004—Ferry Silalahi (Indonesia)
May 9, 2004—Akhmad Kadyrov (Chechnya)
April 12, 2004—Boris Goldman (Russia)
April 5, 2004—Murat Zyazikov (Russia)
March 19, 2004—Chen Shui-bian (Taiwan)
February 27, 2004—Monica Von Borries (Bolivia)
February 13, 2004—Zelimkhan Yandarbiyev (Qatar)
January 4, 2004—Vivencio Bataga (Philippines)
December 25, 2003—Pervez Musharraf (Pakistan)
December 14, 2003—Pervez Musharraf (Pakistan)
December 4, 2003—Jonathan Luna (United States)
October 6, 2003—Maulana Tariq (Pakistan)
September 30, 2003—Jose Castillo (Colombia)
September 11, 2003—Anna Lindh (Sweden)
August 27, 2003—Magomedsalikh Gusayev (Dagestan)
July 23, 2003—James Davis (United States)
July 7, 2003—Boedyharto Angsono (Indonesia)
June 11, 2003—Abdur Khan (Pakistan)
April 17, 2003—Sergei Yushenkov (Russia)
April 5, 2003—Vivencio Bataga (Philippines)
March 28, 2003—Gadzhi Makhachev (Dagestan)
March 24, 2003—Alexandre Martins de Castro Filho (Brazil)
March 15, 2003—Jose Antonio Machado Dias (Brazil)
March 12, 2003—Zoran Djindjic (Serbia)
March 7, 2003—Iliya Pavlov (Bulgaria)
January 25, 2003—Alcebiades Sabino (Brazil)
January 24, 2003—Valdecir Paiva (Brazil)
January 10, 2003—Edward Lampert (United States)
December 29, 2002—Chaudhry Farooq (Pakistan)
December 28, 2002—Nikolay Kolev (Bulgaria)
October 28, 2002—Lawrence Foley (Jordan)
October 25, 2002—Ishii Koki (Japan)
October 18, 2002—Valentin Tsvetkov (Russia)
October 6, 2002—Bertrand Delanoë (France)

September 11, 2002—Mushtaq Ahmad Lone (India)
September 6, 2002—Misir Ashirkulov (Kyrgyzstan)
September 5, 2002—Fernando Mancilla (Colombia)
August 7, 2002—Vladimir Prokhorov (Russia)
July 15, 2002—Jacques Chirac (France)
May 6, 2002—Wilhelmus Petrus Fortuyn (Netherlands)
March 19, 2002—Marco Biagi (Italy)
March 16, 2002—Isaias Duarte Cancino (Colombia)
March 2, 2002—Martha Catalina Daniels (Colombia)
February 28, 2002—Esther Cabezudo (Spain)
February 23, 2002—Ingrid Betancourt (Colombia)
January 25, 2002—Francisco Lins do Rego (Brazil)
January 24, 2002—Elie Hobeika (Lebanon)
January 18, 2002—Celso Daniels (Brazil)
November 7, 2001—Jose Corbi (Spain)
November 1, 2001—Carlos Arturo Pinto (Colombia)
October 17, 2001—Rehavam Ze'evi (Israel)
October 12, 2001—Thomas C. Wales (United States)
October 8, 2001—Luis Comenares (Colombia)
September 28, 2001—Martin O'Hagan (Northern Ireland)
September 20, 2001—Juan Manuel Corzo (Colombia)
September 9, 2001—Ahmad Shah Massoud (Afghanistan)
September 8, 2001—Abdurahim Rahimov (Tajikistan)
September 2, 2001—Jose de Jesus German (Colombia)
August 29, 2001—Yolanda Paternina Negrete (Colombia)
August 10, 2001—Moises Espinosa, Jr. (Philippines)
July 28, 2001—Roseario Silva Rios (Colombia)
July 26, 2001—Muhammad Syaifuddin Kartasasita (Indonesia)
July 25, 2001—Phoolan Devi (India)
July 17, 2001—Karim Yuldashev (Tajikistan)
July 15, 2001—Jose Mugica (Spain)
July 11, 2001—Miguel Ignacio Lora (Colombia)
June 28, 2001—Justo Pedraza (Spain)
June 10, 2001—Luis Eladio Perez (Colombia)
June 8, 2001—Magomedsalikh Gusayev (Dagestan)
June 1, 2001—Ezekiel Alebua (Solomon Islands)
May 24, 2001—Santiago Oleaga (Spain)
May 11, 2001—Marcial Punzalan, Jr. (Philippines)
May 7, 2001—Manuel Abad (Spain)
May 1, 2001—Hector Polania (Colombia)
April 15, 2001—Rodrigo Valencia Restrepo (Colombia)
April 11, 2001—Khabib Sanginov (Tajikistan)
March 20, 2001—Froilan Elexpe (Spain)
February 22, 2001—Chikao Muramatsu (Colombia)
February 22, 2001—Brian Cass (England)

January 24, 2001—Gaffar Okkan (Turkey)
January 21, 2001—Vassilis Michaloliakos (Greece)
January 18, 2001—Henry Torres (Colombia)
December 29, 2000—Diego Turbay (Colombia)
December 19, 2000—Iosif Ordzhonikidze (Russia)
December 15, 2000—Wilson Borja (Colombia)
December 15, 2000—Derwin Brown (United States)
December 14, 2000—Francisco Consuegra (Spain)
December 4, 2000—Fernando Perdomo (Colombia)
November 29, 2000—Carlos Rosas (Colombia)
November 28, 2000—Juliana Villegas (Colombia)
November 27, 2000—Dora Elena Muñoz Pérez and Jorge Betancur Echeverri (Colombia)
November 25, 2000—Lazaro Montes (Colombia)
November 21, 2000—Ernest Lluch Martin (Spain)
November 6, 2000—Malika Gazimiyeva (Russia)
October 30, 2000—Jose Querol Lombardero (Spain)
October 10, 2000—Luis Portero (Spain)
August 30, 2000—Alejandro Vélez Jaramillo (Colombia)
August 7, 2000—Jean-Michel Rossi (France)
August 1, 2000—Leonides Caday (Indonesia)
July 29, 2000—Juan Maria Jauregui (Spain)
July 15, 2000—Jose Carpena (Spain)
June 8, 2000—Stephen Saunders (Greece)
June 5, 2000—Fred Capps (United States)
May 20, 2000—Saifullo Rakhimov (Takikistan)
May 11, 2000—Maria Rondon (Colombia)
April 11, 2000—Miltón Rodriguez (Colombia)
April 3, 2000—Margarita Pulgarín (Colombia)
March 26, 2000—Ilyas Umakhanov (Dagestan)
March 23, 2000—Cuauhtemoc Suastegui (Mexico)
February 28, 2000—James Riley (United States)
February 27, 2000—Crispiniano Quinones (Colombia)
February 27, 2000—Alfredo de la Torre (Mexico)
February 23, 2000—Fernando Buesa Blanco (Spain)
February 8, 2000—Pavle Bulatovic (Yugoslavia)
February 6, 2000—Oscar Aldaba (Philippines)
February 1, 2000—Jesus Leyva Cortz (Colombia)
January 21, 2000—Pedro Antonio Blanco Garcia (Spain)
January 15, 2000—Zelijko Raznatovic (Serbia)
January 7, 2000—Mohammad Marri (Pakistan)
December 30, 1999—Mikhail Dakhya (Russia)
December 17, 1999—Chandrika Kumaratunga (Sri Lanka)
November 29, 1999—S.C. Jamir (India)
November 22, 1999—Abdelkader Hachani (Algeria)
November 2, 1999—Ramesh Nadarajah (Sri Lanka)

October 20, 1999—Viktor Novosyolov (Russia)
July 29, 1999—Neelan Tiruchelvam (Sri Lanka)
July 26, 1999—Pavel Kapysh (Russia)
July 16, 1999—Luagalau Levaula (Samoa)
July 8, 1999—Dragan Simic (Yugoslavia)
May 20, 1999—Massimo D'Antona (Italy)
May 15, 1999—Abdul Kar (India)
April 9, 1999—Nihat Canpolat (Turkey)
March 23, 1999—Luis Maria Argana (Paraguay)
March 18, 1999—H. George Taylor (United States)
March 15, 1999—Rosemary Nelson (Northern Ireland)
March 11, 1999—Dragan Vlahovic (Yugoslavia)
March 5, 1999—Ayhan Cevik (Turkey)
March 1, 1999—Jean-Yvon Toussaint (Haiti)
February 17, 1999—Jaime Hurtado (Ecuador)
December 17, 1998—Ceci Cunha (Brazil)
November 20, 1998—Galina Starovoitova (Russia)
November 18, 1998—Tara Singh Hayer (Canada)
October 23, 1998—Barnett Slepian (United States)
October 19, 1998—Tommy Burks (United States)
October 14, 1998—Dmitry Filipov (Russia)
September 21, 1998—Ahmet Krasniqi (Albania)
September 15, 1998—Jorge Gonzalez (Colombia)
September 12, 1998—Azem Haidari (Albania)
September 2, 1998—Yuri Timoshkov (Russia)
August 11, 1998—Amparo Pallares (Colombia)
July 23, 1998—Aslan Maskhadov (Russia)
June 25, 1998—Manuel Zamarreno (Spain)
June 24, 1989—Marek Papala (Poland)
May 17, 1998—Sarojini Yogeswaran (Sri Lanka)
May 14, 1998—Larry Wijeyaratne (Sri Lanka)
May 6, 1998—Tomas Caballero (Spain)
April 22, 1998—Vadym Hetman (Ukraine)
February 10, 1998—Nicholas Martinelli (United States)
February 9, 1998—Edvard Shevardnadze (Republic of Georgia)
February 6, 1998—Claude Erignac (Corsica)
January 30, 1998—Alberto Jimenez Becèrril (Spain)
January 15, 1998—Ruslan Gitinov (Russia)
January 9, 1998—Jose Goiena (Spain)
December 10, 1997—Vincent Carrozza (Mexico)
November 8, 1997—Nadeem Awan (Pakistan)
November 6, 1997—Alfredo Enrique Vargas (Jamaica)
October 24, 1997—Zoran Todorovic (Yugoslavia)
September 25, 1997—Khaled Mashaal (Jordan)
September 8, 1997—Pierre Rondeau and Robert Corriveau (Canada)

7

August 19, 1997—Vickie Bunnell (United States)
August 18, 1997—Mikhail Manevich (Russia)
August 8, 1997—Jorge Cristo (Colombia)
July 10, 1997—Miguel Blanco (Spain)
June 15, 1997—Larisa Nechayeva (Russia)
May 28, 1997—Costas Peratikos (Greece)
April 30, 1997—Imomali Rakhmonov (Takjikistan)
April 28, 1997—Julio Enrique Acosta (Colombia)
April 10, 1997—Radovan Stojicic (Yugoslavia)
March 21, 1997—Gerardo Bedoya (Colombia)
February 14, 1997—Vincent Nkezabaganwa (Rwanda)
February 11, 1997—Nalanda Ellawala (Sri Lanka)
February 10, 1997—Rafael Emperador (Spain)
February 4, 1997—Benjamin de Jesus (Philippines)
January 3, 1997—Odin Gutierrez Rico (Mexico)
November 3, 1996—Martin Ramirez-Alvarez (Mexico)
November 3, 1996—Paul Tatum (Russia)
October 26, 1996—Kandiah Perinpanathan (France)
October 21, 1996—Ali Boucetta (Algeria)
October 12, 1996—Theodore Miriung (Papua New Guinea)
October 2, 1996—Andrey Karlov Lukanov (Bulgaria)
October 1, 1996—Jakub Fiszman (Germany)
September 14, 1996—Ernesto Ibarra Sante (Mexico)
August 17, 1996—Jesus Romero Magana (Mexico)
August 10, 1996—Mamoru Konno (Mexico)
August 5, 1996—Jaffar Hasso Guly (France)
August 1, 1996—Pierre Claverie (Algeria)
July 16, 1996—Pavlo Lazarenko (Ukraine)
June 13, 1996—Viktor Mosalov (Russia)
June 6, 1996—Valery Shantsev (Russia)
May 28, 1996—Reza Mazlouman (France)
May 15, 1996—Sergio Moreno Perez (Mexico)
April 17, 1996—Arturo Ochoa Palacios (Mexico)
March 25, 1996—Jan Philipp Reemtsma (Germany)
February 23, 1996—Sergio Armando Silva Moreno (Mexico)
February 14, 1996—Francisco Valiente (Spain)
January 5, 1996—Yahaya Ayywash (Palestine)
November 13, 1995—Ahmed Alaa Nazmi (Switzerland)
November 4, 1995—Yitzhak Rabin (Israel)
November 2, 1995—Alvaro Hurtado (Colombia)
October 26, 1995—Fathi Shqaqi (Malta)
October 3, 1995—Kirov Gligorov (Ukraine)
September 27, 1995—Antonio Cancino (Colombia)
September 25, 1995—Paul McLaughlin (United States)
September 20, 1995—Oleg Lobov (Russia)

August 31, 1995—Beant Singh (India)
August 29, 1995—Edvard Shevardnadze (Republic of Georgia)
July 11, 1995—Abdelbaki Sahraoui (France)
June 26, 1995—Hosni Mubarak (Ethiopia)
June 14, 1995—Robert Krueger (Burundi)
April 19, 1995—Jose Aznar (Spain)
March 28, 1995—Mireille Bertin (Haiti)
March 11, 1995—Ernest Kabushemeye (Burundi)
March 8, 1995—Jacqueline Keys Van Landingham and Gary C. Durell (Pakistan)
March 1, 1995—Vlad Listyev (Russia)
February 28, 1995—Tito Espinosa (Philippines)
January 26, 1995—K.V. Krishna Rao (India)
January 24, 1995—Tarsem Singh Purewal (Great Britain)
January 15, 1995—John Paul II (Philippines)
December 3, 1994—Georgy Chanturia (Republic of Georgia)
October 24, 1994—Gamini Dissanayake (Sri Lanka)
September 28, 1994—Francisco Ruiz Massieu (Mexico)
September 5, 1994—John Newman (Australia)
August 9, 1994—Manuel Cepeda (Colombia)
July 29, 1994—John Britton (United States)
July 4, 1994—Omer Haluk Sipahioglu (Greece)
June 18, 1994—Yousef Fathallah (Algeria)
June 7, 1994—Boris Berezovsky (Russia)
May 29, 1994—Khallid Muhammad (United States)
April 28, 1994—Frederico Benitez (Mexico)
April 26, 1994—Andrei Aizderdis (Russia)
April 25, 1994—Angel Losada Moreno (Mexico)
April 1, 1994—Gonzalez Dubon (Guatemala)
March 28, 1994—Belkacem Touati (Algeria)
March 24, 1994—Matthew Flores (United States)
March 23, 1994—Luis Donaldo Colosio (Mexico)
March 19, 1994—Giueseppe Diana (Italy)
March 14, 1994—Alfredo Helu (Mexico)
February 25, 1994—Yann Piat (France)
February 3, 1994—Fernando Sagristano (Italy)
January 29, 1994—Naeb Imran Maaytah (Lebanon)
January 24, 1994—Michalis Vranopoulos (Greece)
December 20, 1993—Antoine Baaklini (Lebanon)
November 25, 1993—Atef Sedki (Egypt)
November 25, 1993—Haynes Mahoney (Yemen)
October 14, 1993—Guy Malary (Haiti)
September 29, 1993—Samuel Motha (South Africa)
September 15, 1993—Giuseppe Puglisi (Sicily)
September 11, 1993—Maninder Singh Bitta (India)
August 19, 1993—George Tiller (United States)

August 18, 1993—Hassan al-Alfi (Egypt)
August 8, 1993—Fred Woodruff (Republic of Georgia)
August 7, 1993—Henri Pharaon (Lebanon)
August 4, 1993—Harvey Weinstein (United States)
August 1, 1993—Viktor Polyanichko and Anatoly Koretsky (Russia)
July, 1993—Benazir Bhutto (Pakistan)
June 2, 1993—Mohammed H. Arbab (Pakistan)
May 24, 1993—Juan Jesus Posada Ocampo (Mexico)
May 14, 1993—Maurizio Costanzo (Italy)
May 1, 1993—Ranashinghe Premadasa (Sri Lanka)
April 23, 1993—Lalith Athulathmudali (Sri Lanka)
April 20, 1993—Safwat Sharif (Egypt)
April 10, 1993—Chris Hani (South Africa)
March 16, 1993—Mohammad Haghdi (Italy)
March 10, 1993—David Gunn (United States)
December 5, 1992—Jiri Svoboda (Czechoslovakia)
November 16, 1992—Clancy Fernando (Sri Lanka)
October 23, 1992—Arthur Kessler (Colombia)
October 1, 1992—Takashi Inoue (Japan)
September 18, 1992—Miriam Rocio Velez Perez (Colombia)
September 17, 1992—Sadiq Sarafkindi (Germany)
August 12, 1992—Eric Stonecipher (United States)
July 27, 1992—Giovanni Lizzio (Italy)
July 19, 1992—Paolo Borsellino (Sicily)
July 14, 1992—Yannis Peleokrassas (Greece)
July 1, 1992—Chris Marshall, John Hill, and Clyde Ashworth (United States)
June 29, 1992—Mohammad Boudiaf (Algeria)
June 9, 1992—Atef Bseiso (France)
June 8, 1992—Farag Foda (Egypt)
June 6, 1992—Danielle Mitterrand (Iraq)
May 26, 1992—Charles Geschke (United States)
May 23, 1992—Giovanni Falconne and Francesca Morvillo (Sicily)
May 5, 1992—Gilchrist Olympio (Togo)
May 5, 1992—Lawrence Jahnke (United States)
April 28, 1992—Sidney Reso (United States)
March 26, 1992—Nareh Rafizadeh (United States)
March 20, 1992—Shin Kanemaru (Japan)
March 12, 1992—Salvo Lima (Sicily)
March 7, 1992—Ehud Sadan (Turkey)
February 15, 1992—María Elena Moyano (Peru)
February 11, 1992—Anthony Quainton (Peru)
January 17, 1992—Micheal Barnes (Philippines)
December 30, 1991—Shafik Wazzan (Lebanon)
November 4, 1991—M. Zaher Shah (Italy)
October 28, 1991—Victor Maverick (Turkey)

October 7, 1991—Cetin Corgu (Greece)
August 9, 1991—Antonio Scopelliti (Calabria)
August 6, 1991—Shapur Bakhtiar (France)
August 4, 1991—Branislav Matic–Beli (Yugoslavia)
July 18, 1991—André Cools (Belgium)
July 16, 1991—Deniz Bolukbasi (Greece)
June 18, 1991—Nabi Sher Junejo (Pakistan)
May 21, 1991—Rajuv Ghandi (India)
April 30, 1991—Enrique Low Murtra (Colombia)
April 27, 1991—V.B. de Chamorro (Nicaragua)
April 8, 1991—Abdol-Rahman Boroumand (France)
April 1, 1991—Detlev Ruhwedder (Germany)
April 1, 1991—Jaime Guzman (Chile)
March 20, 1991—Michael Murr (Lebanon)
March 12, 1991—Ronald Stewart (Greece)
March 2, 1991—Ranjan Wijeratne (Sri Lanka)
February 7, 1991—John Major (England)
January 12, 1991—Al Sharpton (United States)
December 31, 1990—Paul Mariani (Corsica)
November 20, 1990—Vardis Vardinoyannis (Greece)
November 5, 1990—Meir Kahane (United States)
October 23, 1990—Cyrus Elahi (France)
October 12, 1990—Wolfgang Schäuble (Germany)
October 12, 1990—Rifaat al-Mahgoub (Egypt)
September 21, 1990—Rosario Livatino (Italy)
September 18, 1990—Peter Terry (England)
July 30, 1990—Ian Gow (United Kingdom)
July 27, 1990—Hans Neusel (Germany)
July 20, 1990—Antonio Durand (Peru)
May 21, 1990—Federico Velez (Colombia)
May 9, 1990—Giovanni Bonsignore (Sicily)
April 26, 1990—Carlos Pizarro Leon Gomez (Colombia)
April 24, 1990—Kazem Rajavi (Switzerland)
April 10, 1990—Teddy Wang (China)
March 30, 1990—Budgan Zbigniew (Lebanon)
March 22, 1990—Gerald Victor Bull (Belgium)
March 22, 1990—Bernardo Jaramillo (Colombia)
February 25, 1990—Enver Hadri (Belgium)
January 31, 1990—Rashid Khalifa (United States)
January 18, 1990—Motoshima Hitoshi (Japan)
January 5, 1990—Javier Hizon (Philippines)
November 30, 1989—Alfred Herrhausen (Germany)
November 28, 1989—Francisco Jose Guerrero (El Salvador)
November 22, 1989—Rene Moawad (Lebanon)
November 8, 1989—Mohammed Ali Marzouqi (Lebanon)

November 1, 1989—Mariela Espinoza Arango (Colombia)
November 1, 1989—Luis Francisco Madero Forero (Colombia)
October 17, 1989—Hector Rodriguez (Colombia)
October 16, 1989—Abdel Shrewi (Turkey)
October 4, 1989—Joseph Wybran (Belgium)
September 26, 1989—Pavlo Bakoyiannis (Greece)
September 12, 1989—Carmen Tagle (Spain)
September 11, 1989—Pablo Gonzalez (Colombia)
August 18, 1989—Luis Carlos Galan Sarmiento (Colombia)
August 18, 1989—Waldemar Franklin Quintero (Colombia)
August 16, 1989—Carlos Valencia (Colombia)
August 1, 1989—Aleksandr Shkadov (Russia)
July 19, 1989—Jose Posadillas, Ignacio Baraguas, and Fernando Vilces (Spain)
July 13, 1989—Abdul Ghassemlou (Austria)
July 4, 1989—Roldan Betancur (Colombia)
June 9, 1989—Jose Rodriguez Porth (El Salvador)
May 30, 1989—Maza Marquez (Colombia)
May 28, 1989—Michael Aoun (Cyprus)
May 16, 1989—Hassan Khaled (Lebanon)
May 8, 1989—Giorgos Petsos (Greece)
May 1, 1989—David Webster (South Africa)
April 23, 1989—Frank Chikane (South Africa)
April 21, 1989—James Rowe (Philippines)
April 19, 1989—Jose Roberto Garcia Alvarado (San Salvador)
April 10, 1989—Samouil Samouil (Greece)
March 20, 1989—Harry Breen and Robert Buchanan (Ireland)
March 17, 1989—Moises Espinosa (Philippines)
February 12, 1989—Patrick Finucane (Northern Ireland)
January 25, 1989—Gustavo Martinez (Honduras)
January 23, 1989—Anastasios Vernardos (Greece)
January 18, 1989—Panayotis Tarasouleas (Greece)
January 14, 1989—Paul Boeynants (Belgium)
January 11, 1989—Ali al-Marzuki (Lebanon)
January 10, 1989—Konstantinos Androulidakis (Greece)
November 22, 1988—Guerrero Paz (Colombia)
October 20, 1988—Nikola Stedul (Scotland)
September 28, 1988—John Buttle (Colombia)
September 25, 1988—Antonio Saetta (Sicily)
September 20, 1988—Hans Tietmeyer (Germany)
September 14, 1988—Alberto Giacomelli (Italy)
August 17, 1988—Mohammad Zia-ul-Haq, Arnold Raphel, and Herbert Wassom (Pakistan)
August 8, 1988—George Shultz (Bolivia)
June 28, 1988—William Nordeen (Greece)
June 18, 1988—Turgut Özal (Turkey)

May 30, 1988—Mike O'Mara (United States)
May 29, 1988—Alvaro Gómez Hurtado (Colombia)
May 21, 1988—Richard Daronco (United States)
April 16, 1988—Roberto Rufillini (Italy)
April 16, 1988—Khalil al-Wazir (Tunisia)
April 1, 1988—West Germany Attache (France)
March 29, 1988—Dulcie September (France)
March 1, 1988—Alexandros Bodosakis (Greece)
February 17, 1988—William Higgins (Lebanon)
January 25, 1988—Carlos Hoyos (Colombia)
January 14, 1988—Natale Mondo (Sicily)
January 12, 1988—Giuseppe Insalaco (Sicily)
January 4, 1988—Siegfried Weilsputz (France)
October 11, 1987—Jaime Pardo Leal (Colombia)
October 7, 1987—Antanios Hanna (Belgium)
September 14, 1987—Vincent Sherry (United States)
September 9, 1987—Gerrit Jan Heijn (Netherlands)
August 2, 1987—Jaime Ferrer (Philippines)
July 28, 1987—Wilson Bailey (United States)
July 7, 1987—Amir-Hossein Amir-Parviz (England)
July 2, 1987—Mohammed Razi (Spain)
June 26, 1987—Yussef Kherbigh (Italy)
June 1, 1987—Rashind Karami (Lebanon)
May 20, 1987—Ezzedin al-Ghadamsi (Austria)
May 19, 1987—Hamid Chitgar (Austria)
April 25, 1987—Maurice Gibson (Ireland)
April 5, 1987—Gibson Mondlane (Mozambique)
March 20, 1987—George Aronwald (United States)
March 20, 1987—Licio Giorgieri (Italy)
January 20, 1987—Alfred Schmidt (Lebanon)
January 17, 1987—Rudolf Cordes (Lebanon)
January 13, 1987—Enrique Parejo Gonzalez (Hungary)
January 7, 1987—Camille Chamoun (Lebanon)
December 17, 1986—Guillermo Cano Isaza (Colombia)
December 15, 1986—Alain Peyreffite (France)
December 1, 1986—Fabian Ribeiro (South Africa)
November 18, 1986—William Weissich (United States)
November 17, 1986—Jaime Ramirez Gomez (Colombia)
November 17, 1986—George Besse (France)
October 25, 1986—Rafael Garrido Gil (Spain)
October 10, 1986—Gerold von Braunmuhl (Germany)
September 8, 1986—Augusto Pinochet (Chile)
August 17, 1986—Luis Alfredo Macana (Colombia)
August 10, 1986—Arun Vaidya (India)
July 31, 1986—Baquero Borda (Colombia)

13

July 9, 1986—Karl-Heinz Beckurts (Germany)
June 10, 1986—Khalid Nazal (Greece)
April 25, 1986—Arthur Pollick (Yemen)
April 24, 1986—Kenneth Marston (France)
April 15, 1986—William J. Calkins (Sudan)
April 8, 1986—Demitrius Angelopoulos (Greece)
March 19, 1986—Etti Tal-Or (Egypt)
February 28, 1986—Sven Palme (Sweden)
February 22, 1986—Antonio da Empoli (Italy)
February 10, 1986—Lando Conti (Italy)
February 6, 1986—Cristobal Colon (Spain)
January 24, 1986—Tarsem Singh Toor (United Kingdom)
January 16, 1986—Sangtar Singh Sandhu (United Kingdom)
December 16, 1985—Paul Castellano (United States)
August 6, 1985—Ninni Cassara (Sicily)
July 29, 1985—Fausto Estrada (Spain)
July 28, 1985—Beppe Montana (Sicily)
July 24, 1985—Zayed Sati (Turkey)
July 23, 1985—Tulio Manual Castro Gil (Colombia)
June 30, 1985—Haruo Remeliik (Palau)
June 9, 1985—Thomas Sutherland (Lebanon)
May 25, 1985—Shiek Jaber al-Ahmad al-Sabah (Kuwait)
May 14, 1985—Vernon Nkadimeng (Botswana)
April 1, 1985—Giorgos Theofanopoulos (Greece)
March 28, 1985—Viktor Khitrichenki (India)
March 22, 1985—Marcel Carton and Marcel Fontaine (Lebanon)
February 28, 1985—Ghadamsi (Austria)
February 21, 1985—Nikos Momferatos (Greece)
February 7, 1985—Enrique Salazar (Mexico)
January 25, 1985—René Audran (France)
January 13, 1985—Magkjun Farg (Italy)
November 27, 1984—Percy Norris (India)
November 20, 1984—Santiago Brouard (Spain)
November 19, 1984—Evner Ergun (Austria)
October 31, 1984—Indira Gandhi (India)
October 19, 1984—Jerzy Popieluszko (Poland)
October 15, 1984—Henry Liu (United States)
October 12, 1984—Margaret Thatcher (United Kingdom)
August 1, 1984—Srinivasu Dasari (United States)
July 5, 1984—Umaru Dikko (United Kingdom)
June 20, 1984—Erdogan Ozen (Austria)
June 18, 1984—Alan Berg (United States)
April 28, 1984—Isik Yonder (Iran)
April 3, 1984—Rodrigo Lara Bonilla (Colombia)
March 28, 1984—Kenneth Whitty (Greece)

March 16, 1984—William Buckley (Lebanon)
February 15, 1984—Leamon Hunt (Italy)
February 8, 1984—Khalifa Ahmed Aziz al-Mubarak (France)
February 7, 1984—Gholam Ali Oveissi and Gholam Hosein Oveissi (France)
January 29, 1984—Guillermo Lacaci (Spain)
December 16, 1983—Don Tidey (Ireland)
November 22, 1983—Keith McFadden and Zwelakhe Nyanda (Swaziland)
November 15, 1983—George Tsantes (Greece)
October 27, 1983—Taysir Alaedin Toukan (Italy)
October 26, 1983—Mohammad Ali Kourme (India)
October 20, 1983—Henry Gentile (United States)
September 13, 1983—Pierre Massimi (France)
August 21, 1983—Benigno Aquino (Philppines)
August 8, 1983—Mozaffar Ahmad (United States)
July 31, 1983—Rocco Chinnici (Sicily)
July 14, 1983—Dursun Aksov (Belgium)
May 25, 1983—Albert Schaufelberger (El Salvador)
April 12, 1983—Teddy Wang (China)
April 10, 1983—Issam Saartavi (Portugal)
March 9, 1983—Galip Balkar (Yugoslavia)
January 28, 1983—Italy Penitentiary Agent (Italy)
January 13, 1983—Gian Montalto (Italy)
November 4, 1982—Victor Roman (Spain)
September 23, 1982—Esther Milo (Malta)
September 14, 1982—Bashir Gemayel (Lebanon)
September 9, 1982—Bora Süelkan (Bulgaria)
September 3, 1982—Carlo Dalla Chiesa (Sicily)
August 27, 1982—Atilla Altikat (Canada)
August 21, 1982—Roderick Grant (France)
August 12, 1982—Hector Zevallos (United States)
August 11, 1982—Paolo Giaccone (Sicily)
July 23, 1982—Fadl Dani (France)
July 15, 1982—Antonio Ammaturo (Italy)
July 1, 1982—Kemalettin Demirer (Netherlands)
June 17, 1982—Hussein Kamal (Italy)
June 12, 1982—Simon Wiesenthal (Austria)
June 7, 1982—Erkut Akbay (Portugal)
June 4, 1982—Petrus Nzima and Jabu Nzima (Swaziland)
June 3, 1982—Shlomo Argov (United Kingdom)
May 4, 1982—Orvile Gunduz (United States)
April 30, 1982—Pio La Torre (Sicily)
April 27, 1982—Raffaele Delcogliano (Italy)
April 8, 1982—Kani Gungor (Canada)
April 3, 1982—Ya'acov Bar-Simantov (France)
January 28, 1982—Kemal Arikan (United States)

January 19, 1982—Eugene Berry (United States)
January 18, 1982—Charles Ray (France)
January, 1982—Nicola Simone (Italy)
December 18, 1981—James Dozier (Italy)
October 21, 1981—Pierre Michel (France)
October 21, 1981—Francesco Straullu (Italy)
October 19, 1981—Mate Kolic (France)
October 6, 1981—Anwar al-Sadat (Egypt)
September 19, 1981—Pierre Declercq (New Caledonia)
September 15, 1981—Frederick Kroesen (Germany)
September 4, 1981—Louis Delamère (Lebanon)
August 30, 1981—Mohammad Ali Rajai and Mohammad Javad Bahonar (Iran)
July 31, 1981—Joe Gqabi (Zimbabwe)
June 9, 1981—Mehmet Arguz (Switzerland)
June 4, 1981—Renzo Sandrucci (Italy)
May 30, 1981—Ziaur Rahman (Bangladesh)
May 27, 1981—Roger Wheeler (United States)
May 20, 1981—Giuseppe Taliercio (Italy)
May 13, 1981—John Paul II (Vatican City)
May 1, 1981—Heinz Kittel (Austria)
April 27, 1981—Ciro Cirillo (Italy)
April 3, 1981—Carit Demir (Denmark)
March 30, 1981—Ronald Reagan (United States)
March 4, 1981—Tecelli Ari and Resat Morali (France)
February 17, 1981—Luigi Marangoni (Italy)
December 17, 1980—Sarik Ariyak (Australia)
December 13, 1980—Giovanni D'Urso (Italy)
November 12, 1980—Renato Briano (Italy)
September 26, 1980—Selcuk Bakkalbasi (France)
September 17, 1980—Anastasio Somoza Debayle (Paraguay)
August 6, 1980—Gaetano Costa (Italy)
July 31, 1980—Galip Ozmen (Greece)
July 22, 1980—Ali Akbar Tabatabai (United States)
July 21, 1980—Salah al-Din al-Bitar (France)
July 19, 1980—Nihat Erim (Turkey)
July 18, 1980—Shahpour Bakhtiar (France)
July 15, 1980—Abdurrahman Koksaloglu (Turkey)
June 23, 1980—Mario Amato (Italy)
June 17, 1980—Jose A. Lima (Guatemala)
June 14, 1980—El Meshad (France)
May 29, 1980—Vernon Jordan (United States)
May 19, 1980—Pino Amato (Italy)
May 12, 1980—Alfredo Albanese (Italy)
May 5, 1980—Emanuele Basile (Sicily)
April 17, 1980—Vecdi Turel (Vatican City)

March 24, 1980—Oscar Amulfo Romero (El Salvador)
March 19, 1980—Guido Galli (Italy)
March 18, 1980—General Esquivias (Spain)
March 18, 1980—Girolamo Minervini (Italy)
March 16, 1980—Nicola Giacumbi (Italy)
March 14, 1980—Peter Calabro (United States)
February 12, 1980—Vittorio Bachelet (Italy)
February 6, 1980—Dogan Türkman (Switzerland)
January 25, 1980—Emanuele Tuttobene and Antonio Gasu (Italy)
January 16, 1980—Pandelis Petrou (Greece)
January 6, 1980—Piersanti Mattarella (Sicily)
December 22, 1979—Yilmaz Holpen (France)
December 7, 1979—Shahriar Shafik (France)
November 13, 1979—Ephriam Eldar (Portugal)
October 26, 1979—Park Chung Lee (South Korea)
October 12, 1979—Ahmet Benler (Netherlands)
September 25, 1979—Cesare Terranova (Sicily)
September 21, 1979—Carlo Ghiglieno (Italy)
August 27, 1979—Louis Mountbatten (Ireland)
July 21, 1979—Boris Giuliano (Sicily)
July 12, 1979—Carmine Galante (United States)
July 11, 1979—Giorgia Ambrosoli (Italy)
June 25, 1979—Alexander Haig (Belgium)
May 29, 1979—John Wood, Jr. (United States)
May 25, 1979—Luis Hortiguela and Augustin Laso Corral (Spain)
March 30, 1979—Airey Neave (United Kingdom)
March 22, 1979—Richard Sykes (Netherlands)
February 14, 1979—Adolph Dubs (Afghanistan)
January 29, 1979—Emilio Alessandrini (Italy)
January 22, 1979—Ali Hassan Salameh (Lebanon)
January 9, 1979—Miguel Cruz Cuenca (Spain)
January 2, 1979—Costantino Gil (Spain)
December 20, 1978—Barry Leibowitz (United States)
November 27, 1978—Harvey Milk and George Moscone (United States)
November 21, 1978—James Kerr (United States)
November 8, 1978—Fedele Calvosa (Italy)
October 10, 1978—Girolamo Tartaglione (Italy)
September 7, 1978—Georgi Markov (Great Britain)
September 1, 1978—Vladimir Kostov (France)
July 28, 1978—Taha ad-Dawud (Great Britain)
July 9, 1978—Abdul al Naif (Great Britain)
June 24, 1978—Ahmed Hussein al-Ghashmi (North Yemen)
June 21, 1978—Antonio Esposito (Italy)
June 2, 1978—Necla Kuneralp, Zeki Kuneralp, and Besir Balcioglu (Spain)
March 16, 1978—Aldo Moro (Italy)

February 18, 1978—Yussef Seba (Cyprus)
February 15, 1978—Edwin Helfant (United States)
February 14, 1978—Ricardo Palma (Italy)
January 30, 1978—William Zerby (United States)
January 23, 1978—Edouard-Jean Empain (France)
September 12, 1977—Ashraf Pahlavi (France)
September 5, 1977—Hans Martin Schleyer (Germany)
August 20, 1977—Giuseppe Russo (Sicily)
July 30, 1977—Jürgen Pronto (Germany)
July 12, 1977—Salinas Aguirre (El Salvador)
June 9, 1977—Taha Carim (Vatican City)
April 28, 1977—Fulvio Croce (Italy)
April 10, 1977—Qady Ali Hajri (Great Britain)
April 7, 1977—Siegfried Buback (Germany)
February 2, 1977—Jeffrey Agate (Northern Ireland)
January 3, 1977—Mahmud Saleh (France)
January 1977—Pietro Costa (Italy)
December 14, 1976—Alfonso Noce (Italy)
November 14, 1976—Evangelos Mallios (Greece)
October 4, 1976—Juan Maria de Araluce y Villar (Spain)
September 21, 1976—Orlando Letelier (United States)
September 1, 1976—Francesco Cusano (Italy)
August 11, 1976—Margarita Portillo (Mexico)
July 28, 1976—Yvan Tuksor (France)
July 26, 1976—Bulent Ecevit (New York)
July 21, 1976—Christopher Ewart-Biggs (Ireland)
July 10, 1976—Vittorio Occorsio (Italy)
June 16, 1976—Francis Edward Meloy, Jr. (Lebanon)
June 8, 1976—Francesco Coco (Italy)
May 11, 1976—Joacquin Anaya (France)
March 7, 1976—Angel Urbe (Spain)
February 7, 1976—Edwin Zdovc (West Germany)
January 21, 1976—Jack Prizzia (United States)
December 23, 1975—Richard Welch (Greece)
November 27, 1975—Alan Ross McWhirter (Great Britain)
November 3, 1975—Richard Charnley (Great Britain)
October 24, 1975—Ismail Erez (France)
October 23, 1975—Hugh Fraser (Great Britain)
October 22, 1975—Danis Tunaligil (Austria)
October 6, 1975—Bernardo Leighton (Italy)
September 22, 1975—Gerald Ford (United States)
September 5, 1975—Gerald Ford (United States)
March 31, 1975—Laden Djokovic (France)
March 25, 1975—King Faisal (Saudi Arabia)
February 27, 1975—Peter Lorenz (Germany)

February 26, 1975—John Egan (Argentina)
February 13, 1975—Stewart Cunningham (United States)
December 22, 1974—Edward Heath (Great Britain)
November 11, 1974—Allan Quartermaine (Great Britain)
November 10, 1974—Gunther von Drenkmann (Germany)
November 4, 1974—Joseph Crescente (United States)
October 28, 1974—Mrs. Denis Howell (Great Britain)
September 30, 1974—Alfonso Marguerite (Argentina)
September 27, 1974—Barbara Hutchison (Dominican Republic)
September 19, 1974—Juan and Jorge Born (Argentina)
August 28, 1974—Jose Guadalupe Zuno (Mexico)
August 19, 1974—Rodger P. Davies (Cyprus)
August 15, 1974—Mrs. Chung Hee Park (South Korea)
July 21, 1974—Alfredo Marquis (Lebanon)
June 4, 1974—John Michael Henry Hely-Hutchinson (Ireland)
April 18, 1974—Mario Sossi (Italy)
April 12, 1974—Jose Elias de Torriente (United States)
March 20, 1974—Princess Anne (Great Britain)
March 11, 1974—William Fox (Ireland)
February 4, 1974—Patty Hearst (United States)
December 30, 1973—Joseph Sieff (England)
December 27, 1973—Thomas Niedermeyer (Ireland)
December 20, 1973—Luis Carrero Blanco (Spain)
December 6, 1973—Victor Samuelsson (Argentina)
November 22, 1973—John Swint (Argentina)
November 6, 1973—Marcus Foster and Robert Blackburn (United States)
July 1, 1973—Yosef Alon (United States)
May 4, 1973—Terrence Leonhardy (Mexico)
March 10, 1973—Richard Sharples (Bermuda)
March 4, 1973—Golda Meir (United States)
January 27, 1973—Mehmet Baydar and Bahadir Demir (United States)
January 26, 1973—Baruch Cohn (Spain)
December 8, 1972—Mahmoud Hamshari (France)
October 16, 1972—Abdel Zwaiter (Italy)
May 17, 1972—Luigi Calabresi (Italy)
May 15, 1972—George Wallace (United States)
May 15, 1972—Wolfgang Buddenberg (West Germany)
March 21, 1972—Oberdan Sallustro (Argentina)
March 3, 1972—Idalgo Macchiarini (Italy)
December 15, 1971—Zaid Rifai (United Kingdom)
December 12, 1971—Jack Barnhill (Ireland)
December 1, 1971—Victor Breen (United States)
December 29, 1971—Theo Albrecht (Germany)
November 28, 1971—Wasfi al-Tal (Egypt)
August 16, 1971—Viggo Rasmussen (Denmark)

19

May 29, 1971—Henri Wolimer (Spain)
May 17, 1971—Ephraim Elrom (Turkey)
May 5, 1971—Pietro Scaglione (Sicily)
May 1, 1971—Roberto Quintanilla (West Germany)
April 8, 1971—Vladimir Rolovic (Sweden)
January 8, 1971—Geoffrey Jackson (Uruguay)
December 7, 1970—Giovanni Enrico Bucher (Brazil)
November 27, 1970—Pope Paul VI (Philippines)
November 25, 1970—James N. Colasonto (United States)
October 10, 1970—Pierre Laporte (Canada)
October 5, 1970—James Cross (Canada)
September 11, 1970—John Stewart (Jordan)
July 31, 1970—Dan Mitrione (Uruguay)
June 11, 1970—Ehrenfried von Holleben (Brazil)
June 9, 1970—King Hussein (Jordan)
May 29, 1970—Pedro Aramburu (Argentina)
March 30, 1970—Count Karl von Spreti (Guatemala)
September 9, 1969—Murray Jackson (Ethiopia)
September 4, 1969—Charles Burke (Brazil)
May 22, 1969—David Ben-Gurion (Denmark)
January 21, 1969—Leonid Brezhnev (Russia)
August 28, 1968—John G. Mein (Guatemala)
August 2, 1968—Meliton Manzanas (Spain)
June 5, 1968—Robert F. Kennedy (United States)
April 4, 1968—Martin Luther King Jr. (United States)
August 25, 1967—George L. Rockwell (United States)
August 7, 1967—Floyd Hoard (United States)
March 22, 1967—Leopold Senghor (Senegal)
September 6, 1966—Hendrik Verwoerd (South Africa)
June 21, 1966—Arthur Calwell (Australia)
February 21, 1965—Malcolm X (United States)
February 13, 1965—Humberto Delgado (Portugal)
January 21, 1965—Hassanali ali Mansur (Iran)
September 27, 1964—Adib Shishekly (Brazil)
March 24, 1964—Edwin O. Reischauer (Japan)
November 24, 1963—Lee Harvey Oswald (United States)
November 22, 1963—John F. Kennedy (United States)
June 12, 1963—Medgar Evers (United States)
April 10, 1963—Edwin Walker (United States)
August 22, 1962—Charles de Gaulle (France)
September 8, 1961—Charles de Gaulle (France)
May 30, 1961—Rafael Trujillo Molina (Dominican Republic)
August 29, 1960—Hazza Majali (Jordan)
June 24, 1960—Romulo Betancourt (Venezuela)
May 11, 1960—Adolf Eichmann (Argentina)

April 9, 1960—Hendrik Verwoerd (South Africa)
February 8, 1960—Adolph Coors III (United States)
October 15, 1959—Stefan Bandera (Germany)
September 25, 1959—Solomon Bandaranaike (Ceylon)
October 12, 1957—Lev Rebet (Germany)
April 9, 1957—Ante Pavelic (Argentina)
September 21, 1956—Anastasio Somoza Garcia (Nicaragua)
June 15, 1955—C.E. Chillingworth (United States)
January 2, 1955—Jose Antonio Remón (Panama)
October 26, 1954—Gamal Abdel-Nasser (Egypt)
June 18, 1954—Albert Patterson (United States)
January 13, 1954—Allison Wade (United States)
October 16, 1951—Liaquat Ali Khan (Pakistan)
July 20, 1951—Abdullah ibn-Hussein (Israel)
March 7, 1951—Sepahbod Haj Ali Razmara (Iran)
November 13, 1950—Carlos Delgado Chalbaud (Venezuela)
November 1, 1950—Harry Truman (United States)
August 18, 1950—Julien Lahaut (Belgium)

2

Global Statistics

From January 1950 through December 2008 there were a total of nine hundred targeted attacks (assassinations, contract killings, and kidnappings) that were documented to have been perpetrated around the world. It wasn't until the 1970s, however, that these types of attacks came into increasing use. Targeted attacks since then have been on a steady climb over the last three decades. These types of ambushes have been employed by a wide variety of adversaries, ranging from mafia families, to terrorist organizations, to business and political rivals, and even to governments.

The following pages show the statistical breakdown of attacks both worldwide and regionally, which are further reduced by the month in which the attack took place, the day of the week, and even the hour (if able to be determined). The goal is for the reader to obtain an overall understanding of when targeted attacks were staged, and if there was a particular time frame that saw more of this activity than another. By further breaking the numbers down by region, those who work in these areas, either providing protection or within one of the main targeted classes, are provided with a more detailed statistical picture of their immediate environment.

As Figure 2.1 indicates, the first eight years of the 2000s had already exceeded the previous record number of targeted attacks that were documented as occurring during the 1980s. One factor that has probably influenced the numbers of attacks is the advent of the Internet, allowing for information regarding attacks to be almost immediately available, and therefore providing greater recognition of an attack (an obvious terrorist organization goal).

Reviewing the global targeted attacks by the month in which they were staged reveals a fair amount of regularity throughout the calendar year (Figure 2.2). While March documented the greatest number of attacks, it was only by a factor of eleven over the next highest month, September. While the average number of attacks per month was seventy-five, only seven experienced that amount or more.

Targeted attacks have been found to overwhelmingly occur during the traditional workweek of Monday through Friday. This is obviously when most people, especially those in an urban environment, can be found following a more predicable routine of movement. However, as Figure 2.3 reveals, there is a slight concentration between Monday and Wednesday.

Targeted attacks reviewed by the time of day continued the trend of being focused upon a victim's more predictable movement routine. The vast majority of the targeted

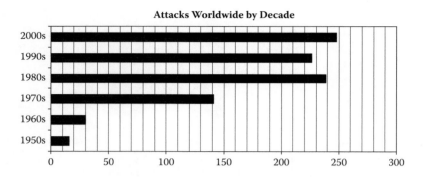

FIGURE 2.1   Attacks worldwide by decade.

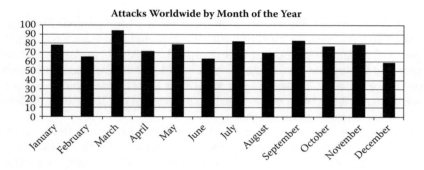

FIGURE 2.2   Attacks worldwide by month of the year.

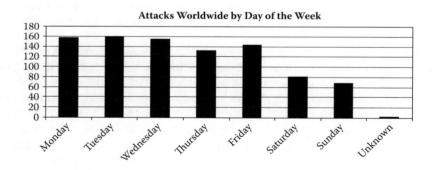

FIGURE 2.3   Attacks worldwide by day of the week.

attacks for which the timing could be determined were found to have occurred during the morning hours between 0601 and 0900 (Figure 2.4). This was followed closely by the evening hours between 1801 and 2100. These two time periods are when people living in the urban environment are generally departing from or arriving to their home or office, or are in transit between these locations.

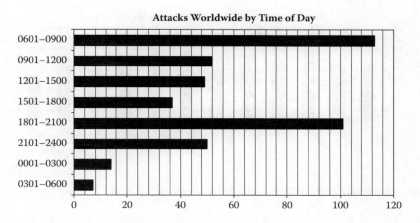

FIGURE 2.4 Attacks worldwide by time of day.

ATTACKS AGAINST VEHICLE-BORNE VICTIMS

Attacks committed strictly against the mobile or vehicle-borne victim over the past fifty-eight years have remained fairly consistent since the 1980s, when there was a dramatic increase (Figure 2.5). The first eight years of the 2000s, however, saw the most of any previous decade.

When targeted attacks were examined exclusively by those staged against vehicle-borne victims, which accounted for 364, a shift in the preferred months of attack was revealed. July documented the most attacks, followed relatively closely by March and August (Figure 2.6). However, the average number of attacks perpetrated against the vehicle-borne victim was thirty per month.

When examined by the day of the week, targeted attacks staged against vehicle-borne victims remained consistent with the global statistics (Figure 2.7). The victim was most often targeted between Monday and Friday. In fact, the same number of attacks was found to have occurred on Mondays, Tuesdays, and Wednesdays.

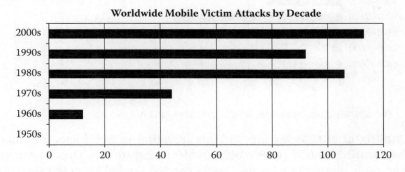

FIGURE 2.5 Worldwide mobile victim attacks by decade.

25

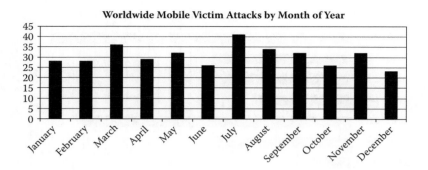

FIGURE 2.6 Worldwide mobile victim attacks by month of the year.

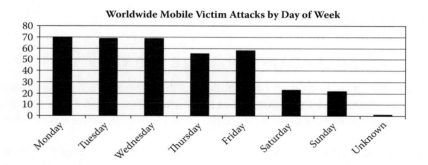

FIGURE 2.7 Worldwide mobile victim attacks by day of the week.

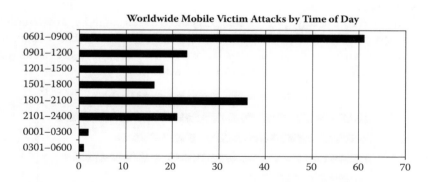

FIGURE 2.8 Worldwide mobile victim attacks by time of day.

In the timing of attacks against victims traveling in a vehicle, the majority were staged in the morning hours between 0601 and 0900 (Figure 2.8). This represented almost double the amount of attacks recorded being carried out between the evening hours of 1801 and 2100.

ATTACKS AGAINST PEDESTRIAN TARGETS

In attacks staged against the pedestrian-based victim since 1950, there has been a steady increase beginning in the 1970s (Figure 2.9). However, as of December 2008, the majority of attacks against pedestrian victims occurred during the 1990s.

In reviewing the 454 pedestrian attacks conducted worldwide, March had the majority documented (Figure 2.10). October followed with the next highest number of attacks. On average there were thirty-eight ambushes conducted against pedestrian-based victims every month.

Attacks perpetrated against pedestrian victims saw consistent numbers throughout the workweek, with Friday recording the most of any given day (Figure 2.11). What is of note was the elevated number of attacks being staged against pedestrian victims during the weekend, especially on Saturday.

In a reversal of the results of attacks against vehicle-borne victims, those conducted against pedestrian-based victims were more common during the evening hours between 1801 and 2100 (Figure 2.12). However, attacks against pedestrians during the hours between 0601 and 0900 still ranked high, with the second most number of attacks.

There were an additional seventy-six targeted attacks that were perpetrated against victims during which their exact position, either on foot or in a vehicle, was not able to

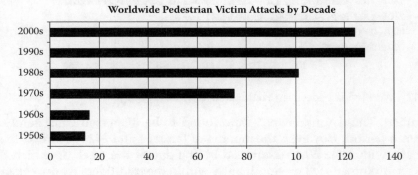

FIGURE 2.9 Worldwide pedestrian victim attacks by decade.

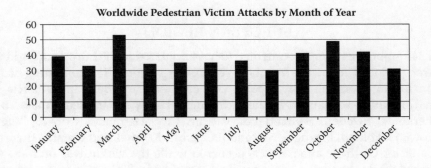

FIGURE 2.10 Worldwide pedestrian victim attacks by month of the year.

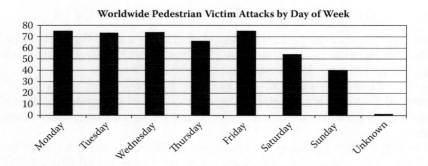

FIGURE 2.11 Worldwide pedestrian attacks by day of the week.

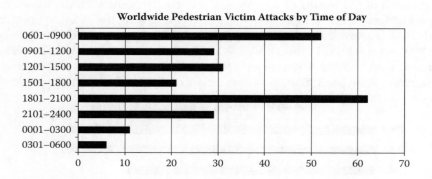

FIGURE 2.12 Worldwide pedestrian victim attacks by time of day.

be determined. These "unknowns" were found to be dispersed consistently over the twelve-month period. However, the months of January and May recorded the greatest number, each with 14%. When examined by the day of the week on which the attack occurred, the unknowns fell predominantly within the traditional workweek of Monday through Friday.

EUROPEAN REGION

A total of 340 ambushes were documented to have occurred in the European region during the research period. There were twenty-seven European countries, consisting of Albania, France (including Corsica), Italy, Spain, Greece, Germany, Belgium, Austria, United Kingdom (England, Scotland, Northern Ireland), Hungary, Ireland, Malta, Bulgaria, the Netherlands, Sweden, Switzerland, Vatican City, Denmark, Corsica, Yugoslavia, Czechoslovakia, Poland, Portugal, Macedonia, Serbia, Kosovo, and Croatia, that recorded targeted attacks. Of those attacks, 52% occurred while the victim was on foot. Another 34% occurred while the victim was traveling in a vehicle. The remaining 14% of attacks were staged when the victim's status could not be determined.

When examined by individual country, Italy documented the greatest number of attacks in the region with 24%. France recorded 15% of the attacks, the second highest number. Spain followed closely behind with 14% of all hits. The United Kingdom and Greece rounded out the top five, with each accounting for 9% of the targeted attacks.

When examined by the decade in which the attacks occurred, the 1980s were the most violent for the European region, with more than 130 attacks (Figure 2.13). Since that record high, Europe has witnessed a gradual decrease in the use of targeted attacks. Much of this can be attributed to the successes obtained by the governments of the individual countries against the various terrorist groups and mafias that were running rampant between the 1970s and early 1990s.

Overall in Europe, the month of July experienced the greatest number of attacks, but accounted for only 11% of the total. August had the least number of attacks, with only 4%. As Figure 2.14 indicates, attacks within the European region occurred with some regularity, averaging twenty-eight a month throughout the year. In examining the 115 attacks staged against vehicle-borne targets, the month of July experienced the single largest number of ambushes, accounting for 17% of all attacks over the twelve-month period.

For pedestrian-based targeted attacks, of which there were 178, the month of October ranked the highest, accounting for 12%. However, the greatest concentration of attacks

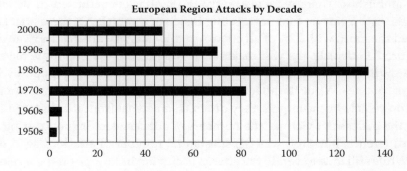

FIGURE 2.13   European region attacks by decade.

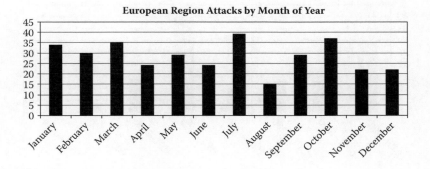

FIGURE 2.14   European region attacks by month of the year.

29

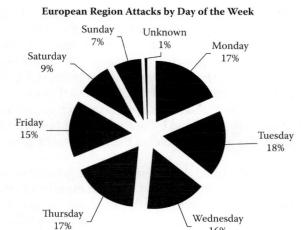

FIGURE 2.15 European region attacks by day of the week.

against pedestrian victims occurred during the winter months and accounted for just over 36% of all ambushes. There were also forty-seven attacks conducted in which it is not known if the victim was on foot or traveling inside of a vehicle. Of these attacks, January documented the most, with 22% of all attacks in this category during the twelve months.

As Figure 2.15 depicts, the vast majority of targeted attacks in Europe have occurred during the traditional workweek, when the victim was generally trapped by his or her employment routines. While the attack percentages in Figure 2.15 are consistent with those for attacks on vehicle-borne targets, they differed somewhat from attacks targeting pedestrians. For the pedestrian victims, the numbers of attacks were highest during the workweek; the difference, however, was the substantial number of attacks staged during the weekend. While still lower overall, the attacks occurring in Europe on the weekends were the highest of any region on earth.

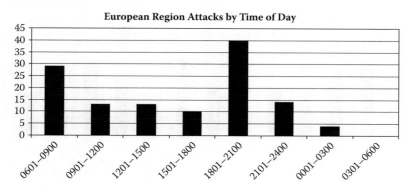

FIGURE 2.16 European region attacks by time of day.

Of the targeted attacks conducted within the European region for which the time of attack was able to be determined, they were discovered to have been staged most often during the evening hours between 1801 and 2100 (Figure 2.16). This was followed by attacks during the morning hours between 0601 and 0900. These hours are generally when victims are in the process of arriving to or departing from their residence or office or in transit between these two locations.

Methods of Attack

The preferred methods of attack in Europe were shootings, which accounted for 63% of all the ambushes. Of these shootings, 17% of them came at the hands of a lone gunman. This was followed by another 17% perpetrated by hit teams consisting of two gunmen. An additional 12% of shooting attacks were carried out by hit teams of between three and five gunmen. Finally, 7% of attacks employing firearms came from motorcycle hit teams (of which most had two riders and were not counted as a two-gunmen hit team). The remaining shooting attacks came in the form of drive-bys, or were carried out by snipers, or an unknown number of gunmen.

Targeted attacks in Europe using explosives were a close second in the total number, accounting for 19%. Of those, the improvised explosive device (IED) was used in 33% of the ambushes. This was followed by the booby-trap device, which was documented as having been deployed 30% of the time. The vehicle-borne improvised explosive device (VBIED) was used in 27% of the attacks. The remaining attacks using explosives came in the form of rocket-propelled grenades, mortars, or hand grenades.

Italy

Italy had the greatest number of targeted attacks of any country in Europe, with eighty-three. Of those, twelve ambushes were conducted employing unknown methods of attack. In the remaining cases in which the methods of attack were able to be determined, shootings ranked as the number one form of attack, accounting for 77%. Of those shooting attacks, 16% were carried out by teams of between three and five gunmen. Motorcycle hit teams, a lone gunman, and two-gunmen hit teams were each responsible for a further 13% of attacks using firearms. The remaining shooting attacks were perpetrated by teams consisting of six or more gunmen or unknown numbers of gunmen.

The next most preferred method of attack in Italy was kidnapping, which was documented in 13% of the ambushes. Explosive-based targeted attacks were used 8% of the time, of which the VBIED was employed on three occasions, followed by the booby-trap device twice, and a single attack by IED.

France (including Corsica)

As with Italy, France experienced a predominance of shootings in the known targeted attacks (four employed an unknown method), ultimately accounting for a total of 74% of all ambushes. Of these firearms-based attacks, 32% of them were carried out by an unknown number of shooters. In the remaining attacks in which the type of shooting could be determined, teams of two gunmen struck 26% of the time. The lone gunman was a close second, responsible for 21% of the shootings. Motorcycle hit teams struck in 12%

31

of the targeted attacks, while attacks by teams of between three and five gunmen were responsible for another 9%.

Explosives were documented in 12% of the known targeted attacks. Of those, the IED was used in three of the attacks, followed by the booby-trap device on two other occasions. A single attack by firebomb (Molotov cocktail) was also recorded. Of the remaining targeted attacks in France, four used edged weapons. There was also a single case of poison being used in a targeted attack, as well as a single kidnapping.

Spain

Spain experienced forty-six targeted attacks over the research period, of which the use of firearms accounted for 61% of the total. Unfortunately, in 54% of these shootings, the exact methods of attack could not be determined. In those attacks where the method was known, 54% came in the form of hit teams consisting of two gunmen. This was followed by another 31% being perpetrated by a lone gunman. The remaining shooting attacks came at the hands of motorcycle hit teams, or in drive-bys.

Explosives were used in a considerable number of targeted attacks in Spain, accounting for 33% of the total. VBIEDs were deployed the most often, with 40% of the attacks. IEDs and booby-trap devices were each used in another 27% of attacks. There was also a single case of a grenade-based attack conducted upon a target. Finally, Spain documented three targeted kidnappings.

United Kingdom (including Scotland and Northern Ireland)

The United Kingdom documented a total of thirty-one attacks during the research period, the bulk of which were staged inside of the borders of England. As with the other nations, firearms-based attacks occurred the most often, accounting for 48%. In these shooting ambushes, a lone gunman was found to be behind five of the attacks. Hit teams of two gunmen were responsible for another three. The remaining shootings consisted of drive-bys, a hit by a team of between three and five gunmen, or could not be determined.

Explosives were documented in 35% of the attacks in the United Kingdom. The booby-trap device saw the most use, being deployed in seven of the attacks. The IED was used in another three, while a single case of a grenade-based ambush was also recorded. There were two targeted kidnappings and two attacks in which poison was the weapon of choice. Finally, there was also a single ambush during which the victim was violently assaulted by men using clubs.

Greece

Greece documented thirty targeted attacks, of which only one used an unknown method. The use of firearms was the dominant method of attack in Greece, responsible for 66% of the total. Of these shootings, there were four attacks conducted by hit teams of between three and five gunmen. Another three ambushes came at the hands of a lone gunman. This was followed by two attacks perpetrated by motorcycle hit teams.

Explosives were also deployed with some regularity in targeted attacks in Greece, accounting for 31% of the attacks. The VBIED saw the greatest amount of use, with five documented attacks. Three ambushes used an IED of some configuration, while one attack was conducted using a rocket-propelled grenade. There was also a single known case of targeted kidnapping.

Germany

Germany documented twenty-three targeted attacks over the fifty-eight-year period. Of those ambushes, eleven involved firearms using a variety of methods. Three of the attacks were perpetrated by hit teams of two gunmen. A lone gunman was recorded as carrying out two of the attacks, as were hit teams of between three and five gunmen. A motorcycle hit team and a sniper were each responsible for single attacks. The remaining attack was carried out by an unknown methodology.

Explosives were used in five of the targeted hits. Two attacks involved an IED being deployed. There was one recorded case of a VBIED-based attack, followed by a single known use of a booby-trap device. Germany also had one of the few targeted attacks using a rocket-propelled grenade. There were four targeted kidnappings, followed by two poison-based attacks, and one attack by edged weapon.

Other Countries

Seventy-six attacks were documented as having occurred in the remaining twenty countries of the region. As with other regions, firearms saw the most use, with 68% of the attacks. Explosives were used in 14% of the targeted attacks, followed by kidnappings occurring 12% of the time. The rest of the attacks interestingly enough came by way of edged weapons.

Regardless of what form the method of attack took in the European region, the adversaries were successful (target kidnapped or killed) 80% of the time. That is just above the average experienced in the five countries with the greatest number of targeted attacks. Italy documented the success rate at 90%. France experienced a 77% rate of success, while Spain documented a 93% success rate. Attacks in the United Kingdom recorded a 55% rate of success, whereas Greece documented a 73% success rate.

Locations of Attack

The locations selected by hostile groups in Europe to spring their ambushes were fairly consistent with the global statistics. Of the known attack locations (fifty could not be determined), at or within close proximity (500 meters or less) of the residence was the most often selected site, accounting for 43% of all attacks. Ambushes staged against victims in transit were the second most popular location (given that a specific place along the victim's route was selected as the ambush point) and accounted for 29% of the attacks. The victim's office came in third, with 10% of the attacks. The remaining ambushes were dispersed over public events, bars/restaurants, hotels, and frequented locations.

Italy

In fifty-nine of the attacks was the location able to be determined. Of those, attacks on victims in transit occurred 44% of the time (in at least two cases, the ambush site was a traffic intersection). This was followed by attacks staged at or near the victim's residence, accounting for 39%. Following distantly were attacks staged at or near the victim's office (when examining judges, this statistic includes attacks occurring at the office as well as those at a courthouse/room, as often they are both located within close proximity to each other or are in the same building) at 8%.

France (including Corsica)
In nine of the attacks, the exact location of the ambush site could not be determined. In the remaining forty-one, the area of the victim's residence was the location most often selected for the ambush, accounting for 46% of the total. This was followed by attacks targeting victims in transit 24% of the time. Attacks staged in the area of the victim's office were a distant third, with only 10% of the ambushes.

Spain
Of the forty-three attacks where the location was able to be determined, 40% occurred at or near the victim's residence. Another 35% occurred while the victim was in transit (one of which was known to have been staged at a traffic intersection). Attacks sprung in the area of the victim's office and restaurants followed distantly, each accounting for 9% of the total.

United Kingdom
Of the thirty attacks wherein the exact location was determined (only one attack was not known), the area of the residence had the most activity, accounting for 53% of the total number of ambushes. Attacks against victims in transit were conducted 23% of the time, followed by attacks at or near the victim's office or while at a hotel, both of which accounted for 10%.

Greece
In five of the attacks, the exact location could not be determined. Of those that were known, 44% of the ambushes were staged while the victim was in transit. At or within close proximity of the victim's residence accounted for another 40% of the attacks, while the area of the victim's office was the site of 12% of the attacks.

Germany
In two of the attacks, the exact location could not be determined. Of those that were known, 48% occurred at or near the residence. Ambushes staged against victims in transit accounted for another 38% of attacks (of which one was known to have occurred at a traffic intersection). Interestingly, there was only one known attack found to have occurred in the area of the victim's office.

Other Countries
In seven of the attacks occurring in the remaining countries of the region, the ambush site could not be determined. Of those that were known, attacks at or near the victim's residence occurred 44% of the time. Attacks on victims in transit occurred 24% of the time (of which two were known to have occurred at traffic intersections). The victim's office was the third most often selected site of attacks, accounting for 15% of the total.

Victims of Attack

In Europe, the number one victim of the targeted assassination, contract killing, or kid-napping was the corporate executive, which recorded 11% of the attacks. Following with 10% of the attacks, the diplomat was the second most often targeted victim. The judge accounted for 8% of all targeted victims, while the law enforcement official rounded out the top four targets at 7%. The remaining attacks targeted every other class of victim, from physician to world leader.

Italy
Italy witnessed the representatives of law and order attacked the most often. Law enforce-ment officials were the target in Italy 20% of the time. Judges fell victim in 17% of the attacks, followed closely by prosecutors being targeted 11% of the time. Federal govern-ment officials followed a distant fourth, accounting for 7% of the victims. The remaining attacks focused upon individuals within eighteen separate categories.

France
World leaders and terrorists tied for the most often targeted victim, each accounting for 14% of attacks. Diplomats and embassy staffers were tied for second, each of which suf-fered 12% of attacks. The remaining ambushes were conducted against twelve other cat-egories of victim.

Spain
Spain saw its military officials targeted 24% of the time, while city/town council members were on the receiving end of another 17% of attacks. Judges rounded out the top three, being attacked 11% of the time. The remaining ambushes were carried out against sixteen other categories of victim.

United Kingdom
In the United Kingdom corporate executives and activists/dissidents suffered the most targeted attacks, each accounting for 19% of the total. World leaders were the next most often targeted victim, documenting 13% of the attacks. Diplomats and lawmakers rounded out the top five, each of which was attacked 9% of the time. The remaining attacks targeted eight other classes of victim.

Greece
As in the United Kingdom, corporate executives in Greece suffered the most attacks, resulting in their being a victim 23% of the time. Embassy staffers from a variety of coun-tries were targeted 17% of the time. Military officials and prosecutors were next in line, each being attacked 13% of the time. The remaining hits were focused upon eight different classes of victim.

Germany
Corporate executives were again the target of choice, falling victim to 30% of the attacks. Government ministers came in next, with 17% of the total, followed by hits carried out

against the activist/dissident 13% of the time. The remaining attacks targeted seven other classes of victim.

Other Countries

In other countries, diplomats were the target of choice, being attacked 21% of the time. They were followed by corporate executives in 11% of the attacks. Embassy staffers fell victim to 9% of the targeted ambushes, with world leaders and the activist/dissident each accounting for another 7% of attacks. The remaining ambushes were staged against eleven other classes of victim.

The Adversaries

In the European region there were fifty-six separate individuals or organizations identified, either by claiming responsibility or found to have been responsible for one or more of the attacks through the investigation. Additionally, there were another forty attacks that were perpetrated by an unknown adversary. Of the known groups, terrorist/extremist organizations were behind the vast majority of the attacks. Organized criminal groups were the second most often encountered adversary, followed by government agents and criminals.

Italy

With the most number of attacks, Italy also experienced the largest number of adversaries. Of the eighty-three attacks in Italy, only eight came at the hands of unknown groups or individuals. Of the remaining seventy-five attacks, 61% were carried out by terrorist/extremist groups. Organized criminal groups were responsible for another 33% of the targeted attacks. The remaining attacks were carried out by government agents, or rivals.

France

In seventeen of the fifty attacks conducted, the adversary was never identified. Of those that were known, 67% were carried out by terrorist/extremist groups or individuals. Another 24% of the attacks came at the hands of government agents, followed by the remaining 9% from criminals.

Spain

Spain is unique among the countries of Europe in that while 100% of its targeted attacks came from terrorist/extremist groups, the vast majority came from a single organization. The Euskadi ta Askatasuna (ETA) accounted for 93% of all known ambushes (the adversaries in two attacks were not known) occurring during the research period.

Greece

In twenty-nine out of thirty attacks in which the perpetrator was known, terrorist/extremist groups struck 93% of the time. The remaining 7% were conducted by government agents, or criminals.

United Kingdom

In five of the attacks the identity of the adversary was never determined. Of the remaining twenty-six, terrorists/extremist groups were responsible for 80% of the ambushes. The remaining 20% were known or believed to have been carried out by government agents.

Germany

In only one case was the perpetrator not known. Of the remaining twenty-two attacks, terrorist/extremist groups were behind 73%. The remaining attacks were evenly split between criminals and government agents.

Other Countries

Of the seventy-six attacks conducted, fifteen came from unknown individuals or groups. Of those that were known, 59% were carried out by terrorist/extremist groups. Government agents were known or believed to be behind another 23% of attacks. Criminals were found to have conducted 10% of the attacks, followed by criminal organizations with 8%.

NORTH AMERICA

Beginning in January 1950 through the end of December 2008, there were 151 urban ambushes known to have occurred in the North American countries of the United States, Canada, Mexico, Haiti, Jamaica, and the Dominican Republic. Of those attacks, 67% occurred while the target was on foot. Another 29% occurred while the target was mobile in a vehicle, with the remaining 4% of attacks occurring while the victim's status was unknown. The United States accounted for far and away the most attacks, with 60%. Mexico came in second at 31% (a large percentage of this increase occurred as a result of the drug cartel wars being experienced in the country in the later 2000s).

As Figure 2.17 indicates, North America has been experiencing a gradual increase in targeted attacks that really began in the 1970s (albeit there was a slight decrease during the 1980s), and if the first few months of 2009 were any indication, that increase will only continue.

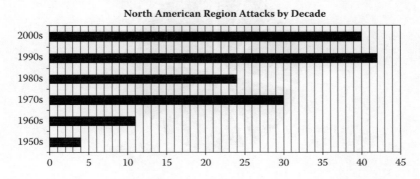

FIGURE 2.17 North American region attacks by decade.

With 15%, the month of May documented the greatest number of attacks (Figure 2.18). When examining the vehicle-borne targets only, the month of May had the single largest number of ambushes, accounting for 22% of all attacks over the twelve-month period. For pedestrian-based targeted attacks, three separate months experienced the bulk of activity. March had the most attacks, accounting for 13%. This was followed by November with 12% and May at 11% of attacks over the twelve-month period.

In North America, the vast majority of targeted attacks have occurred during the traditional workweek, when the victim is generally trapped by his or her employment routine. While the attack percentages in Figure 2.19 are consistent with those in pedestrian-based attacks, the numbers targeting a mobile victim were different. For the mobile victim, Monday experienced the greatest number of attacks at 30%, with Friday coming a close second at 21%.

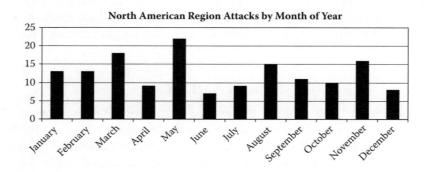

FIGURE 2.18   North American region attacks by month of the year.

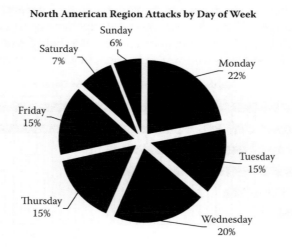

FIGURE 2.19   North American attacks by day of the week.

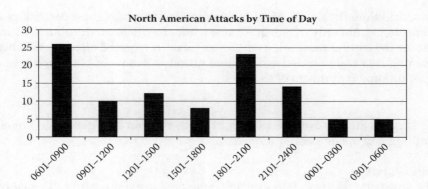

North American Attacks by Time of Day

FIGURE 2.20 North American attacks by time of day.

As noted in other breakdowns, the majority of the targeted attacks occurred while the victim was moving within his or her traditional workweek routine (Figure 2.20). The attacks largely occurred at times when the victim was either in the process of arriving to or departing from his or her residence or office, or in transit between those two locations. Interesting though, was the slight increase around the lunchtime hour. All of these numbers were fairly consistent regardless of whether the targeted victim was mobile or on foot.

Methods of Attack

The preferred method of attack in North America was shootings, accounting for 80% of all the attacks. Of these shootings, 42% of them came at the hands of a lone gunman. Approximately 12% of them took the form of drive-by attacks (in which the number of gunmen could not be confirmed, but would most likely be two or more individuals, including the driver). Another 11% of the shootings came from teams of two gunmen. The remaining hits were carried out by teams of between three and five gunmen, snipers, or an unknown numbers of gunmen.

United States

Consistent with the total North American percentages, shootings were also the number one form of attack, accounting for 81% of all ambushes. Of that 81%, 57% came from a lone gunman. Teams of two gunmen were responsible for 15%, and another 14% from snipers (unknown number of team members). The remaining shooting attacks came at the hands of between three and five gunmen or an unknown number of shooters.

The second most often employed method of targeted attack in the United States came through the use of explosives. However, in the United States the use of explosives, whether in the form of improvised explosive devices (IEDs), vehicle-borne IEDs (VBIEDs), fire-bombs, or booby traps, accounted for only 5% of the attacks.

Mexico

As with the United States, Mexico also experienced a predominance of shooting attacks, accounting for a total of 79%. Of these attacks, 38% of them involved an unknown number of shooters. Additionally, at 35%, Mexico also experienced the highest percentage of drive-by shooting attacks not only in North America, but anywhere on the planet. Kidnappings accounted for the second most often employed tactic in targeted attacks, standing at 15%. The remaining hits were carried out by lone gunmen, teams of between three and five gunmen, or unknown numbers of shooters.

Canada
With only six total attacks over the fifty-eight years, the numbers generated are not useful in determining any major technique/tactic.

Caribbean Islands
With only seven attacks total, the numbers generated are not useful in determining any major technique/tactic.

Regardless of what form the method of attack took in North America, the adversary was successful (target kidnapped or killed) 84% of the time. That is consistent with U.S. statistics, where the success rate stands at 84%. Mexico experienced an 83% rate of success.

Locations of Attack

The locations selected by the adversaries in North America to spring their ambushes were fairly consistent with the global statistics. The residence was the most often selected site, accounting for 33% of all attacks. The office came in second, with 21% of the attacks. Ambushes staged against victims in transit between two locations occurred 20% of the time. Of these, 20% occurred while the victim was stopped or slowed for some type of traffic control point at intersections. Finally, public events were the fourth most often selected site for an ambush at 7%.

United States
As with North America in total, the attacks occurring in the United States occurred most often at the victim's residence, accounting for 36%. This was followed closely by attacks occurring at or near the victim's office (when examining judges, this statistic includes attacks occurring at the office as well as those at a courthouse/room, as generally both are in the same location) at 26%. The public event at 9% was the third most frequent location selected to strike at the victim.

Mexico
Mexico witnessed 36% of its attacks occurring while the victim was in transit between two locations. This percentage is understandable given the high number of drive-by-style attacks experience in the country. The residence, at 21%, was the second most often selected location at which to ambush the victim. The office was a distant third, with only 11% of all attacks.

Canada and the Caribbean Islands
Even with the low total attack numbers, the residence was the number one location to stage the ambush.

Victims of Attack

In North America, the number one victim of the targeted assassination, contract killing, or kidnapping was the law enforcement officer at 19%. At 14%, the prosecutor was the second most often targeted victim. The judge was third, accounting for 12% of all targeted victims. The businessman/corporate executive rounded out the top four targets at 11%. This sequence is largely due to the seventeen law enforcement command officers assassinated in 2008 in Mexico. Without those killings, law enforcement command officers would have sat in fourth place.

United States

There was a slight reversal in the percentages of victims of attack in the United States, in that judges were the most often targeted class of individual, accounting for 19% of the total. This was followed closely by prosecutors at 14%. The businessman/CEO rounded out the top three at 12%. Activists and world leaders were tied for fourth, accounting for 10% of all victims.

Mexico

Mexico was in line with the North American totals, as it was the 2008 targeting in this country that caused law enforcement officers to rise to the top position. In Mexico, law enforcement officers (most holding command positions) accounted for 49% due to the seventeen law enforcement command officers targeted in 2008. While a distant second, prosecutors came in at 17%. The businessman/CEO was the third most targeted class of individual at 10%.

Canada and Caribbean Islands

In these countries there was no single most often targeted class of individual due to their low numbers of targeted attack victims.

The Adversaries

As a result of the dramatic increase in violence experienced in Mexico in 2008, the drug cartel statistically became one of the most often encountered adversaries. While the drug cartel's targeted hits have primarily occurred within the Mexican national boarders, there has been at least one known hit within the United States and several others that are suspected to have been by their hand. Moving away from the drug cartels reveals one of the major issues in studying and preparing for targeted killings. In North America there were thirty-nine separate individuals or organizations either claiming responsibility or found to have been responsible for one or more of the attacks. Further, another thirty-two of the attacks came at the hands of an unknown adversary. That provides an average of almost four attacks per group over the fifty-eight-year period. It is for this reason that it is critical for protective groups to study all types of attacks.

Of the known groups, drug cartels, at 23% of all attacks, were tied for the number one spot with terrorist/extremist organizations, which also accounted for 23% of the ambushes in North America. Individual criminals were the second most often encountered adversary, accounting for 11% of the attacks. Traditional organized crime groups were third overall, with 10% of the attacks.

United States
With the largest number of attacks, the United States also experienced the largest number of adversaries. Of the ninety-one attacks in the United States, seventeen came at the hands of unknown groups or individuals. Of the remaining seventy-four attacks, the general criminal accounted for 22%. The seventeen terrorist/extremist organizations or individuals known to have conducted targeted attacks accounted for another 35% of attacks. Organized criminal groups were the third most active at 19%.

Mexico
The drug cartels, as has been discussed, were the number one adversary, accounting for 49% of all ambushes. The remaining attacks came at the hands of unknown subjects 19% of the time. Three attacks came from rebel/terrorist groups, one from a lone criminal, and one believed to be a government-sponsored hit.

Canada and Caribbean Islands
Of the thirteen total attacks between these countries, six came from unknown groups/individuals. The remaining seven came at the hands of six known groups, five of which could be classified as terrorist/extremist organizations.

CENTRAL/SOUTH AMERICA

There were a total of 123 ambushes found to have occurred within the Central/South American region during the research period. Fifteen countries, consisting of Argentina, Brazil, Bolivia, Chile, Colombia, Ecuador, El Salvador, Guatemala, Honduras, Nicaragua, Panama, Paraguay, Peru, Uruguay, and Venezuela, documented targeted attacks. Of those attacks, 52% occurred while the target was vehicle borne. Another 34% occurred while the target was on foot, with the remaining 14% of attacks occurring while the victim's status

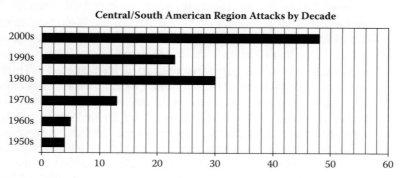

FIGURE 2.21 Central/South American region attacks by decade.

42

was unknown. Colombia documented the majority of attacks with 54%, followed distantly by Brazil with 9%. The countries of Argentina and Guatemala, each of which accounted for 7%, rounded out the top four.

The Central/South American region has witnessed a dramatic increase in targeted attacks during the first eight years of the 2000s, having already doubled what was recorded in the 1990s (Figure 2.21). If this pace continues, then this region may well experience a doubling of the total attacks that were staged during the 1980s.

September recorded the most attacks within the Central/South American region, accounting for 14% of those conducted against both vehicle-borne and pedestrian targets (Figure 2.22). November followed closely with 12%. This was consistent with ambushes staged against vehicle-borne-only targets, with September documenting 15% of the attacks. The majority of attacks against pedestrian targets occurred in November, with 17%.

As Figure 2.23 indicates, targeted violence attacks in the Central/South American region were staged almost equally throughout the workweek, with little in the way of

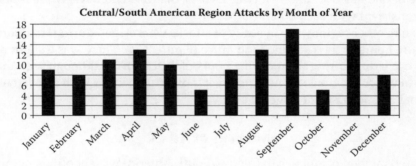

FIGURE 2.22   Central/South American region attacks by month of the year.

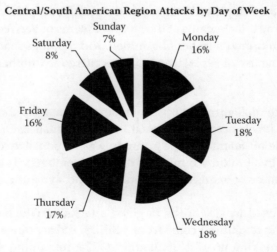

FIGURE 2.23   Central/South American region attacks by day of the week.

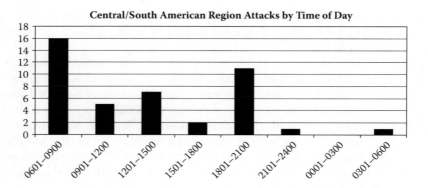

FIGURE 2.24   Central/South American region attacks by time of day.

preference of one day over another. Attacks over the weekend days, while reduced, were also still consistent with each other.

As seen in other regions, the majority of attacks were staged during traditional arrival or departure hours of the residence and office (Figure 2.24). There was a slight preference of attacks occurring during the morning hours of 0601 to 0900, although with the number of attacks in which the time was not known, it is difficult to know with any certainty if this is a regional characteristic of targeted attacks.

Methods of Attack

The preferred method of ambush in Central/South America was shootings, accounting for 67% of all the attacks. Of these shootings, 28% of them came at the hands of motorcycle hit teams. A lone gunman was responsible for 11% of the attacks, as were teams of two gunmen. Drive-bys were also employed in many of the attacks, accounting for 10% of the total. The remaining shooting attacks came at the hands of teams of between three and five gunmen, snipers, or an unknown number of gunmen. Kidnappings made up 22% of the total attacks, followed by the use of explosives, which occurred in another 12%.

Colombia

Consistent with the total Central/South American percentages, shootings were also the number one form of attack, accounting for 68% of all ambushes. Of that percentage, 40% came from motorcycle hit teams. A lone gunman was responsible for 11%, while another 9% came from drive-bys (unknown number of team members). The remaining shooting attacks came at the hands of teams of between three and five gunmen or unknown numbers of gunmen.

Explosives were used in 11% of the targeted attacks, of which the IED was used in 57% of those, while the remaining came from VBIEDs. Kidnappings were also a common tactic in this region, making up 17% of all attacks. The remaining ambushes came in an unknown form.

Brazil

As with Colombia, Brazil also experienced a predominance of shooting attacks, accounting for a total of 72%. Of these attacks, 38% came by way of drive-bys, followed closely by motorcycle hit teams, with 25% of the total. Only one attack was known to have been conducted by a lone gunman, while the remaining firearm attacks came in an unknown form. While no explosive-based attacks were recorded in Brazil, there were three targeted kidnappings documented during the research period.

Guatemala

Seven of the nine targeted attacks recorded the use of firearms. One came by way of a motorcycle hit team and another from a hit team of between three and five shooters. The remaining shooting attacks came in an unknown form or tactic. While no explosive attacks were recorded, two kidnappings were documented.

Argentina

Of the nine targeted attacks documented, seven were kidnappings. The last two were shooting attacks, one of which was perpetrated by a lone gunman.

Other Countries

Of the twenty-six attacks occurring in the remaining countries, seventeen were shooting attacks. Another seven used explosives, while the final two where kidnappings.

Regardless of what form the method of attack took in Central/South America, the adversary was successful (target kidnapped or killed) 87% of the time. That is consistent with Colombia's statistics, where the success rate stands at 89%. Brazil experienced a 91% rate of success, while Guatemala and Argentina each recorded an 89% rate of success.

Locations of Attack

The locations selected by the adversaries in Central/South America to spring their ambushes were fairly consistent with the global statistics. Attacks targeting victims in transit occurred the most often, accounting for 41% of the total. The residence was the second most often selected site, accounting for 17% of all attacks. The office, with 7%, rounded out the top three locations.

Colombia

Attacks occurring in Colombia (twelve occurred at unknown locations) happened most often while the victim was in transit, accounting for 52% (four of which were sprung at traffic congestion points or intersections). This was followed closely by attacks occurring at or near the victim's residence 20% of the time. The victim's office was the site of 11% of the targeted attacks. The remaining were staged at public events, hotels, aircraft/airports, frequented locations, and universities.

Brazil

As with Colombia, victims were ambushed 67% of the time while in transit. The remaining attacks were conducted at the residence, a frequented location, or could not be determined.

Guatemala
Guatemala suffered attacks over a more diverse spectrum of sites, including three at the residence, two each at the office, and while in transit. One attack occurred at a courthouse, while the final one was staged at an unknown location.

Argentina
Unfortunately four of the attacks occurred at an undetermined locale. Of the five known, two occurred at a residence, two were conducted while the victim was in transit, and one at a victim's office.

Other Countries
Thirteen attacks were staged while the victim was in transit. Five attacks were conducted at or near the victim's residence, while the remaining occurred at public events, the victim's office, or could not be determined.

Victims of Attack

In Central/South America, the number one victim of the targeted assassination, contract killing, or kidnapping was the lawmaker at 13%. The judge was second, accounting for 12% of all targeted victims. World leaders and prosecutors each fell victim to 10% of the attacks, while law enforcement officials round out the top four, targeted 8% of the time.

Colombia
Colombia saw nineteen classes of victims targeted for violence during the research period. Of those victims, judges were attacked 17% of the time, the most of any group. Lawmakers were the next most often targeted subjects, accounting for 15% of the total. Prosecutors were next, experiencing 12% of the attacks, followed by law enforcement officials, with 11% of the total.

Brazil
Brazil witnessed its twelve documented attacks perpetrated against six classes of victim. Diplomats suffered the most with three attacks, followed by judges, mayors, and lawmakers, which each had two. World leaders and prosecutors were each recorded as being attacked once.

Guatemala
Guatemala saw only the diplomat attacked more than once. The remaining seven attacks targeted seven separate classes of victim.

Argentina
The corporate executive was targeted in five out of the nine documented targeted attacks. World War II criminals were each attacked twice, followed by one attack on a diplomat and one against a world leader.

The Adversaries

Of the known groups, terrorist/extremist organizations were behind 61% of all targeted attacks in Central/South America. The various drug cartels were behind another 25% of all attacks. Government agents were known or suspected to be behind 8% of the remaining attacks.

Colombia
In only forty-two of the documented attacks was the responsible party able to be determined. Of those, Fuerzas Armadas Revolucionarias de Colombia (FARC) was the most active, conducting 45% of the total known. Drug cartels were behind another 38% of attacks. The remaining attacks were conducted by the Ejército de Liberación Nacional, (ELN) terrorist groups, the National Liberation Army (NLA), Movimiento 19 de abril (M-19), or in the case of two attacks, government agents.

Brazil
Brazil attributed its six targeted attacks in which the adversary was identified to five groups. An Islamic extremist was behind one, a local drug cartel behind another, while organized criminal groups conducted two. The Revolutionary Active Front was behind a single targeted attack, as was the National Liberation Action (ALN).

Guatemala
Unfortunately, all but one of the attacks was conducted by unknown individuals or groups. The one known attack was attributed to the Rebel Armed Forces (FAR) group.

Argentina
The terrorist group Ejército Revolucionario del Pueblo (ERP) was found to be behind four of the nine attacks. Three others were carried out by the Montonerros group, while one was perpetrated by an extremist, and the final one by government agents.

MIDDLE EAST

There were a total of eighty-four targeted attacks documented to have occurred in the Middle East region during the research period. Fourteen countries, consisting of Egypt, Jordan, Iran, Cyprus, Iraq, Israel, Lebanon, Qatar, Saudi Arabia, Turkey, Palestine, Kuwait, Yemen, and Syria, all recorded ambushes. Of these attacks, 36% occurred while the target was on foot. Another 60% occurred while the target was traveling in a vehicle, while the remaining 4% of attacks were staged while the victim's status was unknown. Lebanon documented the most attacks, with just over 40%, followed distantly by Turkey with 15%. Egypt rounded out the top three with 11%.

Over the preceding fifty-eight years, the Middle East region has maintained a steady rate of attacks since the literal explosion of the 1980s (Figure 2.25). While there was somewhat of a decrease in targeted attacks experienced in the 1990s, the first eight years of the 2000s were on pace to have a record number.

Within the Middle Eastern region the month of January experienced the greatest number of attacks, accounting for 13% of the total (Figure 2.26). This was consistent

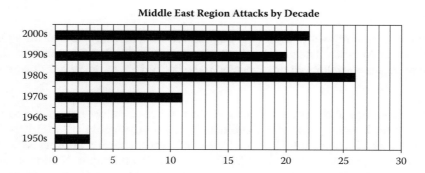

FIGURE 2.25 Middle East region attacks by decade.

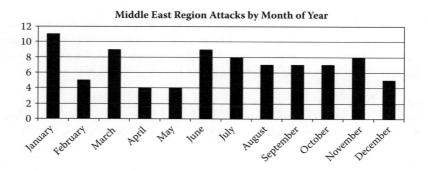

FIGURE 2.26 Middle East region attacks by month of the year.

with the attacks conducted solely upon mobile targets, wherein January also had the single largest number of ambushes, accounting for 16% over the twelve-month period. With pedestrian-based targeted attacks, August documented the bulk of activity, accounting for 19%.

The vast majority of targeted attacks were found to have occurred during the traditional workweek, when the victim was following his or her usual employment routine. While these attack percentages, as listed in Figure 2.27, are consistent with those in pedestrian-based attacks, the numbers targeting a mobile victim were different. For the mobile victim, Monday experienced the greatest number of attacks at 30%, with Friday coming a close second at 21%.

Consistent with the previous breakdown, the majority of the targeted attacks occurred while the victim was within his or her traditional workweek routine. When examined by the time of the day in which the ambush was staged, the attacks were found to largely occur during the "normal" arrival/departure hours (Figure 2.28). This is, of course, the time when victims are in the process of either arriving to or departing from their residence or office, or are in transit between these two locations. All of these numbers were fairly consistent regardless of whether the targeted victim was mobile or on foot.

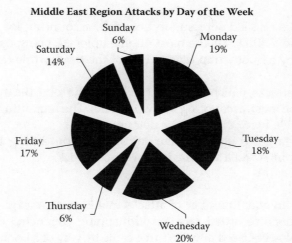

FIGURE 2.27   Middle East region attacks by day of the week.

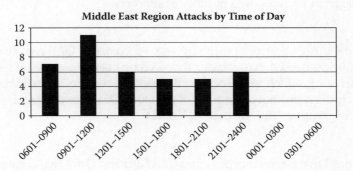

FIGURE 2.28   Middle East region attacks by time of day.

Methods of Attack

The preferred method of attack in the Middle East was explosive-based attacks, which accounted for 42% of all ambushes experienced in the region. Of these attacks, 46% came by way of the VBIED, while another 29% employed a booby-trap device. The suicide bomber was used in 11% of the targeted killings in the Middle East region.

Shootings were found to be involved in 39% of all the documented ambushes. Of these shootings, 24% of them came at the hands of a lone gunman. Approximately 12% of them took the form of drive-by attacks. Snipers were employed in 12% of the attacks, as were motorcycle hit teams. The remaining shooting attacks came at the hands of teams of between three and five gunmen, the two-gunmen hit team, or unknown numbers of gunmen.

Lebanon

The explosive attacks reigned supreme in Lebanon, accounting for 53% of all targeted attacks. Of those, the VBIED was the most often employed, being used 78% of the time. This was followed by a booby-trap device 17% of the time, while the rest were by way of IEDs.

Of the shooting attacks, which accounted for 21% of the total, the three- to five-gunmen hit team was used the most, accounting for two attacks. The remaining were conducted by a lone gunman, a drive-by, or could not be determined.

The rest of the targeted attacks occurring in Lebanon during the research period included six kidnappings and a single-edged weapon attack.

Turkey

Turkey experienced an equal number of attacks making use of explosives and firearms. There was also a single recorded targeted kidnapping conducted during the research period. With the explosive-based attacks, three came by way of a booby-trap device, while the remaining ambushes involved grenades, a suicide bomber, or a VBIED. Of the shooting attacks, a lone gunman was responsible for two, while a drive-by occurred once. The remaining came from an unknown number of shooters.

Egypt

Seven of the nine targeted attacks came by way of firearms. Of those, the three- to five-gunmen hit team was used in two attacks, followed by the motorcycle hit team, a lone gunman, and the drive-by, which were each used once. The remaining two attacks employing firearms came from an unknown number of shooters. Of the two explosive-based attacks, one used a suicide bomber and the other a VBIED.

Jordan

Jordan experienced five separate types of targeted attacks. Only two were shooting based: one by a two-gunmen hit team and the other an unknown number of shooters. There were single cases of a kidnapping, an IED attack, and a poison-based attack.

Iran

Four out of the five targeted attacks used firearms. Two employed motorcycle hit teams, and another two were the work of a lone gunman. A single IED attack was also documented as occurring during the research period.

Israel

As with Iran, four of the five attacks used firearms. Two were the work of a lone gunman, while one attack was carried out by a motorcycle hit team and another by a two-gunmen hit team. There was also a single case of a booby-trap device being deployed in a targeted killing.

Regardless of what form the method of attack took in the Middle East, the adversaries were successful (target kidnapped or killed) 75% of the time. Lebanon documented an 82% rate of success, while Turkey experienced a success rate of 69%.

Locations of Attack

The locations selected by the adversaries in the Middle East to spring their ambushes were fairly consistent with the global statistics. The residence was the most often selected site, accounting for 33% of all attacks. The office came in second, with 21% of the attacks. Ambushes staged against victims in transit between two locations accounted for 20% of the attacks. Of these, 20% occurred while the victim was stopped or slowed for some type of traffic control point at intersections. Finally, public events were the fourth most often site for an ambush at 7%.

Lebanon
Accounting for 53% of the total targeted attacks experienced, those perpetrated against victims in transit occurred most often. This was followed distantly by the residence, which was the site of ambushes 15% of the time. The remaining attacks were dispersed over hotels, offices, frequented locations, public events, or could not be determined.

Turkey
Turkey did not have a clear preference for locations of targeted attacks; however, those occurring against victims in transit occurred 38% of the time (one of which occurred at an intersection). The remaining attack sites included the residence, the office, frequented locations, public events, or could not be determined.

Egypt
Of the nine attacks, four were committed while the victim was in transit and two others at public events. The remaining sites included the residence, the office, and a hotel.

Jordan
Of the five attacks, only the office experienced more than one. The remaining attacks occurred at the residence, while in transit, or could not be determined.

Iran
As with Jordan, of the five attacks, only the office documented more than one. The other attacks sites included public events, while in transit, or could not be determined.

Israel
Israel witnessed five different attack sites. They were staged at the victim's residence, a public event, a hotel, a mosque, or while in transit.

Victims of Attack

In the Middle East, the number one victim of the targeted assassination, contract killing, or kidnapping was the world leader at 30%. Diplomats were hit in 14% of the attacks, making them the second most often targeted victim. Embassy staffers and government ministers each accounted for 8% of all victims.

Lebanon
Attacks were conducted against individuals in thirteen separate classes of target. Of those, the world leader and diplomat each suffered 21% of the attacks. Accounting for 12%, government ministers suffered the next highest number of attacks, followed by lawmakers and corporate executives, each of which recorded 9% of attacks.

Turkey
Attacks here, as elsewhere within the region, targeted a variety of victims, although in these cases there was no clear preference of target. Of the eight classes of victim, only military officials, governor/prefects, embassy staffers, world leaders, and diplomats suffered more than one targeted attack.

Egypt
World leaders were the victim of targeted attacks on four occasions. This was followed by two ambushes perpetrated against government ministers and lawmakers. A diplomat and an activist/dissident each recorded an attack on one occasion.

Jordan
In the five documented targeted attacks, two each were conducted against world leaders and embassy staffers. The fifth attack was targeted against a member of a terrorist organization.

Iran
In this country, three attacks were carried out against world leaders. The two others targeted a judge and an embassy staffer.

Israel
Israel witnessed two world leaders being the focus of targeted violence. The three remaining attacks were conducted against a judge, a government minister, and an underworld figure.

The Adversaries

Of the known groups that carried out targeted attacks in the Middle East region, terrorist/extremist organizations were found to be behind 35% of all ambushes. Government agents were known or believed to have conducted another 14%. The remaining attacks were attributed to rivals, organized criminal groups, or could not be determined.

Lebanon
Of the thirty-four documented targeted attacks, eighteen were conducted by unknown individuals or groups. Of those known, terrorist organizations were behind 56%, with Hizbollah being the most active. Government agents were suspected of being behind the remaining 44% of the attacks (of which the Syrian government is believed to be responsible for the majority).

Turkey
Ten of the thirteen attacks in which the suspects were known were conducted by nine separate groups. Of those ten hits, eight were conducted by terrorist organizations, one by a right-wing extremist, and one attack believed to be the work of government agents.

Egypt
In only five of the nine attacks was the adversary able to be identified. Those five attacks were conducted by the Al-Gama Al-Islamiya, Hizbollah, the Muslim Brotherhood, and the Palestinian Front for the Liberation of Palestine (PFLP).

Jordan
In only three of the five attacks were the responsible groups identified. Of those, one was conducted by government agents, one by the Palestinian Liberation Organization (PLO), and one by Al Qaida.

Iran
Only one attack was attributed to any individual or group, and in this case that group was identified as the work of the Armenian Secret Army for the Liberation of Armenia (ASALA).

Israel
In two of the targeted attacks, the responsible groups were terrorist organizations, the Al Aqsa Martyrs Brigade and the PFLP. One attack was conducted by organized crime, while another was the work of a right-wing extremist. The final attack was perpetrated by an unknown individual or group.

RUSSIA AND THE REPUBLICS

During the research period there were sixty-four urban ambushes found to have occurred in Russia and its republics, consisting of the Republic of Georgia, the Republic of Dagestan, the Republic of South Ossetia, the Ukraine, Chechnya, and the countries of Tajikistan and Kyrgyzstan. Of those attacks, 52% occurred while the victim was traveling in a vehicle. Another 47% occurred while the victim was on foot, while the last 1% of attacks occurred while the victim's status was unknown. Russia documented the most attacks, with just over 61%. The Republic of Dagestan came in second at 14%, and the country of Tajikistan rounded out the top three with 8% of urban ambushes.

Since the 1990s, the Russian region has been experiencing a dramatic increase in targeted attacks (Figure 2.29). That trend continued during the first eight years of the 2000s. It is important to note, however, that information of attacks occurring in the region prior to the 1990s is difficult at best, and the numbers of attacks could be much higher.

The month of August accounted for the greatest number of attacks overall with 14%. August was also the month in which the most attacks were conducted exclusively against vehicle-borne targets, accounting for 24%. Additionally, with the vehicle-borne targets, the month of September was the next most popular, with 15% of attacks. With pedestrian-based targeted attacks, July witnessed the most with 17%. Three separate months were tied

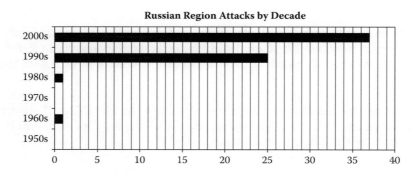

FIGURE 2.29 Russian region attacks by decade.

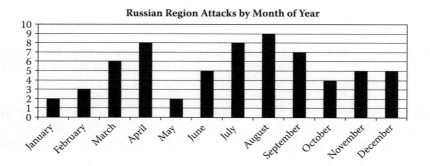

FIGURE 2.30 Russian region attacks by month of the year.

for second greatest number of attacks against pedestrian targets, accounting for 13% each (Figure 2.30).

As Figure 2.31 indicates, the vast majority of targeted attacks have occurred during the traditional workweek, when the victim is within his or her employment routine. Interestingly enough, Wednesday accounted for the greatest number of attacks perpetrated against both vehicle-borne and pedestrian targets.

In each of the previous statistical breakdowns, the majority of the targeted attacks occurred while the victim was within his or her traditional workweek routine. This stayed consistent when examining the total attacks by the time of day. Figure 2.32 illustrates that attacks largely occurred while the victim was in the process of either arriving to or departing from his or her residence or office, or in transit between those two locations. All of these numbers were fairly consistent regardless of whether the targeted victim was mobile or on foot.

Methods of Attack

The preferred method of attack in the Russian region was shootings, accounting for 63% of all the attacks. Of these shootings, 20% of them came at the hands of a lone gunman. Approximately

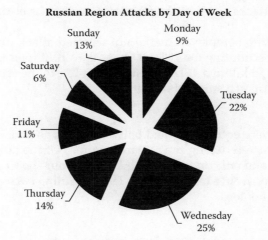

Russian Region Attacks by Day of Week

FIGURE 2.31 Russian region attacks by day of the week.

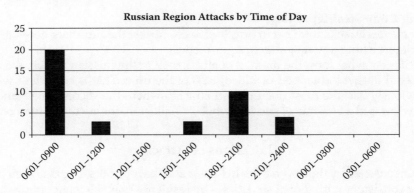

Russian Region Attacks by Time of Day

FIGURE 2.32 Russian region attacks by time of day.

18% of them took the form of sniper-based attacks (in which the number of gunmen could not be confirmed, but would most likely be two). Another 8% of the shooting attacks came from teams of two gunmen. The remaining shooting ambushes were perpetrated by teams of between three and five gunmen, drive-bys, or unknown numbers of gunmen.

Explosives in ambushing targeted victims within the Russian region saw consistent use and accounted for 37% of all attacks. Of those, the IED was deployed the most often at 54%, followed closely by the VBIED at 33%. Grenades were used, interestingly enough, 8% of the time.

Russia

Consistent with the total regional percentages, shootings were also the number one form of attack, accounting for 69% of all ambushes. Of that 69%, 22% came from lone gunmen. Snipers were responsible for 15%, and another 11% from hit teams of two gunmen. The remaining shooting attacks came in the form of drive-bys or at the hands of unknown numbers of gunmen.

The second most often employed method of targeted attack in Russia came through the use of explosives, accounting for 31%. Of these, the VBIED was employed in 50% of all explosive-based targeted killings. IEDs accounted for 42% of the remaining attacks, while the rest came in the form of a suicide bomber.

Republic of Dagestan

Eight attacks, which were equally divided between firearms and explosives, were documented as having occurred during the research period. Of the attacks using explosives, three were IED based, and only one was a VBIED. In the four shooting attacks, one was the work of a sniper and one from a lone gunman. The remaining two came at the hands of an unknown number of shooters.

Tajikistan

With only five total attacks over the fifty-eight years, the numbers generated are not useful in determining any major technique/tactic.

Remaining Countries/Republics

With only eleven attacks total occurring in five countries, the numbers generated are not useful in determining any major technique/tactic.

Regardless of what form the method of attack took in the Russian region, the adversary was successful (target kidnapped or killed) 64% of the time. That is consistent with Russia (which obviously had the most documented attacks), where the success rate stands at 67%. Dagestan witnessed a 56% rate of success, while in Tajikistan, the success rate stood at 100%.

Locations of Attack

The locations selected by the adversaries in Russia and the republics to spring their ambushes were fairly consistent with global statistics. The residence was the most often selected site, accounting for 42% of all attacks. Coming in a close second, with 41%, were attacks conducted while the victim was in transit. The remaining 17% of attacks were dispersed over locations, including the office, courthouse, frequented places, and public events.

Russia

As with the region as a whole, the attacks occurring in Russia occurred most often while the victim was in transit, accounting for 46%. This was followed closely by attacks occurring at or near the victim's residence, at 38%. The office ranked a distant third, accounting for only 8% of attacks.

Republic of Dagestan

The Republic of Dagestan witnessed four of its attacks occurring while the victim was at or near his or her residence. Another four were staged while the victim was in transit, one of which is known to have taken place at a traffic intersection. Only one attack was found to have been carried out at the victim's office.

Tajikistan
Three of the five recorded attacks were perpetrated at or near the victim's residence. One was staged while the victim was in transit, while the last known targeted attack occurred at a public event.

Remaining Countries/Republics
While individually the numbers of attacks were low, of the five remaining countries, the most selected location for a targeted attack was the residence, which had five attacks. This was followed by three attacks on victims in transit. One attack was staged at a public event, another at the victim's office, and yet another attack was found to have occurred at a courthouse.

Victims of Attack

In Russia and the republics, the number one victim of the targeted assassination, contract killing, or kidnapping was the corporate executive at 20%. With 17% of the attacks, the world leader was the second most often targeted victim. The mayor was third, accounting for 13% of all targeted victims. The government minister and the federal government official tied for the fourth position, having 9% of the attacks.

Russia
Corporate executives were on the receiving end of targeted attacks 28% of the time. Mayors were ambushed 21% of the time, while lawmakers and world leaders tied for third, each suffering 13% of the attacks.

Republic of Dagestan
Government ministers found themselves the target of an assassin in four attacks. The remaining five ambushes targeted a world leader, a prosecutor, a lawmaker, a judge, and a local government official.

Tajikistan
Federal government officials and government ministers each fell victim to two attacks, while a world leader was attacked once.

Remaining Countries/Republics
World leaders were the victims in four of the attacks occurring within these five countries/republics, followed closely by federal government officials, who were attacked on three occasions. The remaining attacks targeted an intelligence officer, a lawmaker, and two corporate executives.

The Adversaries

Russia and the republics have found themselves in a unique situation since the 1990s. Facing a variety of adversaries, from rebels of the breakaway regions, to Islamic extremism, to mafia groups running out of control, this area of the planet never knew when or where the next attack might occur. Unfortunately, the vast majority of attacks within the region came from unknown subjects.

Russia
The vast majority of attacks came at the hand of unknown assailants. However, given the timing (referring to the upheaval following the collapse of the former Soviet Union government) of the attacks, it could be fair to assume that organized crime was behind a majority of them. Of the eleven known attacks, four are known to have been at the hands of organized crime and another two by Islamic extremists. The last five attacks are believed to have been perpetrated by government agents.

Republic of Dagestan
In all but one of the attacks that occurred in Dagestan, the adversary was not able to be determined. The one attack that was known was found to have been perpetrated by a Chechen extremist.

Tajikistan and Remaining Countries/Republics
In all but one of the documented attacks, the assailant was not known. The remaining attack, which occurred in Chechnya, was strongly believed to have come from a government agent.

SOUTH ASIA

There were a total of sixty-one ambushes found to have occurred in the South Asia region during the research period. Five countries, consisting of Afghanistan, Bangladesh, India, Pakistan, and Sri Lanka, each documented targeted attacks. Of those attacks, 57% occurred while the target was vehicle borne. Another 41% were staged while the victim was on foot, with only one attack occurring when the victim's status was unknown. Pakistan documented the most attacks, with just over 41%, followed very closely by Sri Lanka with 26%. India rounded out the top three with 25%.

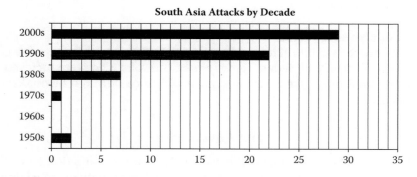

FIGURE 2.33 South Asia attacks by decade.

Since the 1990s the region of South Asia has witnessed a moderate increase in targeted attacks occurring during the first eight years of the 2000s (Figure 2.33). However, there was a dramatic increase in targeted attacks since the 1980s.

With 13%, the month of October had the greatest number of ambushes in the South Asian region (Figure 2.34). Of note is the relatively low number of attacks occurring during the first part of the calendar year through early spring. With the mobile targets, the month of November experienced the single largest number of ambushes, accounting for 14% of attacks over the twelve-month period. With pedestrian-based targeted attacks, two separate months experienced the bulk of activity. The months of October and May had the most attacks, each accounting for 20%.

As Figure 2.35 indicates, the vast majority of targeted attacks have occurred during the traditional workweek, although in this region the concentration of attacks was toward the end of the week. When examined solely by attacks on pedestrian targets, Friday stood

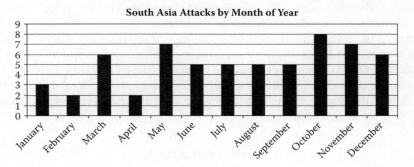

FIGURE 2.34 South Asia attacks by month of the year.

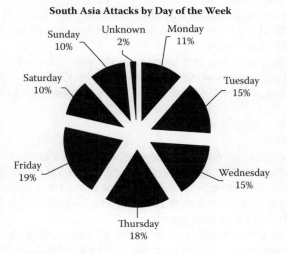

FIGURE 2.35 South Asia attacks by day of the week.

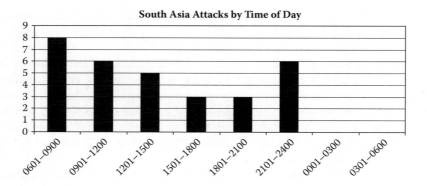

South Asia Attacks by Time of Day

FIGURE 2.36 South Asia attacks by time of day.

out, with 28% of the ambush activity. For the mobile victim, Thursday had the most attacks with 26%, followed by Tuesday with 17% of the total.

Continuing the trend, the timing of the majority of the targeted attacks occurred while the victim was within his or her traditional workweek routine (Figure 2.36). The attacks largely occurred while the victim was in the process of either arriving to or departing from his or her residence or office, or in transit between those two locations. Interesting was the concentration of attacks occurring during the morning hours decreasing by late afternoon, only to spike after 2101 hours.

Methods of Attack

The preferred method of attack in the region of South Asia was shootings, accounting for 56% of all the attacks. Of these shootings, 15% of them came at the hands of motorcycle hit teams. Approximately 18% of them took the form of two-gunmen hit team attacks. Another 12% of the shooting attacks came from a lone gunman. The remaining shooting attacks came at the hands of teams of between three and five gunmen, drive-bys, snipers, or unknown numbers of gunmen.

Explosives were also an often employed tactic in which to carry out a targeted killing. In this region, explosives were used in 41% of the attacks. Of those, the suicide bomber was deployed in 68% of attacks. The IED was used in 16% of these types of attacks, followed by the VBIED with 16%.

Pakistan

Consistent with the total South Asia percentages, shootings were also the number one form of attack in Pakistan, accounting for 60% of all ambushes. Of the nine shooting attacks in which the method was able to be determined, three came from motorcycle hit teams. The drive-by and two-gunmen hit team were each used in two attacks, followed by a lone gunman and sniper, each recording a single attack.

The second most often employed method of targeted attack in Pakistan came through the use of explosives, accounting for 36% of the total. In those attacks, the suicide bomber was far and away the most active, responsible for 67% of the total. The IED was used in 22%, with VBIEDs making the remaining attacks. Finally, there was a single attack that used poison, but there was strong evidence that a small explosive was used in the dispersal of the toxin.

Sri Lanka

Sri Lanka was one of the only countries on the planet to experience a predominance of explosive-based attacks, accounting for a total of 56%. Of these attacks, 89% of them involved a suicide bomber. Only one attack using explosives involved a prepositioned IED.

In shooting attacks, which accounted for 44% of targeted hits, a variety of methods were employed. Lone gunmen struck twice, and in another two attacks the total number of gunmen could not be determined. The remaining attacks using firearms were conducted by a sniper, a drive-by, and a two-gunmen hit team.

India

Accounting for 73% of all attacks, the firearm was used the most often in targeted attacks in India. Of those, the two-gunmen hit team was responsible for 27% of attacks. They were followed by the motorcycle hit team with 18%. The remaining ambushes were carried out by a lone gunman, teams of between three to five gunmen, or could not be determined. In explosive-based attacks, two came by way of suicide bomber, while the IED and VBIED were each used once.

Afghanistan/Bangladesh

With only five attacks total, the numbers generated are not useful in determining any major technique/tactic.

Regardless of what form the method of attack took in the region of South Asia, the adversary was successful (target kidnapped or killed) 72% of the time. Pakistan did not record that high of a success rate, which stands at 60%, Sri Lanka witnessed an astounding 94% rate of success in targeted attacks. India documented a 67% rate of success in targeted attacks carried out in its country.

Locations of Attack

The locations selected by the adversaries in the region of South Asia to spring their ambushes were fairly consistent with the global statistics. Ambushes staged against victims while in transit between two locations accounted for 44% of the total. Public events were the second most often selected site for an ambush, with 20%. This was followed by the residence, which was witness to 18% of all attacks.

Pakistan

Targeted attacks occurred 60% of the time while the victim was in transit (one of which was staged at a traffic intersection). This was followed distantly by attacks occurring at or near the victim's residence 16% of the time. Rounding out the top three spots were public events, with a documented 12% of the ambushes.

Sri Lanka

Sri Lanka witnessed 44% of its attacks occurring while the victim was traveling in a vehicle between locations. Public events, with 25%, was the second most frequent location selected to ambush the victim. The residence was a distant third, at only 19% of all attacks.

India

India experienced its attacks almost equally between the four main locations. Five attacks were carried out against targets in transit (one of which was staged at a traffic intersection), while four occurred at public events. The victim's residence and office were each the scene of three other targeted attacks.

Victims of Attack

In South Asia, the number one victim of the targeted assassination, contract killing, or kidnapping was the world leader, accounting for 18% of attacks. At 15%, the lawmaker was the second most often targeted victim. The military official was third, accounting for 11% of all targeted victims. The government minister, with 10% of the attacks, rounded out the top four most often targeted individuals.

Pakistan

As with the region as a whole, world leaders were the most often targeted class of individual in Pakistan, accounting for 20% of all attacks. Lawmakers, judges, and candidates for prime minister each accounted for 12% of the victims. The remaining attacks were carried out against nine other classes of victim.

Sri Lanka

Military and world leaders suffered the most attacks, totaling 19%. Government ministers, lawmakers, and political leaders accounted for 13% of the targets. The rest of the victims fell into four different categories.

India

Lawmakers and government ministers each found themselves the focus of targeted attacks in India 20% of the time. World leaders and federal government officials were each attacked 13% of the time, while the remaining attacks targeted five other classes of victim.

The Adversaries

In the South Asian region there were ten separate individuals or organizations either claiming responsibility or found to have been responsible for one or more of the attacks. Of those, seven were terrorist organizations, with the other three conducted by criminals, a rival, and government agents. In twenty-five of the attacks, the group or individual behind it could not be determined. Of the known groups, terrorist/extremist organizations were responsible for 54% of the targeted attacks.

Pakistan

Perhaps not surprisingly, 44% of the attacks came from Islamic extremists with no known links to any particular group. Known terrorist groups Al Qaida and the Abu Nidal Organization each claimed responsibility for a single attack, while another was believed to have been carried out by government agents. The remaining attacks were carried out by unknown individuals or groups.

Sri Lanka

The Tamil Tigers were found or known to be responsible for 75% of all targeted attacks within Sri Lanka. The remaining attacks came by unknown individuals or groups.

India

Of the seven targeted attacks in which the adversary was known, seven different adversaries were responsible. Six of these were by terrorist organizations and only one from a criminal group.

ASIA/PACIFIC

There were a total of forty-six ambushes found to have occurred in the Asia/Pacific region during the research period. Twelve countries, consisting of Australia, China, Philippines, South Korea, Indonesia, New Caledonia, Taiwan, Papua New Guinea, Palau Island, Japan, Solomon Islands, and Samoa, documented targeted attacks. Of those attacks, 72% occurred while the target was on foot. Another 28% occurred while the target was mobile in a vehicle. The Philippines documented the most attacks, with just over 41%, followed distantly by Japan with 17%. Indonesia rounded out the top three, with 11% of the recorded attacks.

The Asia/Pacific region has witnessed a trend of steadily increasing violence, commencing in the 1960s. However, the first eight years of the 2000s documented a substantial rise in these types of attacks, which is on pace to double that which was experienced during the 1990s (Figure 2.37).

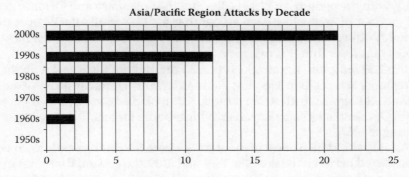

FIGURE 2.37 Asia/Pacific region attacks by decade.

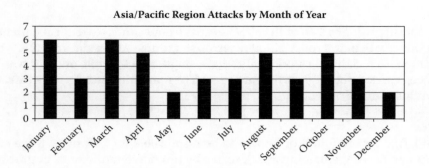

FIGURE 2.38 Asia/Pacific attacks by month of the year.

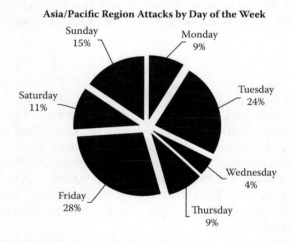

FIGURE 2.39 Asia/Pacific region attacks by day of the week.

Overall with six each, the months of January and March had the greatest number of attacks, the bulk of which were conducted against pedestrian targets (Figure 2.38). Additionally, with the pedestrian targets, the months of January and October experienced the largest number of ambushes, each accounting for 15% of all attacks over the twelve-month period. With vehicle-borne targeted attacks, April experienced the most, accounting for 23% of attacks within this category.

As Figure 2.39 indicates, the attacks occurred throughout the week, with the weekend experiencing more attacks than Monday, Wednesday, and Thursday. When examining the thirty-three attacks against pedestrian targets, 33% took place on Fridays, followed by 18% on Tuesdays. Of the attacks staged against vehicle-borne targets, Tuesdays were the highest, accounting for 38%.

In the Asia/Pacific region, most of the attacks where the timing was known were found to have been staged between the hours of 1801 and 2100, the general time one departs from his or her office or arrives at his or her residence (Figure 2.40). It is interesting to note the increase of attack activity during the lunch to early afternoon hours.

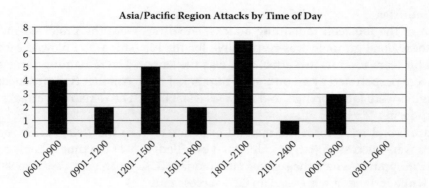

FIGURE 2.40 Asia/Pacific region attacks by time of day.

Methods of Attack

The preferred method of attack in the Asia/Pacific region was shootings, accounting for 67% of all the attacks. Of these shootings, 32% of them came at the hands of lone gunmen. Approximately 16% of them took the form of the two-gunmen hit team. The remaining shooting attacks came at the hands of teams of between three and five gunmen, from snipers, drive-bys, or unknown numbers of gunmen.

Philippines

Consistent with the regional percentages, shootings were also the number one form of attack in the Philippines, accounting for 74% of all ambushes. While five of these shooting attacks were conducted by unknown groups or individuals, the remaining used a variety of methods. Three attacks were conducted by the two-gunmen hit team, while a lone gunman and a team of between three and five shooters were each responsible for two attacks. Drive-by and sniper attacks were each used in a single targeted hit.

Explosives were only known to have been deployed in three targeted attacks, and each time a different method was used. Of the three attacks, one used the suicide bomber, another used a prepostioned IED, and the last used a VBIED. Of the two remaining attacks, one used an edge weapon and another was a kidnapping.

Japan

Japan is unique among the countries experiencing targeted attacks in that the majority, four of the eight, were perpetrated using edged weapons. Three attacks were perpetrated by lone gunmen, while one ambush employed an IED.

Indonesia

Indonesia had five total targeted attacks over the fifty-eight-year period, each of which employed a different method. Of the three shooting attacks, one employed the motorcycle hit team, one was a drive-by, and the last came at the hand of a lone gunman. Of the two remaining attacks, one used poison against the victim while the other involved a VBIED.

Other Countries

In eleven of the fourteen remaining attacks, shootings were the preferred method. In four of these, lone gunmen was responsible for the hit. This was followed by the two-gunmen hit team used in two attacks, as was the sniper. The remaining three shooting attacks were perpetrated by an unknown number of men. Another two attacks occurring in the region were kidnappings, and one was a stabbing. The remaining attacks came in unknown forms.

Regardless of what form the method of attack took in the Asia/Pacific region, the adversary were successful (target kidnapped or killed) 74% of the time. That is consistent with the Philippines, where the success rate stands at 84%. Japan experienced a 38% rate of success, while Indonesia witnessed an 80% success rate.

Locations of Attack

The locations selected by the adversaries in the Asia/Pacific region to spring their ambushes were consistent with the global statistics. The residence was the most often selected site, accounting for 26% of all attacks. Ambushes staged against victims in transit between two locations accounted for 22% of the attacks. The victim's office came in third, with 15% of the attacks.

Philippines

The Philippines recorded nineteen attacks over a variety of locations, with no one particular place seemingly preferred over another. Attacks at or near of the office as well as against victims in transit each accounted for 21%. This was followed by ambushes staged at an airport as well as public events, each documenting 16% of the total attacks. The remaining were carried out at churches, residences, or frequented locations.

Japan

Japan documented eight attacks in one of three locations. The victim's residence was the site of four such attacks, followed by the office with three. A single attack occurred at a public event.

Indonesia

As with Japan, attacks in Indonesia occurred in only one of three locales. Attacks in transit ranked number one, with three of the five. This was followed by single attacks on an aircraft and a frequented location.

Other Countries

In the remaining countries in the region, attacks were predominantly staged at or near the victim's residence, followed by while in transit. Other attacks were set at a hotel, a college, a public event, or could not be determined.

Victims of Attack

In the Asia/Pacific region, the number one victim of the targeted assassination, contract killing, or kidnapping was the lawmaker, with 20%. At 17%, the mayor was the second most often targeted victim. The world leader was third, accounting for 11% of all targeted victims.

Philippines
Mayors fell victim to the highest number of attacks, accounting for 32% of the total. This was followed by lawmakers, who were attacked 26% of the time. Members of clergy rounded out the top three most often targeted people, recording 21%. Corporate executives, military officials, and federal government officials were also targeted during the research period.

Japan
Japan did not witness one class of subject overwhelmingly targeted over another. Of the eight attacks, the targets fell within six different classes. Government ministers and mayors each recorded two attacks, while diplomats, lawmakers, federal government officials, and political leaders were each attacked once.

Indonesia
In Indonesia there was no single most often targeted class of individual due to the low number of targeted attacks.

Other Countries
In attacks occurring in the other countries within the region, world leaders were targeted in five instances. Lawmakers were targeted in three other attacks, followed by corporate executives in two attacks.

The Adversaries

Of the known groups, terrorist/extremist organizations were behind 24% of the attacks. In the remaining ambushes, criminals or criminal organizations were responsible for four, while rivals to the victim were behind three of the attacks. Two attacks were staged by government agents, while the remaining ones were perpetrated by unknown individuals or groups.

Philippines
In only ten of the attacks were the perpetrators known either through investigation or by claims of responsibility. Of those, three came from the hands of Abu Sayyaf terrorists. The New People's Army laid claim in two attacks, and Al Qaida and the Red Scorpion group were each behind a single attack. Political rivals were found to be responsible for two attacks, while a criminal was behind the last.

Japan
In the four attacks in which the responsible party was known, each came from a different adversary. One attack was attributed to the Yakuza crime group, one to an extremist

organization known as Chukaku, one to a regular criminal, and the last to a right-wing extremist member.

Indonesia

Of the four known responsible parties of targeted attacks, Jemaah Islamiya was behind one, while Moro Islamic Liberation Front (MILF) was behind another. A government agent perpetrated a single attack, as did a regular criminal.

AFRICA

There were a total of thirty documented ambushes found to have occurred on the African continent during the research period. Fourteen countries, consisting of Algeria, Botswana, Burundi, Ethiopia, Gambia, Mozambique, Rwanda, Senegal, South Africa, Sudan, Swaziland, Togo, Tunisia, and Zimbabwe, documented targeted attacks. Of those attacks, 57% occurred while the target was on foot. Another 40% occurred while the target was mobile in a vehicle, with the remaining 3% of attacks occurring while the victim's status was unknown. Algeria documented the most attacks, with just over 27%, followed very closely by South Africa with 23%. The countries of Burundi, Ethiopia, and Swaziland, each of which accounted for 7%, rounded out the top three.

The African region of late has seen a fairly substantial decrease in targeted attacks (although to be fair, obtaining information on attack activity has been difficult). The 1990s recorded the most targeted attacks, followed closely by the 1980s (Figure 2.41).

Overall, the month of April had the greatest number of attacks, of which all but one were conducted against pedestrian-based targets (Figure 2.42). With mobile targets, June experienced the single largest number of ambushes, accounting for three of the five attacks perpetrated that month.

As Figure 2.43 indicates, the vast majority of targeted attacks have occurred during the traditional workweek, when the victim is forced to move by his or her employment routine. When examining just the pedestrian-based attacks, a concentration was found on

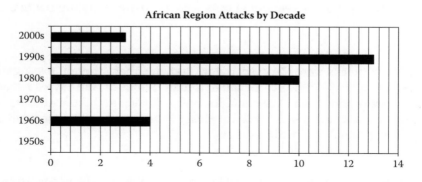

FIGURE 2.41 African region attacks by decade.

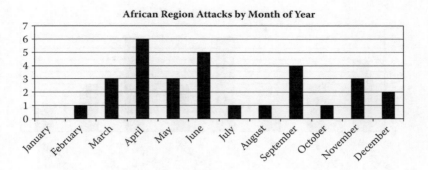

African Region Attacks by Month of Year

FIGURE 2.42   African region attacks by month of the year.

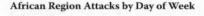

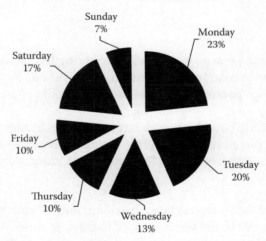

African Region Attacks by Day of Week

FIGURE 2.43   African region attacks by day of the week.

Mondays and Saturdays, each of which documented five attacks. Of the attacks on vehicle-borne targets, there was no clear preference for a day, although there were no attacks registered as having taken place on Saturday or Sunday.

Targeted attacks within the African region were found to have been staged at all hours of the day, with the most activity occurring equally between the hours of 1501 and 1800, and 2101 and 2400 (Figure 2.44).

Methods of Attack

The preferred methods of attack in the African region were shootings, accounting for 67% of all the ambushes. Of these shootings, 30% of them came at the hands of lone gunmen. While some of the attacks were perpetrated by teams of between three and five shooters,

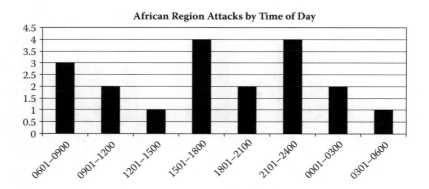

FIGURE 2.44   African region attacks by time of day.

or a drive-by, the rest of the shooting attacks were conducted by an unknown number of gunmen.

Algeria

Shootings were the number one form of attack, accounting for four of the seven ambushes. Of these attacks, two were conducted by lone gunmen and one by a team of three to five gunmen. The remaining shooting attacks came at the hands of an unknown number of shooters or tactic.

Explosives were used in two of the seven targeted attacks in Algeria. One came through the use of a booby trap placed upon the victim's vehicle, while the second was by way of a suicide bomber. The last attack was found to have been a kidnapping.

South Africa

As with the other countries in the region, a predominance of shooting attacks was experienced, accounting for five of the seven attacks. In three of these attacks, a lone gunman was responsible, while in another it was a team of six gunmen. The last shooting attack came at the hands of an unknown number of gunmen. South Africa also documented a stabbing attack as well as one of the rare poison-based attacks.

Regardless of what form the method of attack took in the African region, the adversary was successful (target kidnapped or killed) 73% of the time. Algeria documented a success rate of 88%, while South Africa witnessed a 71% rate of success.

Locations of Attack

The locations selected by the adversaries in Africa to spring their ambushes stayed consistent with the global statistics. The residence was the most often selected site, accounting for 40% of all attacks. Ambushes staged against victims in transit documented 23% of the attacks. Another 10% of the attacks were staged at or near the victim's office, while the remaining were staged at mosques, a dentist office, or could not be determined.

Algeria
Targeted attacks staged in this country occurred at a more varied amount of locations. Attacks were documented twice at a victim's residence as well as during public events. Another two attacks struck victims while they were in transit, of which one was found to have taken place at a traffic intersection.

South Africa
South Africa witnessed four of the seven attacks at the victim's residence, while the remaining were sprung at the office, an airport, and once at a public event.

Other Countries
Even with the low total attack numbers, the residence was the number one location to stage the ambush. This was followed by attacks on targets in transit.

Victims of Attack

In the African region, the number one victim of the targeted assassination, contract killing, or kidnapping was the activist, with 27% of the attacks. At 20%, the world leader was the second most often targeted victim. The remaining targets fell into ten different categories of victim.

Algeria
As with the locations of the ambushes, assassins in this country also focused their attacks on a diverse set of victims. World leaders and mayors were each attacked twice, while the remaining victims included a clergy member, an activist, a government minister, and a terrorist.

South Africa
Attacks here were focused upon four targeted classes of individual. World leaders, federal government officials, and activists each documented two attacks during the research period. One member of clergy was the victim of a targeted attack during this period.

Other Countries
Activists were attacked the most in the remaining countries (five times). World leaders and diplomats each documented two attacks, each of which was staged in a different country.

The Adversaries

Interestingly, the majority of attacks in Africa were known to be or strongly believed to have been conducted by government agents. This was followed by Islamic extremist groups, or the attacking group/individual could not be determined.

Algeria
With the largest number of attacks, Algeria also experienced the largest number of adversaries in this region. The terrorist group Armed Islamic Group (GIA) was responsible for three of the targeted attacks, while Islamic extremists were behind two other attacks.

Government agents were believed to be behind one attack, and the remaining two came from unknown individuals/groups.

South Africa
Of the seven attacks occurring in this country, five were found or strongly believed to have been conducted by government agents. The remaining two attacks came from extremists targeting the government representatives.

Other Countries
As with South Africa, the other countries in the region experienced a substantial amount of attacks, seven of the fifteen, by government agents. One ambush was conducted by the Islamic terrorist group Al-Gama Al-Islamiya, while the rest were perpetrated by unknown groups or individuals.

3

Attack Methodology

In this chapter the methods employed by adversaries in order to accomplish their goal will be examined with the purpose of obtaining an understanding of their strengths and weaknesses. The carrying out of an assassination/kidnapping is a major operation for any individual or group that requires a great deal of preparation if there is to be any hope of success. Fortunately, these attacks are generally a rare occurrence, given the world's population, but happen often enough to be of concern for those within the most often targeted classes of victims, as well as those assigned to a protective function. While the tactics used in these types of operations can vary considerably given the region, target class, adversary, availability of resources, etc., when taken as a whole it is possible to develop a better understanding as to why and how they were employed, thus allowing for the development of preattack indicators as well as immediate action responses.

Figure 3.1 references the top eleven primary methods of attack (which will be further explained in the coming pages) employing a specific tactic or technique and the number of times they were used during the perpetration of a targeted ambush. It is important to keep in mind that in some instances more than one method was used at the time, i.e., a two-man hit team wearing masks or some type of disguise in order to either protect their identity

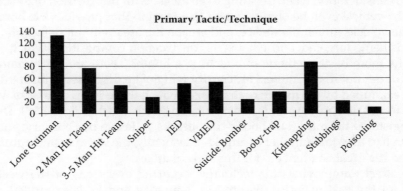

FIGURE 3.1 Primary tactic/technique.

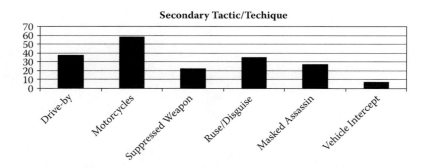

FIGURE 3.2   Secondary tactic/technique.

or assist them in closing the distance with their target prior to attacking. Figure 3.2 details six secondary techniques (also further explained in the following pages) used in carrying out the killing or kidnapping.

BOOBY TRAP

There were thirty-five attacks found in which a booby-trap explosive device was the common factor. In all but one of these attacks, the device was attached to a vehicle (the last was packed inside of a desk that detonated upon the opening of a drawer). This style of assassination really exploded (if you forgive the pun) onto the world stage during the 1970s, which experienced nine such attacks. Prior to that, only one attack was documented to have occurred during the 1960s and none during the 1950s. There was a slight drop in the use of this attack method during the 1980s, with eight attacks, and into the 1990s, with seven. However, as of December 2008, there had already been eleven attacks by booby-trap explosive device recorded during that decade.

There is a certain amount of risk of early discovery when assassins decide to attach an explosive device to a target's vehicle. It therefore requires the adversary to take a number of factors into consideration when deciding to go ahead with this method of attack. First, can access to the vehicle even be obtained, and in a fashion that provides the bomber(s) time to reach the vehicle, attach the device, and escape the area without detection? What type of vehicle is being targeted, and what is its construction composition, which can impede many of the more basic methods of attaching a bomb? There are many more considerations, of course, but in the interest of security will not be discussed within this work.

When examined by the month of the year in which these types of attacks were carried out, it was found that only April did not record any such attacks (Figure 3.3). The month of October registered the most total booby-trap attacks, followed by February, June, and July, all of which had an equal number of attacks. Seasonally, the summer and autumn months experienced the greatest numbers for this style of attack.

While attacks employing this technique occurred every day of the week, Monday accounted for the vast majority (Figure 3.4). Thursday and Friday rounded out the top three days, respectively.

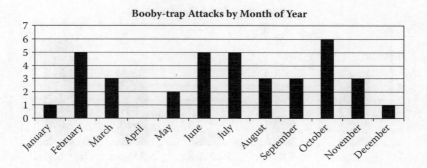

FIGURE 3.3 Booby-trap attacks by month of the year.

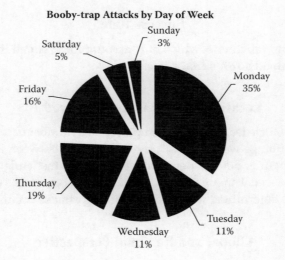

FIGURE 3.4 Booby-trap attacks by day of the week.

For this style of attack to even begin first requires one or more individuals to gain access to the victim's vehicle without being detected. It stands to reason then that most of these devices are attached to vehicles during the nighttime hours, when most vehicles are left unattended for extended periods of time. The type of device and the triggering mechanism being employed will partially determine the amount of time the bombers will need to spend at the car itself, as well as the potential noise that could arise during installation. As a result, it goes without saying that the bomber will want as many factors as possible in his or her favor in order to succeed.

One of those factors would be a decrease in the overall ambient light, thereby lessening the chance of being spotted. It was found that 57% of attacks by a booby-trap device occurred within seven days plus or minus of a new moon (Figure 3.5). Inclement weather may have also played a factor in this method, but could not be determined with any degree of certainty.

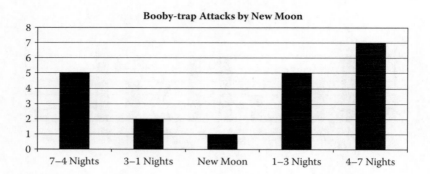

FIGURE 3.5 Booby-trap attacks by new moon.

Success Rate

Attacks using a booby-trap device, which only account for 4% of all the attacks during the research period, obtained a 76% success rate.

Locations Most Likely Employed At

The booby-trapped vehicle technique was employed at a number of locations. Not surprisingly, 59% of the bombings were against targets traveling between locations. Interesting enough though, booby-trap devices detonated 44% of the time while at the residence. The victim's office experienced a small amount, recording 19% of attacks employing this technique. It could not be determined where the remaining attacks occurred.

Global and Regional Perspective

The United Kingdom (including Northern Ireland) was the dominant location for this tactic, accounting for 26% of all booby-trap attacks. It was followed by Spain, which recorded 15% of this style of ambush. The European region documented the most booby-trap device detonations, with 67%, followed by the Middle East with 37%.

Most Likely Employed By

The Irish Republican Army (and its variants) was the dominant user of the booby-trap device, but only accounted for 18% of the attacks. They were followed by Spain's ETA (Euskadi ta Askatasuna) with 11%. Interestingly enough, 22% of the booby-trap device attacks are known or strongly believed to have come at the hands of government agents. Overall, terrorist groups were the single most dominant employer of this tactic, claiming responsibility for 59% of all attacks. Only 11% were found to have come from criminal organizations. Responsibility for the remaining attacks could not be determined.

Most Likely Employed Against

The activist/dissident fell victim to the booby-trap device attack 19% of the time, the most of any of the target classes. The next most common victims were lawmakers with 15%, and then prosecutors, world leaders, embassy staffers, and terrorist leaders, each of which accounted for 11% of attacks. The remaining attacks targeted individuals falling within thirteen other target classes.

DRIVE-BY

There were a total of thirty-seven attacks by way of drive-by shooting from a vehicle against a victim. Thirty-two of the attacks took place against a moving target, with the remaining five targeting pedestrian victims. The drive-by attack was also found to be a more modern tactic, which first appeared during the 1980s, when ten were conducted. While the 1990s had only six such attacks, the first eight years of the 2000s saw the number of drive-by ambushes spike to twenty-one.

The month of September recorded six drive-by attacks, the most during the calendar year (Figure 3.6). April and May followed closely behind, each having five such attacks. However, this tactic was found to have been employed throughout the calendar year.

Mondays and Wednesdays witnessed the vast majority of drive-by ambush attacks, followed, interestingly enough, by Saturday (Figure 3.7). Sundays and Thursdays had an equal number of attacks, as well as having the least number during the week period.

While fourteen of the attacks occurred at an unknown hour, eight were staged between the hours of 1801 and 2100, the most of any time period. This was followed by three attacks between 2101 and 2400. The morning hours of 0601 to 0900 recorded five such attacks. During the six-hour period between 1201 and 1800 only four drive-by attacks were documented. The final three are known only to have occurred during hours of darkness.

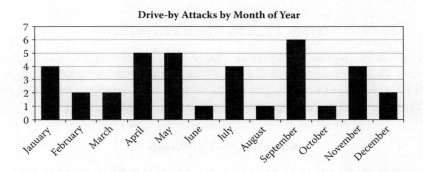

FIGURE 3.6 Drive-by attacks by month of the year.

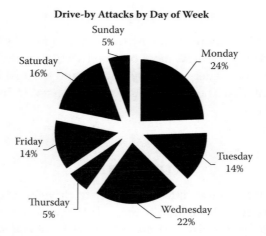

Drive-by Attacks by Day of Week

FIGURE 3.7 Drive-by attacks by day of the week.

Success Rate

While the drive-by tactic represented only a small percentage of total firearms-based attacks, it had a very high success rate. Overall, the tactic has recorded an 89% success rate in that the target was killed by the assassin(s). Against the thirty-two mobile targets, the drive-by was successful 86% of the time. Against the five pedestrian targets the success rate was 100%.

Locations Most Likely Employed At

Drive-by attacks were found to have been conducted at only four known locations. With 73% of attacks, the most preferred was while the victim was traveling in a vehicle. This was followed by attacks at or within close proximity to the victim's residence 16% of the time. The remaining attack sites were at the office or a frequented location.

Global and Regional Perspective

Mexico was witness to the most prolific use of the drive-by tactic, accounting for 35% of all attacks. This is in comparison to Colombia, which had the second highest use, but accounted for only 11% of attacks. The remaining drive-by attacks occurred in more than seventeen countries encompassing every region on the planet.

Most Likely Employed By

The drug cartels of Mexico and Colombia employed this tactic more often than any other group, accounting for a total of fourteen attacks. Attacks by government agents were responsible for another three, while six came from six separate terrorist organizations. The remaining attacks were perpetrated by unknown groups or individuals.

Most Likely Employed Against

Ironically, it was the law enforcement official that was the target of this style of attack most frequently, accounting for 35% of all victims. Lawmakers were the next most often targeted class of victims, documenting 11% of the total, followed by judges with 8%. The remaining attacks were conducted against eleven different targeted classes.

Protective Details

In only 30% of attacks in which the drive-by method was used was a protective detail of some form present. As with other attacks, the training, experience, and availability of weapons to the protective force could not be determined. Given the high fatality rate of the target in this style of attack, it can be inferred that most, if not all, of the victim's vehicles were not armored. Whether such vehicles were available to the victims prior to the attacks was also not able to be determined.

IMPROVISED EXPLOSIVE DEVICE

There were a total of fifty-one attacks in which the use of an improvised explosive device (IED) was the common factor. In those attacks, the technique was employed twenty-six times against victims traveling in a motor vehicle and twenty-five times against pedestrians. Beginning in the 1960s, which experienced two IED attacks, there has been a steady rise in their use in targeted attacks. Six such attacks were staged during the 1970s, which doubled to twelve in the 1980s, while the 1990s suffered thirteen attacks. The first eight years of the 2000s recorded eighteen ambushes employing the IED tactic.

The attack method saw use throughout the calendar year, with August and July recording the most (Figure 3.8). This was followed by March, April, October, and December,

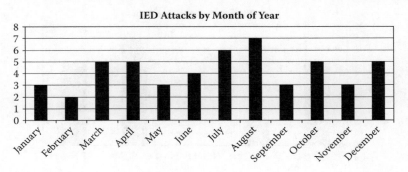

FIGURE 3.8 IED attacks by month of the year.

which each saw five IED attacks. Seasonally, the use of IED-based targeted attacks was concentrated in the spring and summer months.

As with other attacks methods, most of the IED ambushes occurred during the traditional workweek, with Tuesday having the most of any day (Figure 3.9). Thursday and Friday rounded out the top three, each with 16% of attacks.

Given the nature of the IED, many are placed in advance of the arrival of the targeted victim. As with the booby-trap explosive device, it stands to reason that bombers would want to take advantage of increased hours of darkness, especially around a new moon phase. Figure 3.10 details twenty-five IED-based attacks that fell within seven days plus or minus of the new moon. These numbers do not include the four known roof bombs, two bombs that were known to have been buried or set up during the daylight hours, and one bomb that was placed inside of an office. The remaining nineteen IED attacks occurred within seven or less

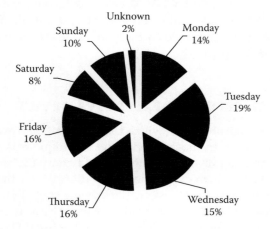

FIGURE 3.9 IED attacks by day of the week.

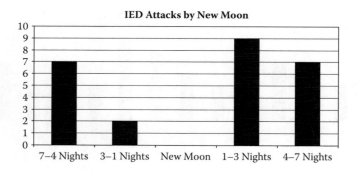

FIGURE 3.10 IED attacks by new moon.

days of the full moon, although in all cases the weather at the time—inclement, overcast, or clear—could not be determined with any degree of certainty.

Success Rate

Ambushes making use of IEDs had only a 41% success rate overall. Attacks targeting pedestrian-based targets experienced success 40% of the time, while mobile targets only achieved 38% success.

Locations Most Likely Employed At

The area in and around the victim's residence sustained the most attacks by IED, accounting for 45%. Attacks staged while the target was in transit were the second most often selected site, recording 39% of the total. The remaining ambushes were staged at locations such as the victim's office, frequented locations, a public event, a bus terminal, and a hotel.

Global and Regional Perspective

The European region experienced the greatest number of attacks by way of the IED, documenting 41% of the total known. Russia and its republics (Dagestan, Ukraine, South Ossetia, and Chechnya) experienced the next highest use, with 25%. The Middle East region witnessed 20% of the IED-based attacks. When examined by individual country, Russia recorded the most attacks by IED, with five. The countries of Spain, Colombia, and the Republic of Dagestan each had four attacks, while Greece, France, and the United Kingdom experienced three IED detonations.

Most Likely Employed By

Improvised explosive device attacks have been employed by a large number of groups and individuals over the years, displaying some remarkable creativity in their design and placement. Twenty-four of the attacks were attributed to terrorist organizations, while only three were known to have been conducted by organized criminal groups. Four of the attacks are known or strongly believed to have been carried out by government agents. Spain's ETA and Northern Ireland's Irish Republican Army (IRA) each were responsible for four targeted attacks using IEDs.

Most Likely Employed Against

With thirteen of the attacks, world leaders fell victim to IEDs the most often. They were followed in suit by government ministers, accounting for seven. The top three classes of victims were completed by corporate executives, with five such attacks. Prosecutors, judges, diplomats, and military officials each suffered three IED-based attacks. The remaining ambushes targeted eight other classes of victim.

Protective Details

Only 41% of the victims had protective details at the time these attacks were perpetrated. Ambushes using an IED are an effective way to deal with the presence of a protective detail. While there is no way to know with any certainty if the presence of a detail leads to the initiation of this type of attack, it would have to be a factor. Beyond the use of an armored vehicle, the only real benefit of a protective team relative to this method of attack is their training, experience, and dedication to ensuring a variety of routes and speeds are followed when traveling.

Unusual IED Tactics

On four occasions the target vehicle was rapidly approached by an adversary whereupon an improvised explosive device was placed on the roof of the vehicle. The assassin then quickly fled while almost simultaneously detonating the device (in one instance the device was believed to have been remote detonated at the time of placement, thereby killing the assassin as well). In all four of these attacks, the victim was killed. Additionally, in only one instance was the car the victim was traveling in armored.

On three occasions the IED was buried under the roadway known to be traveled by the target. In two of these attacks, the bombers employed a ruse in order to justify the amount of time spent at the ambush point. In another four of the attacks, the IED had been positioned under a bridge that the victim was known to be traveling upon.

LONE GUNMAN

There were a total of 132 attacks stemming from the classic lone gunman. This method of assassination was employed 78% of the time against pedestrian targets and another 20% against motor-vehicle-bound targets, with the remaining occurring at an unknown target position. Attacks perpetrated by the lone gunman have been on the rise since the 1970s, which documented seventeen such attacks. Interestingly, this was the same number of gunman attacks during the preceding twenty-year period of the 1950s and 1960s. The number nearly doubled during the 1980s to thirty attacks. In the 1990s the number of lone gunman ambushes rose to thirty-nine, while by December 31, 2008, the assassin had struck twenty-eight times.

In only eighty of the attacks were the type of weapons employed by the assassin known. In fifty-three of those cases, the gunman used a pistol or revolver, while in seventeen of the ambushes the weapon of choice was an automatic rifle or submachine gun. In only one known case did a gunman use both an automatic weapon and a pistol. In five of the attacks the gunman used a rifle (not including sniper attacks), and in four a shotgun was the weapon of choice.

The months of January and March saw the highest use of lone gunman ambushes, followed very closely by July and October (Figure 3.11). The month of August recorded the least amount of total attacks using this tactic. Seasonally, winter through early spring had the most instances of this style of attack.

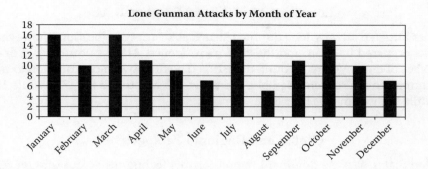

FIGURE 3.11   Lone gunman attacks by month of the year.

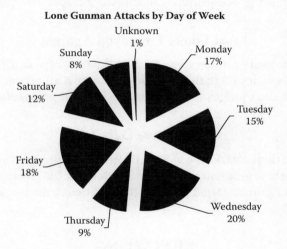

FIGURE 3.12   Lone gunman attacks by day of the week.

The majority of lone gunman attacks were found to have taken place on Wednesday, followed closely by Friday, then Monday (Figure 3.12). As with most attack activity, the bulk has taken place during the traditional Western world workweek.

Success Rate

Ambushes stemming from the classic lone gunman accounted for the largest number of total attacks. Overall, 78% of all attacks by a lone gunman were successful in that the target of the hit was killed. Not surprisingly, the attacks against pedestrian-based targets had the highest rate of success, at 82%, while attacks conducted against mobile-based targets was successful only 62% of the time.

Locations Most Likely Employed At

As in other targeted attacks, lone gunmen struck at a variety of locations; however, 33% of the attacks occurred in or around the victim's residence. Attacks occurring at or near the target's place of employment accounted for 19%. The final two most common locations for a lone gunman to strike were at public events, which accounted for 17%, while 14% were staged while the victim was in transit.

Global and Regional Perspective

The United States was the dominant region for this technique, accounting for 32% of all known attacks. France and Italy were next, but each only documented a lone gunman in 7% of the attacks. Russia and Colombia rounded out of the top five, accounting for 5% and 4%, respectively. The remaining lone gunman attacks were dispersed over forty countries.

Most Likely Employed Against

Worldwide attacks by lone gunmen were used against twenty-six different target classes. However, four classes of individuals were targeted above all others. World leaders were ambushed 18% of the time, judges 13%, lawmakers 8%, and prosecutors 6%.

Protective Details

In the vast majority of these attacks the victim did not have a protective detail; in fact, in only 22% of the attacks by a lone gunman was a protective team of some sort present. Additionally, in most of the attacks against a target with a protective detail, the target was on foot.

KIDNAPPING

There were a total of eighty-eight known kidnappings of targeted individuals during the fifty-eight-year research period. While a relatively rare occurrence during the 1950s with one and 1960s with three kidnappings, the 1970s witnessed a massive spike, with thirty-three kidnapping-based ambushes. The 1980s experienced a slight decrease, but still accounted for twenty-three such attacks. Since then, the numbers have continued to decrease, with the 1990s having fifteen targeted kidnappings and the first eight years of the 2000s having thirteen.

Kidnappings require a considerable amount of planning—beyond that which would normally be called for in attacks employing firearms or explosives. This level of planning is only compounded when the target to be ambushed will be mobile. There is the need to overcome any resistance stemming from potential protective personnel or the target itself. This requires a certain amount of time at the ambush point, which will almost always exceed the time required at a site where an explosive or shooting is to take place. There is the need to have a viable escape route, which can again go beyond what is needed in other attack methods. Finally, to have a captive for any extended duration will result in a multitude of extended problems and issues.

As Figure 3.13 depicts, with the exception of July, kidnappings were conducted with almost no regard as to the month of the calendar year. Seasonally, however, the concentration of kidnappings was during the winter and spring months.

The traditional workweek, as with most attack tactics, continues to have the most activity in regard to kidnappings (Figure 3.14). Thursday and Monday stood out with the most total kidnapping-based ambushes, followed closely by Friday and Tuesday.

Success Rate

As complicated an operation as a kidnapping can be, it enjoyed an astonishing success rate of 98%, during which the victim was abducted regardless of the presence of a protective detail. When conducted against pedestrian targets, the success rate was 100%, while

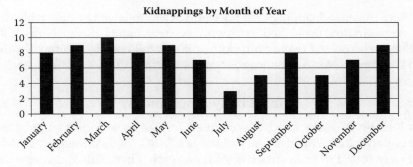

FIGURE 3.13 Kidnappings by month of the year.

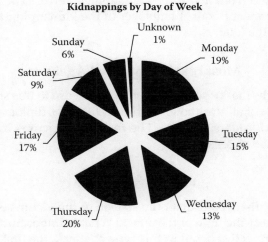

FIGURE 3.14 Kidnappings by day of the week.

against mobile targets a 94% rate of success was obtained. Additionally, there were twenty kidnappings that occurred at a point at which it could not be determined if the victim was a pedestrian or mobile. Of those unknowns, the rate of success was 100%.

Location Most Likely Used At

Kidnappings were found to have been conducted primarily at one of two locations: while in transit (30% of the time) or at the residence (28% of the time). The office was also a common location, albeit to a much lesser degree, only accounting for 7% of the kidnapping ambush sites. Unfortunately, 26% of the attacks occurred at locations that could not be determined. The remaining known kidnapping sites included frequented locations, public events, a hotel, a restaurant/bar, and a university.

Global and Regional Perspective

Colombia, with eleven kidnappings, led the world. It was followed by Italy with nine, Mexico with eight, Argentina and the United States with seven each, and Lebanon with six. Regionally, however, Europe witnessed twenty-nine kidnappings, followed by Central/South America, which had twenty-six. North America rounded out the top three with eighteen.

Most Likely Employed By

Criminals looking to make a profit accounted for the most kidnapping-based attacks, with twelve. Italy's Red Brigades and Colombia's FARC (Revolutionary Armed Forces of Colombia) were found to have struck eight times each. Hizbollah and suspected government agents were determined by authorities to be behind four kidnappings each. The remaining attacks employing this methodology were spread out over twenty-three groups, each documenting between one and three kidnappings. Terrorist organizations as a whole were far and away the most frequent employer of the kidnapping ambush, known to be responsible for 63% of the total.

Most Likely Employed Against

Perhaps not surprisingly, the corporate executive fell victim to this style of attack the most often, representing 44% of all the known victims. With 15%, diplomats were a distant second, followed by world leaders with 6%. The remaining victims included subjects from sixteen different targeted classes.

Protective Details

In kidnappings, it was discovered that only sixteen of the victims employed a protective detail of some measure at the time of the attack. What is important to note is that should one find oneself in a protective detail in this type of attack, the first priority of the adversary will be the removal of the protectors.

MASKED ATTACKER

There were twenty-seven known attacks during which a mask, such as a balaclava or ski mask, was used to prevent the easy identification of the attacker(s) by the target or any witnesses. Eighteen of the attacks were against pedestrian-based targets, while nine targeted vehicle-borne victims. As with other secondary attack methods, there has been an increase in the employment of wearing masks while conducting a targeted attack. Fourteen of the total number of attacks where a mask was employed took place during the first eight years of the 2000s, four of which occurred in 2008. The 1990s accounted for seven attacks by masked adversaries, and another four during the 1980s. Only two attacks by masked attackers were documented to have taken place during the 1970s. There was no known usage during the 1950s and 1960s.

In the targeted attacks during which the adversary employed a mask of some sort, the following were commonalities:

- Seventeen of the targeted victims were government employees or politicians.
- Six of the attacks were perpetrated by a lone gunman.
- Six of the attacks were perpetrated by hit teams of two assassins.
- Eleven occurred at or inside of the victim's residence.
- Nine occurred while the targeted subject was in transit.
- Eighty-nine percent of the attacks were successful.

Overall, the use of masks was relatively low and, being spread out over seventeen countries, did not appear to favor one country over another. Regionally, however, Europe, with 56%, recorded the most known use of a mask during an assassination or kidnapping. North America stood second, with 15% of the known usage.

In twelve of the attacks, the group or individual behind the mask was never identified (their goal was apparently accomplished). Ten of the masked attacks came from terrorist organizations, with Spain's ETA having the most (three). Six of the masked attacks came from criminals or criminal organizations.

MOTORCYCLE HIT TEAMS

The employment of motorcycle in conducting assassinations and contract killings has been used with a considerable amount of lethality in just about every corner of the world, from Europe to South America, from the Middle East to Indonesia, from North America to Asia; all have been witness to the devastating effectiveness of a motorcycle hit team. The attack method has been used by a number of organizations, to include governments, but its most profound admirers are with European and Middle Eastern terrorist organizations, Italian organized crime syndicates, Colombian cartels, Brazilian rebel factions, Asian organized crime, and Philippine death squads.

The use of motorcycle-borne hit teams provides assassins with a number of advantages, all of which are generally not suspicious in and of themselves. One of the biggest advantages comes through the use of protective leathers and a full-coverage helmet (all of which would be considered common safety measures regardless of the time of year): the identity, race, and even sex in some cases are all concealed from victims or witnesses. While motorcycles with two riders are not extremely common, they are not unusual enough to raise the suspicions of the average citizen. By using a pistol, or compact submachine gun, the weapon can easily be concealed between the bodies of the driver and passenger, again without being suspicious. Finally, the motorcycle provides the opportunity for rapid advance and escape from the attack site, regardless of the level of traffic or the presence of roadways.

In this study there were a total of fifty-eight attacks in which the use of motorcycles was a common factor, accounting for approximately 7% of all attack tactics. Of those, the technique was employed 62% of the time against motor-vehicle-bound targets. Pedestrian targets accounted for 34% of the attacks, with 3% occurring at an unknown target position. In 72% of motorcycle-based attacks, there were two riders. Employing two riders is optimum, as it allows the operator of the bike to focus on keeping it upright and in play and the passenger/shooter to focus on the target. In nine of the attacks by motorcycle teams, five employed a pistol while another four made use of automatic weapons, either submachine guns or rifles.

Dr. Siegfried Buback, Germany's chief federal prosecutor, has the dubious honor to be the first known victim of a motorcycle-borne attack. It was this attack in the spring of 1977 that set the mold for the tactic as it has been employed, and which has remained largely unchanged today. As recently as March 2009, a "hitman training camp" was discovered in the mountain region of the Central American country of Guatemala. At that camp were found weapons and motorcycles along with other items that allowed authorities to deduce that the camp was training motorcycle-bound hit teams.

As depicted in Figure 3.15, the attacks have spiked during the months of March, April, and August. While it is difficult to know with any certainty what the reasoning for this is, the spike in March could merely be the result of the passing of the more harsh winter weather in the northern regions, thereby allowing more motorcycle use.

As with other types of attacks, most occurred during the traditional workweek, with Monday and Tuesday having a slight lead on the other days (Figure 3.16). Considering the flexibility the motorcycle provides a hit team, they still must rely upon their target following a somewhat predictable schedule.

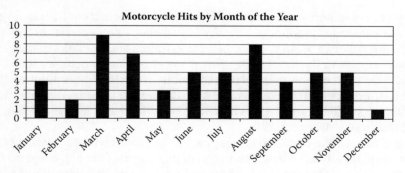

FIGURE 3.15 Motorcycle hits by month of the year.

88

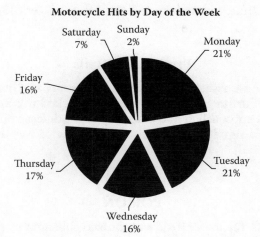

Motorcycle Hits by Day of the Week

FIGURE 3.16   Motorcycle hits by day of the week.

Success Rate

While only accounting for a small percentage of total attacks, motorcycle hit teams have one of the highest success rates of all documented attack styles. Overall, the tactic has a 97% success rate, meaning the target was successfully killed. Against mobile targets that number drops slightly to 94%, while against pedestrian targets it stands at 100%.

Global and Regional Perspective

The motorcycle technique was employed at a number of locations, but the vast majority of strikes were against targets traveling between locations, accounting for 48%. Of those, 38% occurred at unknown points along the route. Approximately 8% occurred at traffic intersections. The victim's residence accounted for the second most often used location for motorcycle-based attacks at 16%.

Most Likely Employed By

Colombia was far and away the most dominant user of the motorcycle hit team, accounting for a full 34% of all known attacks. This is in comparison to Italy, which has the second highest use, but accounting for only 13% of all attacks. Those percentages also echo the regional numbers of South/Central America, accounting for 45% of all attacks, and Europe, standing at 29%.

Most Likely Employed Against

Worldwide the motorcycle technique was used to attack fifteen different target classes. However, four classes of individuals were targeted above all others. Judges were ambushed 17% of the time, lawmakers 15%, military officers 13%, and businessmen/CEOs 11%.

Protective Details

Most of the victims in these assassinations did not have any sort of protective detail, short of perhaps a chauffeur. Further, only one of the cars attacked was armored, and in that situation, the motorcyclist approached and placed an IED briefcase on the roof of the vehicle while it was waiting at a signal light (in this case the device was detonated immediately, killing the assassin as well).

POISON

With only eleven attacks, the use of toxic weaponized substances ranked as the least often employed method of assassination (at least of those known). In all but one of these cases, the individual employing the weapon was known to be or strongly believed to be an agent of a government service. In all but one case, the target of the attack was an activist/dissident against the government suspected of being behind the attack. In the last case the target was a member of a terrorist organization.

In terms of the timing of poison attacks, they were found to have occurred in only six of the calendar months, with September recording the most, with four. This tactic was also conducted on every day of the week except for Tuesday. Wednesday accounted for the most poison-based attacks, with three. There was no preferred time of day in which to strike, although the vast majority occurred during the daylight hours between 0600 and 1800.

Success Rate

Given the amount of planning and preparation involved with a poison-based assassination attack, it had only a 64% rate of success.

Locations Most Likely Employed At

This style of attack was deployed at several locations, but interestingly enough, the airport/airplane accounted for the most, with three attacks. Other locations in order of the frequency include the office, while in transit, the residence, court, a restaurant, and one case in which it could not be determined.

Global and Regional Perspective

Given the low known total of poison-based attacks, it is difficult to determine a country were this type of ambush is more apt to occur. However, the United Kingdom and Germany each had two such attacks, putting them at the top of the list of countries in which poison was used. This also pushed the European region to the top, with five of the total attacks. Two attacks were found to have taken place on the African continent, one in

South Africa and one in Mozambique. The remaining countries known to have experienced such an attack were Jordan, Indonesia, Pakistan, and the United States.

Most Likely Employed By

In one case the suspect behind the case was never discovered; the other ten attacks were all found to have been or strongly believed to be government agents.

Most Likely Employed Against

The activist/dissident fell victim to this style of attack the most, accounting for six of the eleven attacks. This was followed by victims in the targeted classes of intelligence officer, clergy, prosecutor, terrorist, and one attack that successfully killed a world leader, a diplomat, and a military official.

Types of Poison and Delivery Methods

In four of the attacks, the toxic substances remain unknown to any degree of certainty (in two of these attacks, the delivery device was a mist-spraying gun that dispersed the unknown agent into the face of the target). With the remaining attacks, six substances were employed. Ricin was used in two of the attacks, both times injecting the substance into the subject with a specially modified umbrella. In one of the attacks, a toxic known as Paraoxen was applied to the underwear of the target; this was later absorbed into the skin of the victim. In an attack using cyanide, pistol rounds were dipped into the toxic substance. Fortunately for the victim, the bulk of the cyanide burned off when the round was fired. In one case a radiological substance known as polonium-210 was introduced into the victim's tea. A similar method was employed when the toxin arsenic was added to a drink of a target while traveling on board an aircraft. Finally, there was a single attack that is strongly believed to have employed a deadly nerve agent that successfully killed a world leader, diplomat, and military official.

RUSE

The use of a ruse or disguise was known to have been employed in thirty-five attacks. The primary use of this tactic is that it allows the assassin(s) to close the distance with the target, as well as reduce the level of scrutiny and suspicion from the target and protective detail, if present. This method was used in twenty-six attacks against pedestrian-based targets and nine mobile targets. The 1990s witnessed the most use of this tactic, with ten such attacks. Prior to that, during the 1980s there were nine ruse-based attacks, while seven took place during the 1970s. During the 1960s only one such attack was found, but none where found during the 1950s. By December 2008, there had been eight attacks using the ruse during the 2000s.

Success Rate

The use of a ruse/disguise by the assassin or kidnapper to get within striking distance of his or her target allowed for an 89% success rate regardless of the type of attack being staged.

Locations Most Likely Employed At

The residence saw 43% of the total usage of the ruse/disguise tactic. Attacks employing a ruse/disguise targeted subjects while they were in transit 20% of the time. The remaining locations included public events, the office, a restaurant, a sporting event, an airport, or could not be determined.

Global and Regional Perspective

There were nineteen countries discovered to have known attacks during which a ruse or disguise was used. Italy led the pack with five of these attacks, followed by Germany and the United States each with four. India and Afghanistan wrapped up the top five, each of which experiencing three such attacks. With fifteen attacks making use of this tactic, the European region led the world. This was followed by South Asia, which accounted for seven of the attacks, and North America with six.

Most Likely Employed By

Twenty-three of the groups known to have made use of a ruse/disguise when conducting a targeted attack were found to be terrorists. Five were found to be criminals or organized criminal groups, while two were believed to be government agents. The remaining five came at the hands of unknown groups or individuals.

Most Likely Employed Against

With six attacks each, the world leader and corporate executive were most often the victims of the ruse/disguise-applied attack. The diplomat suffered four such attacks. The remaining attacks targeted twelve different victim classes.

Types of Disguises/Ruses Employed

While there were a variety of different ruses or disguises known to have been employed in order to ambush a target, only eight were found to have been used more than once. The following is a list of the different ruses and disguises along with the number of times they were used:

- Disguise of police officers inside a patrol vehicle conducting a traffic stop (four occasions)
- Ruse of journalists seeking an interview (three occasions)
- Disguise of a priest (two occasions)
- Ruse of a business meeting with the victim (two occasions)

- Disguise of a postman delivering mail (two occasions)
- Ruse of selling flowers door to door (two occasions)
- Disguise consisting of wigs, mustaches, and glasses (two occasions)
- Ruse of a family/friendship visit (two occasions)
- Ruse of a flat tire/vehicle problems (two occasions)
- Disguise of plumbers needing to repair a leak (one occasion)
- Ruse of asking for directions (one occasion)
- Disguise of a deliveryman (one occasion)
- Ruse of a fellow tenant in elevator (one occasion)
- Disguise of a woman in a burka, but worn by a man (one occasion)
- Ruse of an innocent-looking flower girl (one occasion)
- Disguise consisting of a fake beard (one occasion)
- Ruse of a fan seeking a photo/autograph (one occasion)
- Disguise of a telephone repairman (one occasion)
- Ruse of a highway construction crew making repairs (one occasion)
- Disguise of airline pilots awaiting transport to the airport (one occasion)
- Ruse of land surveyors working on a roadway (one occasion)
- Ruse of members of a sporting event crowd (one occasion)
- Disguise of a military member in uniform (one occasion)

Type of Attack Conducted in Conjunction with Ruse/Disguise

In targeted attacks by way of ruse or disguise, seventeen were shootings. Eight came from lone gunmen, while another four were carried out by hit teams of three to five gunmen. The remaining shooting attacks came from an undetermined number of shooters. In eight of the targeted attacks employing a ruse or disguise, the goal was the kidnapping of the victim. Five of these were against mobile targets.

Six of the targeted attacks occurred by way of explosive device, four of which were suicide bombers. The remaining two explosive attacks occurred when the bombers used a ruse of highway construction crew or land surveyors in order to preposition the device; both attacks were ultimately successful. Four of the attacks, all of which were pedestrian based, were stabbing ones, which for obvious reasons required a disguise or ruse in order to close the distance.

SNIPERS

Often depicted in the movies as the quintessential assassin, the sniper was found to have been employed in only twenty-seven attacks worldwide. Of these hits, four were perpetrated against vehicle-borne targets, while the remaining twenty-three were against pedestrian-based victims. While a relatively rare occurrence, there has been a consistent amount of sniper attacks over the previous fifty years, beginning during the 1960s. The decades of the 1960s, 1970s, and 1990s each witnessed five of these attacks, while the 1980s suffered four. The first eight years of the 2000s, however, experienced the greatest number of assassinations by way of the sniper's bullet, with eight.

One great attribute the sniper's rifle affords the assassin is the distance in which he or she needs to be prior to striking. Second, the nature of the scoped large-caliber rifle allows the assassin to reach into a protective detail's circle and kill a target even if he or she is wearing soft body armor. While today's technology allows for attacks up to more than a mile away, even an average caliber rifle in the hands of an average shooter can allow shots from 100 to 500 meters, all of which are beyond the ranges of sidearms and submachine guns. As a result, they are and remain of the greatest concern to the competent protective detail.

Interestingly enough, two of the attacks were against a moving motorcade, both of which were positioned in a location where the motorcade would be making a turn, thereby forcing the speed of the vehicles to be slowed considerably. Additionally, both of the sniper nest positions were at a considerable elevation in relation to the target. In one of the attacks, the target was traveling inside of a convertible vehicle, allowing for correct target identification. The second attack forced the sniper to fire through the roof, which he did eight times; however, since five of the rounds found their mark, the sniper apparently had some inclination as to the location within the vehicle of his target.

In the first attack on the convertible vehicle, only one man was ever directly linked to the killing. However, it is believed by many to have been conducted by more than one sniper team. In the second attack, it was found to be the work of a two-man team. Both sniper teams were within approximately 100 meters of their target. While the distance of the shot was relatively short, the fact that the shots were made from elevated positions against moving targets required snipers with considerable training and experience (or just plain lucky).

In attacks against pedestrians, most appear to have been conducted by military-trained teams, evidenced by the traditional use of the sniper/spotter concept. However, two were conducted by nontrained individuals, one late at night, in which he was able to lay undetected for approximately four hours prior to completing his mission, and the other early in the morning.

The attack method was only found to have been employed in nine separate months (Figure 3.17). Seven attacks were documented as occurring in August, followed by March with six. Seasonally, the attacks were concentrated in the spring.

As with other attacks, most of the sniper-based attacks were staged during the traditional workweek (Figure 3.18). However, Friday, with 36% of all attacks, had far and away the most activity.

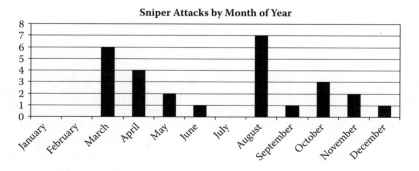

FIGURE 3.17 Sniper attacks by month of the year.

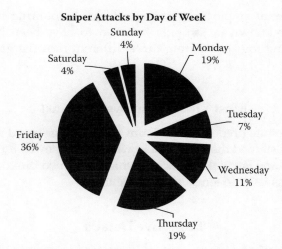

FIGURE 3.18   Sniper attacks by day of the week.

Success Rate

Given the nature of this method of attack, it should come as no surprise that assassinations by way of sniper resulted in a 93% kill ratio. However, the art of the sniper requires a more highly trained assassin, especially when the distance or elevation increases, and especially when the target is traveling in a vehicle. This is a likely reason for the high success rate, but also the relatively low use.

Locations Most Likely Employed At

With 33% of all attacks, the victim's residence and office were equally selected by the sniper as the optimal place to strike. This was followed by attacks on targets in transit, with 11% of the total. The remaining 23% of sniper attacks occurred at four other locations, including an airport, hotels, a public event, and frequented locations.

Global and Regional Perspective

The United States had the most sniper-based attacks over the fifty-eight-year period, accounting for a full 41%. The only other country to record more than one sniper attack was Russia (including the Republics of Dagestan, Georgia, and the Ukraine), with 26% of known hits. The remaining attacks were dispersed over nine other countries.

Most Likely Employed By

Unfortunately in thirteen of the attacks, the group or individual behind the ambush was not or could not be determined. Of those that are known, the right-wing extremist/

racist was the dominant employer of sniper attacks, accounting for six. Government agencies were either known or strongly believed to have been behind three of the attacks. The remaining four came from three different terrorist groups and one organized crime group.

Most Likely Employed Against

Globally there was no one predominant victim of the sniper-based attack. However, the corporate executive sustained the most attacks with four, followed by world leaders, activists, military officials, and lawmakers, each of which sustained three sniper-based attacks. The remaining victims fell into ten separate categories.

Protective Details

The majority of the victims of assassination by way of sniper did not have a protective detail; in fact, in only seven of the attacks was a protective presence of some sort known to have been involved. Given the type of threat a sniper represents, there is perhaps little a protective detail can offer short of an awareness of where the potential sniper nest position could lay, and therefore divert some resources to covering those areas.

EDGED WEAPONS

There were a total of twenty-one known edged weapon attacks occurring over the fifty-eight-year period of review. Understandably, edged weapon attacks represent a relatively small percentage of attacks, but enough to warrant a more through review. Unlike the other forms of ambush, the use of an edged weapon, while a very quiet style of attack, requires the adversary to get extremely close to his or her victim. While the background of the attackers isn't known, an edged weapon in the hands of someone knowledgeable is extremely formidable, even against someone armed with a firearm.

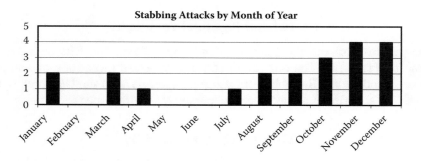

FIGURE 3.19 Stabbing attacks by month of the year.

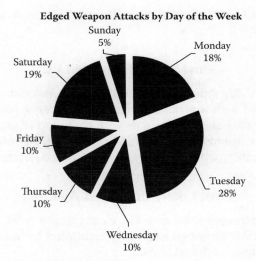

Edged Weapon Attacks by Day of the Week

FIGURE 3.20   Edged weapon attacks by day of the week.

Statistically, the majority of edged weapon attacks occurred in November and December, each of which recorded four such attacks (Figure 3.19). Stabbing attacks were concentrated in the late summer through mid winter months, with the most attacks occurring in November and December. Given the preferred location of attack, this could be due to the decreased hours of light in these months.

Tuesdays documented the majority of edged weapon attacks, followed interestingly enough by Saturdays (Figure 3.20). Mondays rounded out the top three days for this style of attack. The remaining were spread primarily through the workweek.

Success Rate

Of the twenty-one attacks, only twelve were successful in that the victim was killed. However, with the exception of a single attack in which no injury occurred, all were successful in that the victim received at least some sort of slashing or stabbing wound.

Locations Most Likely Employed At

With almost 50% of the edged weapon attacks, the residence was the most often selected location for this style of ambush. The office was a distant second, with 19% of edged-weapon-based attacks. The remaining were dispersed over five other locations or could not be determined.

Global and Regional Perspective

While still a small total number, the countries of Japan and France recorded the most edged-weapon attacks, with four each. The United States rounded out the top three countries, with three edged-weapon attacks. The remaining occurred in ten separate countries.

The European region, interestingly enough, witnessed the most attacks by way of stabbings, accounting for 43%.

Most Likely Employed By

Unfortunately in nine of the attacks, the identity of the assassin or the group he or she may have been associated with was never discovered. However, the majority of the edged-weapon attacks came at the hand of criminals with some sort of grudge against the target. They were followed by extremist-based attacks (right wing, Islamic, etc.), representing no specific group. The remaining attacks came at the hands of a government agent and rivals.

Most Likely Employed Against

World leaders and government ministers fell victim to the most edged-weapon attacks during the research period, although each only accounted for three. The remaining targeted individuals were in ten other classes.

Protective Details

In only eight of the attacks was a protective detail of some sort present at the time. However, given the nature of an edged-weapon attack, the assassin needs to get within extremely close range in order to strike, which should be rather difficult if a protective detail is present. In order for that to occur, the assassin must, through either disguise or ruse, cause protective personal to lower their guard. Once within striking distance, the stabbing assassin will be in a position to strike repeatedly and with potentially great lethality before a detail can react to stop the attack. However, similar to a suicide bomber targeted attack, the assassin would have to go into the operation with the realization that he or she will not survive.

SUICIDE BOMBERS

A total of twenty-four attacks in which the use of a suicide bomber was the common factor were found to have been conducted during the research period. Of those attacks, the technique was employed sixteen times against motor vehicle targets and eight times against pedestrians. The first known use of a suicide bomber to conduct a targeted killing occurred during the 1980s. There would not be a repeat of this technique until during the 1990s, which witnessed twelve such attacks. As of December 2008, a total of eleven such attacks had occurred in the 2000s.

The months of May, October, and December each recorded four suicide-bomber-based attacks (Figure 3.21). Seasonally, the suicide bomber was deployed throughout the late spring through early autumn.

Thursday, with 33% of suicide bomber attacks, had far and away the most such activity (Figure 3.22). This was followed by Mondays with 21% and Fridays with 17%. Interestingly,

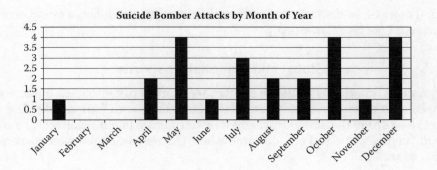

FIGURE 3.21 Suicide bomber attacks by month of the year.

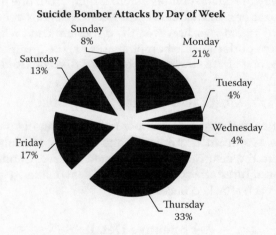

FIGURE 3.22 Suicide bomber attacks by day of the week.

there was a sharp decline in this method of attack during Tuesday and Wednesday, both of which documented less attacks by a suicide bomber than those occurring on a Sunday.

Success Rate

Attacks by way of suicide bomber only had a 46% overall success rate. Somewhat surprisingly, against pedestrian-based targets the success rate sat at only 75%. Targeted attacks against vehicle-borne victims were successful 31% of the time.

Locations Most Likely Employed At

The suicide bomber struck 50% of the time while the target was in transit. This was followed by attacks occurring at public events, which accounted for 29%. The remaining 21%

of suicide-bomber-based attacks occurred at the office, the residence, a mosque, or at locations that could not be determined.

Global and Regional Perspective

Not surprisingly, attacks by a suicide bomber were primarily restricted to the regions of South Asia, with seventeen attacks, and the Middle East, with four attacks. The country of Sri Lanka recorded the most, with eight targeted suicide bombing attacks. Pakistan followed suit, having witnessed six such ambushes. The remaining ten were dispersed over nine other countries.

Most Likely Employed By

Targeted killings by way of suicide bombers stem largely from one group. Several Islamic fundamentalist organizations/individuals employed this tactic over eleven separate occasions. Sri Lanka's Tamil Tigers was; however, the dominant user, with nine attacks attributed to them. With three of the suicide bombing attacks, the group responsible could not be determined. Finally, one of the attacks was believed to come from a criminal group.

Most Likely Employed Against

World leaders fell victim to the suicide bomber target killing the most often, accounting for nine of the attacks. Government ministers and military officials, each of whom suffered four attacks, were the next most often targeted classes. Candidates for president/prime minister witnessed three attacks, while clergy, a lawmaker, a governor/prefect, and a political leader were each attacked once.

Protective Detail

In 83% of the attacks, a protective detail was present at the time. Unfortunately, given the nature of this tactic, only the detection of the bomber while still at a relatively safe distance can save a principal. Once the bomber has closed to within twenty or so feet (given that devices are often constructed of approximately 10 pounds of explosive material), the blast force coupled with the shrapnel will have very lethal effects.

SUPPRESSED WEAPONS

There were twenty-two documented attacks that were known or reasonably believed to have occurred using suppressed weapons. Eighteen of these attacks were against pedestrian-based victims, while four were perpetrated against vehicle-borne targets. The use of suppressors has been on the rise, with twelve occurring during the first eight years of the 2000s, half of which occurred during 2008. The 1990s only recorded suppressors being used in six attacks, and two were found to have been used during the 1980s.

Of those attacks, the following were commonalities:

- Twenty-one of the victims did not have any sort of protective detail.
- Twenty of the attacks were at close range with multiple rounds fired.
- Thirteen of the victims were government employees or politicians.
- Five of the victims were activists/dissidents.
- Eight of the attacks were perpetrated by teams of two assassins.
- Fourteen occurred at or inside of the victim's residence.
- Four occurred at or inside of a hotel.
- Four occurred in the morning hours.
- All of the attacks were successful.

Overall, the use of suppressed weapons was relatively low and did not appear to favor one region over another. However, the country of Russia was found to have had the most attacks using this tactic, with four. Mexico followed with three such attacks. The United States, France, and Belgium each witnessed two attacks using suppressed weapons. The remaining were staged in nine other countries.

Generally the type of suppressed weapon used in the attacks was that of the pistol, which accounted for 83% of the total (there were eighteen attacks where the type of weapon was known). The pistol calibers included .22, .22LR, .380, 7.65, and 9 mm. A suppressed rifle was deployed and accounted for two sniper-based attacks. Finally, one case of a suppressed submachine gun was discovered, taking the form of a MAC-10 in .45 caliber.

In eight of the attacks using suppressed weapons, it was known or there were strong indications to believe that the attack came from governmental agents. This is certainly reasonable given the general difficulty in obtaining suppressors. Islamic extremist groups were found to be behind three of the attacks, as were the Mexican drug cartels. The remaining attackers were neo-Nazis, criminals, or could not be determined.

A suppressed weapon provides a number of benefits for the would-be assassin. First, it allows a shooting to occur in an area where bystanders are in close proximity to the ambush site, such as a hotel or apartment, without drawing unwanted attention. By reducing the noise, there is less likelihood for witnesses, thereby making a clean escape more probable. One problem suppressors do present to the assassin is the decrease in overall concealability. When attached to even the smallest pistol, the length of the weapon will nearly double. The presence of the suppressors can also indicate a more sophisticated adversary who has access to more advanced hardware.

THE THREE- TO FIVE-GUNMEN HIT TEAM

A total of forty-seven attacks were found to have been perpetrated by hit teams consisting of between three and five assassins. Sixty-eight percent of the attacks targeted the pedestrian-based victim, while 21% were against a mobile victim. The remaining attacks were staged against a target whose exact positioning could not be determined.

The three- to five-person hit team has seen documented use since the 1960s, which recorded two such attacks. During the 1970s the number spiked to eleven such attacks. The decade of the 1980s witnessed the most usage of this tactic, accounting for fourteen. This carried through the 1990s, when thirteen attacks were staged by the three- to five-person hit team. There was some decrease in the usage of this tactic during the first eight years of the 2000s, as only seven attacks were documented.

In thirty-six of the attacks perpetrated by these hit teams, the type of weapon was known. In fifteen of those, automatic weapons were employed. In thirteen others, a pistol was the weapon of choice. In three attacks, the assassins made use of a combination of both weapons. In five of the attacks, the weapon of choice was a shotgun.

The month of July, with nine, documented the most attacks employing this tactic (Figure 3.23). This was followed by February, during which six attacks were recorded. However, this tactic was employed throughout the calendar year with some consistency, with the sole exception of December, which recorded only one known instance of an attack by this method.

Fridays, with 21%, and Wednesdays, with 19%, witnessed the vast majority of ambush attacks by this style of hit team (Figure 3.24). Sundays and Tuesdays each documented 17%

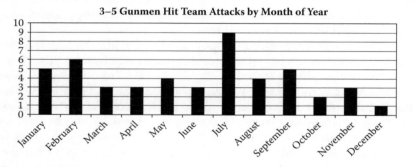

FIGURE 3.23   Three- to five-gunmen hit team attacks by month of the year.

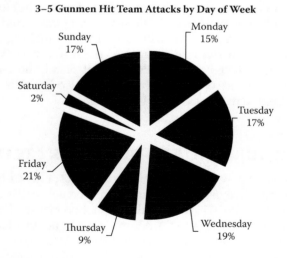

FIGURE 3.24   Three- to five-gunmen hit team attacks by day of the week.

of all of the attacks. The remaining were spread out over the other days; however, only 2% of all attacks were found to take place on a Saturday.

Unfortunately, twenty-six of the attacks occurred at an unknown hour. Of the known times, the morning hours of 0601 to 0900 recorded seven such attacks, the most of any time frame. This was followed by five attacks during the hours of 1801 to 2100. Another four attacks were sprung between 2101 and 2400. During the nine-hour period between 0901 and 1800, only four attacks are known to have occurred. Finally, one attack was documented to have taken place between 0001 and 0300.

Success Rate

Not surprisingly given the number of shooters, attacks by hit teams of between three and five gunmen had a very high rate of success. In total, the tactic had an 89% rate of success. In the ten attacks against vehicle-borne targets, the rate was 80%, while against thirty-two pedestrian targets it sat at 94%. Additionally, there were five attacks perpetrated against a target during which its positioning, either mobile or pedestrian, could not be determined. Of those five attacks, the success rate was 80%.

Locations Most Likely Employed At

The three- to five-gunman hit team ambush was conducted at a variety of locations, but the residence was witness to 53% of the total usage. This technique was employed against victims in transit 11% of the time, followed by the office 9% of the time. The remaining attacks were staged at four other locations, including public events, a restaurant, hotels, and a university, or could not be determined.

Global and Regional Perspective

With 19% of the attacks, Italy recorded the most use of the three- to five-gunman hit team. This was followed by Greece, which had 9% of the attacks. Mexico, France, and Colombia each documented 6% of targeted attacks employing a hit team of this configuration. The remaining attacks employing this methodology occurred in twenty countries. With 49% of the total attacks by this style of hit team, the European region ranked number one. This was followed by the region of Central/South America, with 13% of known usage.

Most Likely Employed By

Italy's Red Brigades and Greece's November 17 used the three- to five-gunman hit team the most often of any one group. They each were known to have employed it on four occasions. All told, twenty-four different groups have made use of the tactic (nineteen were terrorist organizations, both international and regionally domestic), all of which conducted twenty-six such attacks. With thirteen of the attacks, the group or individuals responsible were neither claimed nor determined by investigation.

Most Likely Employed Against

The world leader fell victim to this method the most often, suffering six of the total known attacks. Federal government officials fell second most often, accounting for five of the attacks. Judges, government ministers, law enforcement officials, diplomats, and activists/dissidents were next in recorded ambushes by this style of hit team, each of which suffered four. The remaining usage was spread out over eight different targeted classes.

Protective Details

In only 21% of these attacks was a protective detail of some sort present. Given the high fatality rate of the target in this style of attack, we can infer that the detail was simply overwhelmed (although it was not able to be determined if the individuals assigned to protection were even armed at the time, or their level of training). However, during this research the protective detail was found to consist most often of a single man. Even if two protective detail members were present, engaging a hit team of this size would require significant skill at arms.

TWO-GUNMEN HIT TEAM

There were a total of seventy-six attacks documented as being conducted by the two-gunmen hit team. Only twelve such attacks were employed against vehicle-borne targets, with another sixty-one targeting pedestrian-based victims. In three cases, the exact location of the victim at the time of the attack could not be determined. The use of this tactic has been on the increase, resulting in considerable lethality since the 1970s, which recorded fourteen known attacks. That number jumped to twenty-two attacks during the 1980s, before falling to fifteen during the 1990s. As has been seen in other attack methods, the first eight years of the 2000s recorded a steady rise in its use, having witnessed twenty-one such attacks by way of the two-person hit team.

In thirty-six of the attacks, the type of weapon used was known. Of those, nineteen made use of a pistol or revolver. Another eleven attacks employed automatic weapons of some configuration. In only two cases was a combination of both weapons known to have been employed in the attack. In three of the ambushes, a shotgun was used, and in one known case a rifle.

While attacks by the two-gunmen hit team have been employed throughout the calendar year, November recorded the most, with 16% of the total number committed (Figure 3.25). Seasonally, the greatest numbers of this style of attack were carried out during the autumn and winter months.

The largest percentages of this attack style were recorded during the middle of the workweek, with Wednesday having the most of any single day, with 20% (Figure 3.26). Tuesday, with 19% of the total number, followed closely behind by Thursday, with 17% of the attacks. Interestingly enough, Saturday, with 14%, had the next highest percentage of attacks during the seven-day period.

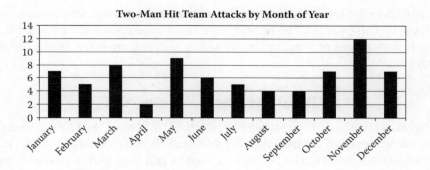

Two-Man Hit Team Attacks by Month of Year

FIGURE 3.25 Two-gunmen hit team attacks by month of the year.

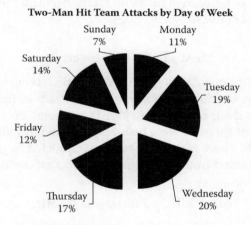

Two-Man Hit Team Attacks by Day of Week

FIGURE 3.26 Two-gunmen hit team attacks by day of the week.

Success Rate

Two-person hit teams have proven to be an extremely effective and deadly way of conducting targeted killings, being successful 92% of the time regardless of the presence of a protective detail. Against the twelve vehicle-borne victims, the two-gunmen hit team had a 75% success rate. When employed against the pedestrian victim, the rate of success stood at 97%. In three of the attacks, the position of the victims could not be determined, but of those, two were successful.

Location Most Likely Used At

The victim's residence was the scene of the majority of the attacks by the two-gunmen hit team, accounting for 33% of the total number. This was followed by the office in 20% of the attacks, and against a victim in transit 13% of the time. Interestingly, the location with the next highest percentage was a bar or restaurant, which documented 9% of the attacks by this method. The remaining attacks were staged at a variety of locations, including hotels, places of worship, universities, sports complexes, hotels, or could not be determined.

Global and Regional Perspective

The United States ranked as the number one country for use of the two-gunmen hit team tactic, recording eleven of the total number known. Following closely behind, France documented eight such attacks. The countries of Spain and Italy each witnessed seven such attacks during the fifty-eight-year period. The remaining use of this tactic was dispersed over twenty-seven countries worldwide. Regionally, Europe ranked number one, with 49% of all attacks by the two-gunmen hit team. North America ranked a distance second, accounting for only 17% of attacks.

Most Likely Employed By

Terrorists/extremist groups made strong use of this tactic, having been found to be behind thirty-two of the attacks. Organized criminal groups (such as the Cosa Nostra, and the Mexican and Colombian drug cartels) were a distant second, accounting for only twelve such attacks. Government agencies were believed to be behind another seven attacks by the two-gunmen hit team. Three of the attacks were conducted by general street criminals, while the remaining stemmed from groups/individuals that could not be determined.

Most Likely Employed Against

The victims of this tactic ran the gamut of the targeted classes. The diplomat, however, was the victim the most often, recording thirteen attacks. They were followed by lawmakers, who suffered eight such attacks. Mayors and activists each fell victim to six attacks, while judges rounded out the top five victim classes, with five attacks.

Protective Details

Details were only present in eighteen of the attacks by the two-gunmen hit team. However, they were successful in keeping their principal from being killed 72% of the time.

VEHICLE-BORNE IMPROVISED EXPLOSIVE DEVICE

The vehicle-borne improvised explosive device (VBIED) was documented in fifty-three targeted attacks, representing only 6% of all ambushes. Of those attacks, the technique was perpetrated forty-one times against vehicle-borne victims. Another twelve were carried out against pedestrian victims.

With twenty documented VBIED attacks, the first eight years of the 2000s experienced the same number as occurred during the entire decade of the 1990s. This was followed by the 1980s, which recorded ten such attacks using this methodology, with only two occurring during the 1970s, and only one during the 1960s.

The VBIED attack method was employed throughout the year, but January, March, and July recorded the most, each accounting for 13% of the total known usage (Figure 3.27). The months of June and September rounded out the top five months, with six each. Seasonally, the winter months accounted for 40% of the VBIED attacks.

As with other targeted ambushes, most VBIED attacks were staged between Monday and Friday, with Tuesday accounting for 27% of the total (Figure 3.28). Monday and Wednesday followed suit, with 17% and 15%, respectively. Sunday was also found to have recorded a fairly large number of VBIED attacks, having an equal percentage with Thursday and Friday.

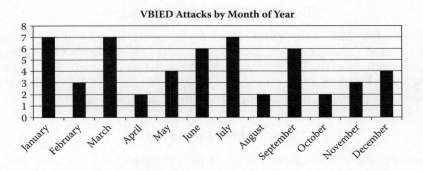

FIGURE 3.27   VBIED attacks by month of the year.

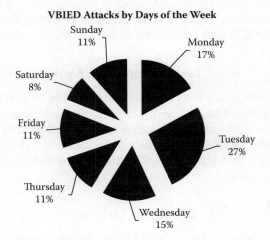

FIGURE 3.28   VBIED attacks by day of the week.

Success Rate

Given the potential power of VBIEDs it is somewhat surprising that this technique was only successful 42% of the time. When employed against pedestrian-based targets, the VBIED is understandably far more lethal, recording a 75% success rate. This rate, however, drops considerably when the target is mobile inside some sort of vehicle, at only 40%.

Locations Most Likely Employed At

As perhaps would be expected, the VBIED-based ambush occurred most often while the victim was in transit, accounting for 58% of the attacks. This provides a strong indication that routes of travel were either limited or not changed up often enough. The area in and around the target's residence documented 26% of all VBIED attacks. The remaining attacks occurred at the office, frequented locations, and public events.

Global and Regional Perspective

Lebanon, recording 28% of the VBIED attacks, witnessed the most of any country. Spain and Russia shared the second spot, each experiencing 11% of attacks. Greece rounded out the top spots, with 9% of the VBIED-based ambushes. Seventeen countries documented the remaining VBIED attacks during the research period. Regionally, Europe and the Middle East shared the top spot, each recording 32% of the total VBIED activity.

Most Likely Employed By

In twenty-two of the VBIED attacks, the group behind the ambush was never discovered by either claims of responsibility or subsequent investigation (or never released to the public). Government agencies were known or believed to be behind eight of the VBIED attacks, followed by Spain's ETA with five. Greece's November 17 organization claimed four of the attacks, while Italy's Sicilian mafia was found to be responsible for three. The remaining ambushes were undertaken by nine different organizations, both terrorist and organized crime.

Most Likely Employed Against

World leaders were far and away the predominant victim to this style of attack, recording thirteen in fifty-eight years. They were distantly followed by corporate executives, who were attacked five times, and judges and mayors, each of which fell victim to four VBIED attacks. Military officials, lawmakers, government ministers, and federal government officials were each ambushed three times by VBIEDs. The remaining attacks targeted subjects in eleven other victim classes.

Protective Details

Seventy-four percent of targets of the VBIED-based attack employed protective details of some sort. In many of these attacks, the protective operation was a long-running one that often traveled between work and the residence. Herein lies the strength of the VBIED tactic in that by its very nature it can be parked in a location and, if done properly, be left for a fairly long period of time. This requires only for the adversary to patiently wait for the target to travel the route where the device is located.

VEHICLE INTERCEPT

The vehicle intercept, while only documented in seven attacks (but more likely exceedingly higher), is nonetheless an important tactic for protective details and victims to be aware of. Given the high number of kidnappings that are known to have occurred against victims that were traveling in a vehicle, the interception of said vehicle had to have occurred at some point. In these attacks, in which the target to be kidnapped has a protective detail, the adversary must obviously deal with them first. This results in an extremely dangerous encounter for the detail, whether prepared or not. Perhaps no case better exemplifies this than the kidnapping of Aldo Moro in Italy (covered in detail in the case summaries).

Of the seven known instances of a vehicle being intercepted, three had a protective detail, all of whom were killed by the adversaries. While the exact method of intercept can vary, it is often facilitated when a vehicle pulls in front of the targeted vehicle/motorcade and immediately slams on the brakes, causing one or both of the motorcade vehicles to rear-end each other. This is then generally followed by a second suspect car, which acts as a cutoff vehicle. Oftentimes the suspects rapidly deploy from both vehicles and immediately open fire upon the target vehicle.

While a vehicle intercept tactic provides the adversary with a certain amount of flexibility in where and when it is staged, it has an inherent weakness that can be exploited by the observant protective detail or target. For the intercept to work, a hostile vehicle must first position itself in front of the target vehicle. This positioning requirement is what the detail/target must be alert to and prepared to act accordingly.

The intercept tactic is known to have taken place in Lebanon, Italy, Peru, Switzerland, and Mexico at several different times of the year and week. The groups known or believed to have been behind the attacks include the Sicilian mafia, Shining Path, rebels, and possibly government agents. The targets have included government ministers, a judge, a diplomat, an activist, and on three occasions, corporate executives.

4

Attack Locations

Perhaps the most important factor for any ambush is the location it is to take place. For the adversary there are a number of factors that must be taken into consideration during the planning phase. Does the potential ambush site allow for the type of attack being considered? Does it allow for the attacker to wait for the victim to arrive without being detected, and in the case of the urban setting, without people becoming suspicious? Does the site provide for a quick and efficient escape after the attack has been conducted (which applies for all but the suicide bomber)? Finally, the most important factor, will the target be at the ambush site within a known time frame?

Just about every adult on this planet has two locations that he or she can be expected to be found at certain times of the day within a twenty-four-hour period. This is generally the residence and the place of business (hereafter referred to as the office). It is for this reason that the vast majority of targeted attacks are staged at one of these two locations. Most often the office is the one location that is known to an adversary. With this knowledge, it only requires a little patience and effort to locate the residence (which has become infinitely easier to obtain with the advent of the Internet). Generally speaking, people are safe inside of these two locations, but the moment they step out the door, they are at immense risk, if they are being targeted.

A professional assassin or kidnapper (someone willing to take the time to research and plan an attack) will generally want more than just these two potential ambush sites to select from. It is therefore critical to understand what the adversary looks for in potential ambush locations. Each time a target frequents a location, or travels the same route, increases the potential ambush site selections available to the adversary.

Figure 4.1 details the eight most often selected sites used in ambushes around the world. Of note is the number of attacks occurring while the targeted victim was in transit (generally while traveling between the residence and office). This statistic indicates that a great many victims had been traveling the same routes, which is a habit of most humans that requires a great deal of dedication to break. Of all of the attacks occurring while the victim was in transit between locations, thirty-nine are known to have been staged at intersections (often while waiting for a signal light to switch to green), or areas of known traffic congestion.

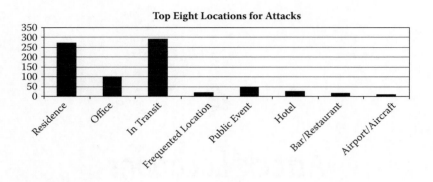

FIGURE 4.1 Locations of attacks.

The following pages will detail each of the eight locations where the greatest numbers of attacks were known to have occurred during the research period. In the case of the attacks while in transit, a separate section details those occurring at intersections or traffic congestion points. Finally, one section details ambushes staged while the victim was in the process of entering or exiting a vehicle. Sixty-three of the attacks are known to have taken place at this vulnerable time.

AIRPORT/AIRCRAFT

Ten attacks were found to have been staged against a victim while at an airport or onboard an aircraft (only two have been conducted since September 11, 2001, only one of which actually occurred on an aircraft, but was at the hand of a government agent). While representing an extremely low number of attacks given the total reviewed, this is a very unusual and even difficult location in which to strike. However, the beating death of a Hell's Angel by a rival biker gang, which initially began verbally onboard an aircraft and actually occurred at the major airport in Sydney, Australia in 2009, provides further proof of the need to examine this location.

Timing of Attack

In the four attacks in which the time was known, three occurred between the hours of 1801 and 2100. One was found to have been staged between the morning hours of 0901 and 1200.

Type of Attack

Six of the attacks employed firearms, a lone gunman accounting for two of these. The sniper and the two-gunmen hit team were each responsible for a single attack. The last two shootings came in an unknown form. Interestingly, poison was used in three of the ten attacks, two of which occurred onboard the aircraft while in flight. The remaining victim was attacked by an assassin armed with an edged weapon.

Success Rate

Overall, attacks staged at an airport or onboard an aircraft resulted in an 80% success rate. Seven of the attacks were sprung against pedestrian targets (including those onboard an aircraft), resulting in a 71% rate of success. Of the three ambushes on mobile targets (arriving to or departing from an airport), the rate of success was 100%.

Global and Regional Perspective

These ten attacks were discovered to have occurred in seven countries. Only the Philippines, with three, and Colombia, with two, experienced greater than a single attack at an airport or aircraft. The remaining attacks occurred in Pakistan, Indonesia, South Africa, Mexico, and Corsica.

Most Likely Employed By

The drug cartels of Colombia and Mexico were each found to be responsible for three of the attacks. Another three ambushes at these locations were found to be or strongly believed to have been perpetrated by government agents. Of the remaining two attacks in which the responsible party was known or determined, a criminal was behind one and a political rival behind the other.

Most Likely Employed Against

Members of clergy fell victim to ambushes at this location the most often, with three documented attacks. Lawmakers and presidential candidates were the next most frequent, each of which victims in two attacks. The remaining three attacks targeted a world leader, an activist/dissident, and a federal government official. In the single successful attack against the world leader, a diplomat and a military official were also killed.

BAR/RESTAURANT

There were a total of seventeen ambushes that were documented as having occurred at a bar or restaurant. These locations represent an interesting place for staging an ambush, as while they can be visited with some frequency, there is not generally any regularity. They are also very public locations requiring the assassin to enter the establishment, approach his or her target, and in full view of the other patrons, strike.

Timing of Ambush

Of the attacks at these locations in which the time was able to be determined, twelve occurred during the hours of 0601 to 2400, or the general hours of operation of the establishment. Four of the attacks were staged between 1801 and 2100, with only one occurring after that. Two attacks were found to have taken place in the morning hours between 0601 and 0900. During the nine hours between 0901 and 1800 there were five attacks recorded. The remaining could not be determined.

Type of Attack

The attack by the two-gunmen hit team was responsible for seven ambushes staged at a bar or restaurant. Lone gunmen struck three times, while hit teams of three to five gunmen were behind two other attacks. In three of the ambushes, the type of the shooting tactic employed could not be determined. In a single attack, poison was used, while the last attack was a kidnapping.

Success Rate

Strikes at a bar or restaurant had a 100% success rate (all of the attacks were perpetrated against pedestrian-based victims). It is perhaps the boldness of the attack that serves to increase the level of surprise, or the fact that the victim is generally seated and the attacker must be within close proximity prior to attacking, that led to the high success rate.

Global and Regional Perspective

Ten countries witnessed ambushes being sprung while the victim was at a bar or restaurant. Spain documented the most with four attacks, followed by the United States with three. The remaining such ambushes occurred in Yugoslavia, Mexico (each of which experienced two), the United Kingdom, Peru, Bulgaria, France, Germany, and Italy. The European region had the most attack activity occurring at or inside of a restaurant.

Most Likely Employed By

With more than half of the total ambushes at a bar or restaurant, organized criminal groups, from the Mexican drug cartels to Sicilian and Serbian mafia families to American mafia, were responsible for nine of the attacks. Spain's ETA (Euskadi ta Askatasuna) was responsible for another three of the attacks, the most of any single terrorist organization. The remaining came from other terrorist organizations, government agents, or could not be determined.

Most Likely Employed Against

Interestingly enough, underworld figures and law enforcement officials fell victim to attacks at these locations more than any other targeted class, but only accounted for three each. Judges, intelligence agents, and corporate executives each suffered two attacks. The remaining attacks targeted subjects from five other classes of victim.

ENTERING/EXITING A VEHICLE

When watching a quality professional protective team leave in a vehicle motorcade, one would notice that the driver is inside of the vehicle with the engine running prior to the arrival of the protectee and his or her detail. The team then waits until the protectee is safely inside of the car with the door shut before all the remaining members quickly enter the vehicle and immediately drive off. Professional protective teams emphasize that their drivers are to remain in the car with the engine running until the protectee is safely inside of his or her destination, or just prior to the protectee exiting a location. The reason for this is that protecting a target when in the process of entering or exiting a vehicle unprepared can be extremely precarious.

This location or timing of an ambush was known to have been employed on at least sixty-three separate occasions with lethal results. Striking a target while in the process of entering or exiting a vehicle makes use of a natural lull in the target's movement. The potential victims can often find themselves trapped in one of two places. They are seated inside of the vehicle but the engine is not on, and perhaps the keys aren't even in the ignition; either way, they are prevented from, or at the very least extremely delayed in, executing a rapid flight by vehicle out of the kill zone. In the other position, the victim is outside of the vehicle in the open with no immediate cover options to move to. There will not be enough time to enter the vehicle and escape, and he or she is generally too far away from the entrance of his or her home or office to make a run for it.

Add to this the possibility that the victim has complicated his or her situation by the simplest of ways. He or she has subconsciously tunneled his or her focus on getting into and out of the vehicle. His or her hands may be clutching a briefcase or purse, a cup of coffee, even keys. His or her mind and thoughts are not on what is going on around them, but rather, he or she is distracted by the upcoming or past days' events, meetings, family issues—anything and everything but his or her surroundings.

The assassin(s), meanwhile, takes advantage of this and rapidly approaches the target, leaving the victim with less than a second or two, if he or she even notices the adversary, in which to take some action. At this point, if either the detail or target is armed, the only option remaining is to act instantly and respond the way any competently trained military unit would—by closing the distance and charging the attacking force with extreme violence. Generally speaking, this only would work if the protective personnel or targeted individual were armed at the time of the attack.

Location of Ambush

For 60% of the attacks, the residence was the number one location in which a victim was targeted while entering or exiting his or her vehicle. By staging the attack here, the assassin can potentially increase the chance of success by taking advantage of human nature in the morning. The area in which the home is located can also provide benefits.

In the case of high-density housing, often the victim can be struck while in a covered and often dark parking garage. In a suburban area, there is generally an increase in vegetation, fencing, etc., which can facilitate an attacker's ability to hide within close proximity and wait for the opportunity to strike. There also tends to be less general pedestrian traffic in residential areas, thereby reducing the number of potential witnesses.

While ten of the attacks occurred at unknown locations, the office was used 16% of the time. The remaining attacks against a victim in the process of entering or exiting his or her vehicle occurred on two occasions at hotels, twice at frequented locations, and once at an airport.

Timing of Ambush

When conducted at the residence, 50% of the attacks occurred in the evening between 1801 and 2100. The morning hours between 0601 and 0900 were selected 24% of the time. By striking during these hours, the assassin gains the benefits of decreased ambient light, further adding to his or her ability to approach and strike. These times can also see a potential decrease in the target's general alertness, given a long day. The remaining ten attacks at a residence occurred at unknown hours.

Of the attacks staged at the office, 40% occurred in the morning between 0601 and 0900. This is a risky time and location in which to strike given the increased mobile and pedestrian traffic found in corporate and industrial areas. However, of the attacks studied, these tended to be staged at the earlier side of the time gap and indicated a substantial knowledge of the target's activities. Two occurred in the evening, and another four were at an unknown time.

Type of Attack

As would be expected, 84% of the attacks staged at this time/location involved firearms. Teams of two gunmen perpetrated 30% of the ambushes. Lone gunmen accounted for another 24% of the attacks. The remaining ambushes were documented as having come at the hands of either teams of between three and five shooters, or an unknown number of gunmen. A single attack was found to have employed a sniper, and in that instance the target had a heavily armed protective detail. Kidnappings were documented in 10% of the attacks at this time/location. Finally, explosives were recorded as being employed on only two occasions, once by way of an IED and once with a suicide bomber attack.

Protective Details

Of the sixty-three attacks, only thirteen had protective details consisting of a driver or protective team. In those attacks, the adversary was successful 99% of the time, with the target being killed. This is not to say the protective team made an error, as the level of training isn't known, but it does further reveal how dangerous attacks at this time/location can be.

Global and Regional Perspective

Twenty-nine countries witnessed ambushes staged while the victim was entering or exiting a vehicle. The United States documented the most, with 21%, followed by Colombia with 11%. The countries of Mexico and Spain rounded out the top four spots with 6% each.

Most Likely Employed Against

Eighteen classes of individuals fell victim to attacks at this time. The businessman/CEO was targeted 22% of the time, the most of any class of victim. Judges documented the second highest number of victims, accounting for 11%. Diplomats rounded out the top three most often targeted with 10%. World leaders and lawmakers were tied for fourth, each having 8% of the attacks.

FREQUENTED LOCATIONS

There were twenty targeted attacks known to have occurred at or inside of a location frequented by the victim. These proved to be places worship, schools attended by the victim's children, health clubs and golf courses, and even dry cleaning establishments. Given the total number of attacks researched for this work, this represents an exceedingly low number. However, frequented locations provide the adversary just one more potential area in which to target the victim beyond the office and residence. Additionally, they also serve to increase potential routes habitually traveled, thereby providing other areas to be assessed by the assassin(s). It is therefore important to understand the attacks that have occurred at these areas.

Timing of Ambush

The majority of these attacks were staged during the morning hours, with seven occurring between 0601 and 1200. Another five occurred between 1201 and 1800. Only two attacks were found to have taken place after 1801. The timing of the remaining six could not be determined with any specificity.

Type of Attack

As with other locations, a variety of attack methods were employed. Firearms were used in twelve of the ambushes, while explosives were used in only five of the cases. There were known to have been two kidnappings from the frequented location, and in a single case, the victim was stabbed. The shooting-based attacks included the use of a sniper, drive-bys, a motorcycle-based hit team, a lone gunman, or could not be determined. The explosives included only the VBIED and IED types of attacks.

Success Rate

Attacks staged at frequented locations had an overall success rate of 95%. With fourteen of the attacks targeting pedestrian-based victims, the success rate was at 93%. The rate of success was 100% in attacks carried out against vehicle-borne victims.

Global and Regional Perspective

The United States led the world in attacks at frequented locations, with five. The remaining fifteen were dispersed over eleven countries in all of the regions but South Asia. Regionally, North America was in the top position with seven of the attacks. Europe was second, accounting for five of the attacks.

Most Likely Employed By

Interestingly, organized criminal groups, including the drug cartels of Mexico and Colombia, as well as the mafia families of Sicily and the Russian mafiya groups, most often staged attacks at frequented locations. Only two terrorist organizations are known to have staged attacks at these locations: Spain's ETA and Turkey's Dev Sol. The remaining attacks came from rivals, government agents, or could not be determined.

Most Likely Employed Against

Corporate executives were the target of the attack on five occasions while at a frequented location. Prosecutors were the victims in another three of the attacks. The remaining were dispersed over nine of the targeted classes.

HOTELS

There were a total of twenty-seven attacks that occurred at or inside of a hotel. One of the interesting issues with hotels (as with restaurants) is that it requires an adversary to have some sort of intelligence that the target will be at a specific hotel at a specific time. In the case of at least one world leader, the information was publicly available due to it being the location for a high-level governmental conference. However, even in this case, the bomber needed advance intelligence as to the room to be occupied. In a separate case involving a sniper attack against an activist, the hotel and room were a common stop location. It may have also been advertised in the local media, or just commonly known to the local population.

Attacks staged at or inside of a hotel impose some considerable problems for an assassin or kidnapper. Namely, hotels are an area that generally has a large population of people, all potential witnesses moving in and around. Even on the individual floors where the pedestrian traffic is lessened to a considerable degree, there is no control or knowledge of when an anonymous guest may exit his or her room. The noise created as a result of an attack could be quickly detected by other guests and reported. Where inside of the hotel the room is located can also be a factor in a successful attack. The ambush site's location in relation to a stairway or elevator can also factor into a successful escape by the assassin after the attack.

Timing of Ambush

Of the fifteen attacks of which the time of day was known, it was found that there were three periods that had the most attack activity. The morning hours between 0601 and 0900 recorded three attacks. The bulk of the attack activity, however, occurred after 1200. Between 1201 and 1500, another three attacks were documented. This was followed by the hours of between 1801 and 2100, which also witnessed another four attacks. All total, though, during the twelve hours between 1201 and 2400 there were ten recorded ambushes. The remaining two occurred between the hours of 0001 and 0300.

Type of Attack

Eighty-five percent of the ambushes occurring at or inside of a hotel were shooting attacks. A lone gunman was found to have conducted five of the attacks, followed by the two-gun-men hit team being responsible for another four. In two of the ambushes, a sniper targeted the victim. Hit teams of between three and five gunmen were responsible for another two of the attacks. Unfortunately in nine of the attacks, the number of shooters involved could not be determined. In one interesting case, the shooting attack took the form of a motorcy-cle-based hit team firing upon their target as he walked just outside of the hotel.

There were three explosive-based targeted attacks occurring at a frequented hotel. Two of these took the form of an improvised explosive device, and another one from a grenade that was thrown at the victim. In the remaining two attacks occurring at a hotel, one employed an edged weapon and one was a kidnapping.

Global and Regional Perspective

The European region documented the most ambushes occurring at hotels, with a total of nine. This was followed by the North American region, which recorded a total of eight. The Middle Eastern region rounded out the top three spots with six attacks staged at a hotel.

The United States documented five attacks conducted at a hotel, the most of any single country. Following closely behind were the countries of Mexico, Lebanon, and the United Kingdom, each of which experienced three such attacks. The remaining ambushes staged at or inside of hotels occurred at twelve different countries in every region but Africa.

Most Likely Employed Against

The world leader was the victim most often in attacks in or around hotels, with a total of eight. Terrorist leaders were the next most often ambushed at a hotel, with four known attacks, followed by the activist/dissident, with three. The remaining ambushes were per-petrated against nine other targeted classes, each accounting for only one or two attacks.

Groups Responsible for the Attack

In five of the attacks, the group or individual responsible was never determined with any degree of certainty. Of the remaining twenty-two attacks, it was discovered or strongly believed that government agents carried out five. Next in line of responsibility were the drug cartels of Mexico, with three known attacks at a hotel. The remaining ambushes stemmed from eleven different groups, nine of which were terrorist organizations, and all but three were Islamic extremist-based.

IN TRANSIT

There were a total of 292 attacks that occurred while the victim was in transit. In thirty-nine of those attacks, the ambush site was at an intersection or point of traffic congestion and these attacks are detailed in a later section. Of the remaining 253 attacks, the exact location either could not be determined or simply occurred at some point along the route (most likely at some other unknown choke point). In all but nineteen of the attacks, the target was in transit while in a vehicle of some type. Of those nineteen, the target was walking between locations at the time of the attack.

The high number of attacks provides some indication that a majority of victims traveled the same route(s) habitually, thereby increasing the number of places they could be ambushed. This is a very interesting statistic, in that changing one's route of travel is one of the most often emphasized suggestions given to those who might be targeted. It is also one of the easiest methods of prevention, while at the same time requiring possibly the greatest amount of self-discipline to perform.

Timing of Ambush

In 106 of these attacks, the time frame was known. Of these the majority occurred during the morning hours of 0601 and 0900, accounting for 36% of the total. This was followed by another 12% between 0901 and 1200. The evening hours of between 1801 and 2100 witnessed 23% of the total attacks. Another 9% were staged between 2101 and 2400. Attacks occurring during the afternoon hours of 1201 to 1800 accounted for 19% of the attacks.

Type of Attack

The shooting-based attack reigned supreme against vehicle-borne targets, representing 57% of the total. Unfortunately in 28% of the ambushes, the exact type of shooting method could not be determined. Of those known, the drive-by shooting method was the most preferred, accounting for 35% of the attacks. This was followed by motorcycle-based hit teams 28% of the time. These two methods of attack are of note, as their inherent flexibility does not require that a specific attack site be selected beyond where the victim's vehicle is to be initially picked up. Once the victim is picked up, it is simply a matter of time for the adversary to pull up within striking distance without raising the suspicions of the target.

Further, the changing up of the travel routes is not an effective countermeasure, as the attack site will occur whenever the adversary is in range.

Ambushes by a lone gunman accounted for 18% of the known attacks, while the two-gunmen hit team was responsible for another 8%. The remaining attacks were perpetrated by snipers, hit teams of between three and five gunmen, and teams of eight or more shooters. In all of these attacks, the gunmen were positioned along the route of their target's travel. The lone gunman and hit teams conducted their attacks while on foot. It is with these that changing up of the travel routes have the greatest effect.

Explosive-based ambushes were used in 32% of the attacks against a victim in transit. The VBIED tactic saw the most use, with 35% of the total. Accounting for another 22% of the explosive attacks, the IED was the second most often used method. The booby-trap device was documented as being employed 20% of the time, while the suicide bomber attacks occurred 13% of the time. The remaining explosive attacks, in order of frequency, took the form of grenades, rockets, and a Molotov cocktail.

In 10% of the attacks against a vehicle-borne target, kidnapping was the goal. Kidnappings from mobile targets require a considerable amount of planning (covered more in-depth within the attack methodology sections), beyond that which would normally be called for in other attacks. Because of the level of planning, there are many more opportunities for their detection if the target or protective detail is alert.

Success Rate

Ambushes staged against targets in transit resulted in a 69% overall success rate. In those attacks perpetrated against pedestrian victims in transit on foot, the success rate was 89%, while against targets in vehicles it stood at 68%. Ambushes employing firearms against in-transit victims resulted in an 80% success rate. Those attacks making use of explosives obtained only a 42% rate of success. Of the kidnappings, the success rate was 92%.

Global and Regional Perspective

Attacks against targets while in transit were staged in sixty-one separate countries, representing every region on the planet. Only nine countries experienced attacks into the double digits. Italy and Colombia ranked number one, each accounting for twenty-four attacks, or 9% of the total. Lebanon recorded nineteen in-transit attacks, while Russia and Mexico each had seventeen. Spain and Pakistan are each known to have had thirteen such attacks, with France and Greece finishing up with twelve and ten, respectively.

Regionally, Europe ranked number one, accounting for 34% of the total attacks dispersed over eighteen countries. The Central/South American region witnessed 18%, which occurred in ten countries. The region of the Middle East had 13% of the attacks on transitory targets, spread out over nine countries, while the North American region documented 10% over four countries. Russia and its republics rounded out the top five regions with 9%, staged in six countries.

121

Most Likely Employed By

In 104 of the attacks against transitory targets, the groups responsible were found to be terrorist organizations. In twenty-two of the attacks, the groups were Islamic extremists. Spain's ETA staged ten attacks against transitory targets, while Colombia's FARC and Italy's Red Brigades each carried out eight such attacks. Germany's Red Army Faction and Greece's November 17 organization were each behind another seven attacks on targets in transit.

Thirty of the attacks were staged by organized criminal groups, ranging from the drug cartels of Mexico and Colombia to the Italian mafia groups of Sicily and Naples. Criminals not associated with any identifiable group conducted five of the attacks. Seventeen of the attacks were known or strongly believed to have been perpetrated by government agents. Unfortunately, in ninety-seven of the attacks, the groups or individuals could not be determined.

Most Likely Employed Against

While ambushes staged against individuals in transit targeted twenty-five classes of victim, 74% were focused upon nine groups. Of those, world leaders experienced the most, with thirty-four attacks. Diplomats witnessed the second highest number of attacks, with twenty-six. Law enforcement officials rounded out the top three with twenty-three documented ambushes. Corporate executives and military officials each experienced twenty attacks. Lawmakers, government ministers, and judges each documented between sixteen and seventeen attacks. Finally, prosecutors wrapped up the last of the nine, accounting for twelve of the attacks while in transit.

TRAFFIC AND INTERSECTIONS

Of those attacks staged against victims while in transit, thirty-nine occurred at traffic intersections, or at points of known traffic congestion. (While this number is mostly likely much higher, these were the only ones found to be specifically identified as occurring at these points.) These locations of attack provide an adversary with some valuable benefits that can enhance his or her chance of success. First and foremost, these locations, by their nature, force a vehicle-borne target to slow the vehicle down in order to make a turn or come to a stop for the traffic control device. This decrease in speed offers the bomber a vastly greater chance of success in triggering the device at the correct moment, allowing the blast wave to strike at the desired portion of the vehicle.

Similarly, it provides the gunmen with a target that is effectively locked in a static location, with little to no immediate way of escape (if the vehicle/driver has not or was prevented from positioning the vehicle properly). If the vehicle is not armored (and in one case the assassins knew of a method to circumvent), then the victims are sitting inside one large kill zone. All that remains is for the gunmen to pour fire into their victim's vehicle.

How an intersection doesn't favor the assassin is in knowing when their target will be at the attack site, unless of course the route is followed habitually, within a narrow window of opportunity. In those cases when the target travels a predictable route at a predictable time, the assassin is provided a number of potential attack sites, limited only by the distance traveled. Additionally, with traffic congestion as well as intersections controlled by a traffic signal, it is very difficult for the perpetrators to ensure that the target vehicle will be stopped at the correct location (although in one attack, it was discovered that the assassins had a remote device, allowing them to manipulate the traffic signal lights as they saw fit). Stop signs obviously increase the likelihood of a stop at the precise location, and therefore should be approached with more caution.

Timing of Ambush

In only twenty-five of the attacks was the timing able to be determined. Of these, 40% occurred during the morning hours between 0601 and 0900. Another 28% occurred between 0901 and 1200. Attacks staged between the hours of 1501 and 1800 recorded the next highest number, accounting for 16%. Only 8% were found to have occurred between 1201 and 1500, as well as between 1801 and 2400.

Type of Attack

Ambushes staged at these points along the route employed firearms twenty-eight times, followed by explosives in nine of the attacks. In the remaining two attacks, kidnapping was the goal. Of the shootings, motorcycle gunmen ranked number one, accounting for 21% of the total. This was followed by lone gunmen, who were found to be behind another 18% of the ambushes. Shooting attacks staged by two-gunmen hit teams rounded out the top three with 14%. The remaining attacks came in the form of drive-bys, teams of three to five gunmen, or could not be determined. In those attacks using explosives, the VBIED and IED were deployed equally, accounting for a total of eight. In only one of the attacks was a suicide bomber documented as having struck.

Success Rate

Attacks staged at these locations regardless of the method employed had an 87% rate of success. This is a very high rate considering that 49% of the time a protective detail of some sort was present during the time of attack.

Global and Regional Perspective

Twenty-three countries are known to have been witness to attacks at intersections or points of traffic congestion. While there was no one country found to have a clear dominant number of attacks occurring at these locations, Colombia had the most with four, followed closely by Mexico, Spain, Greece, and Germany, each of which are known to have had three. Regionally, Europe experienced the most use of this location, with 41%. Central/ South America witnessed 21%, followed by North America with 18%.

Most Likely Employed By

Twenty-one different groups are known to have staged attacks at these points. In twelve of the attacks, the groups or individuals responsible were not able to be determined. Of those that were known, 81% were found to have been conducted by terrorist organizations. These groups ranged from Colombia's FARC to Greece's November 17 to Spain's ETA to a variety of the Islamic extremist groups. Only 20% of attacks at traffic intersections or congestion points were known to have been conducted by organized crime groups.

Most Likely Employed Against

The lawmaker was the victim in the majority of these attacks, but at only 15% still represented a small total number. Prosecutors, world leaders, judges, and military officials each accounted for 10% of the victims. The remaining victims fell into one of ten other targeted classes.

OFFICE

A total of 102 attacks were documented to have occurred at or inside of an office. The office is perhaps the most often generally known location of a target, but presents problems for the assassin or kidnapper. Most professional work locations tend to be concentrated in certain areas of a city or town, resulting in high foot and vehicle traffic. This is especially true with targets working with the government. Mayors, judges, prosecutors, city council members, government ministers, and others traditionally work in areas with a well-established security or a law enforcement presence. Given the large amount of foot and vehicle traffic found in work areas, the assassin/kidnapper is faced with numerous potential witnesses. At the same time, the assassin/kidnapper is provided with an increased ability to blend in during the surveillance/reconnaissance phase of the operation.

Timing of Ambush

The traditional arrival hours of 0601 to 0900 accounted for the most attacks at this location, accounting for 26% of the fifty-eight attacks in which the exact timing was known. Following closely, with 22%, were attacks staged during the traditional departure hours of between 1801 and 2100. Finally, during the common lunch hours between 1201 and 1500, another 21% of attacks were committed. The late morning hours of between 0901 and 1200 documented 14% of the attacks, while the rest were dispersed throughout the remaining hours of the day. No attacks, however, were found to have taken place between the hours of 0301 and 0600.

Success Rate

Attacks staged at the office location recorded an 84% success rate overall. Attacks staged at these locations, but targeting pedestrian-based victims only, accounted for eighty-six of

124

the attacks and had a 91% success rate. In the sixteen attacks against vehicle-borne targets occurring at this location, a 50% rate of success was achieved.

Type of Attack

The use of firearms during an ambush upon a target while at the office accounted for 75% of all attacks. Of these, the lone gunman was the predominant method, known to be responsible for twenty-five attacks. Hit teams of two gunmen were found to be behind sixteen of the attacks, while a sniper was involved in another eight. In fourteen of the shooting attacks, the exact method of attack could not be determined. The remaining ambushes employing firearms, listed in order of frequency (all of which had less than five known), include motorcycle hit teams, teams of between three and five gunmen, drive-bys, and teams of six or more gunmen.

The use of explosives to ambush a target at the office accounted for only 14% of the total. The VBIED and booby-trap device were each employed five times, the most of any explosive-based attack. The suicide bomber and the IED device were used in two attacks each. The remaining ambushes came in the forms of kidnapping, with 6% of the total; edged-weapon attacks with 4%; and poison in 2% of the attacks.

Global and Regional Perspective

Forty-one countries witnessed targeted subjects being attacked while at an office location. However, the United States suffered the most, accounting for 23% of the total number. Mexico, Italy, and Colombia tied for second, each of which experienced 6% of the attacks. Finishing up third with the greatest number of ambushes, the countries of Spain, the Philippines, and France each documented 4% of the attacks. Regionally, North America and Europe tied for the top position, each with 30% of the documented attacks, while Central/South America recorded another 12%.

Most Likely Employed By

No one group was found to have a particular preference for attacks at the office. Thirty-five of the attacks came at the hands of terrorist/extremist organizations such as FARC, Party of God, Abu Sayyaf, the Abu Nidal Organization, and twenty-one others. Organized criminal organizations and solo criminals were found to be behind another twenty-three of the attacks occurring at the office. Government agents were known or strongly believed to be responsible for five attacks, while courtroom defendants attacked on three occasions and political/office rivals were behind two. The remaining came from unknown groups or individuals.

Most Likely Employed Against

There were twenty-two targeted classes of individuals that were victims of an ambush at their place of employment. The corporate executive was attacked 15% of the time, the most of any class. Judges, with 14% of attacks at the office, were a close second. Lawmakers were a victim in 9% of the attacks, while with 8% of the attacks each, diplomats and mayors were the next most often targeted. World leaders found themselves being attacked while at the office 7% of the time, while clergy members and activists/dissidents each fell victim 6% of the time.

PUBLIC EVENT

There were a total of forty-seven ambushes staged at a public event (most often rallies for candidates for election, but also including sporting events, weddings, dedications, and other celebratory events). Generally speaking, public events are the quintessential location, at least for the public at large, for an assassination to occur. Many of the most high-profile attacks on world leaders have taken place here, only to be further imprinted on society's collective memory through modern action movies. In reality, public events are one of the worst concerns for protective details, and rightly so. The massive crowds, the open venues, and the well-publicized detailing of whom will be in attendance and when, all provide for massive security concerns.

Timing of Attacks

The timing of ambushes in this category is really irrelevant, as it is based primarily upon when the target will be at the location, either arriving, departing, or speaking. That being said, with thirteen attacks, the majority occurred between 1500 and 2400. The next most common time for an attack was between 0901 and 1200, which also experienced four.

Type of Attack

Sixty-six percent of attacks staged at public events employed firearms of some configuration. The lone gunman accounted for 69% of all shooting attacks. Interestingly enough, there was only one documented attack occurring at a public event that involved a sniper. The remaining shooting attacks were in the form of hit teams consisting of between three and five gunmen, motorcycle attack teams, two-gunmen hit teams, or could not be determined.

Explosives were deployed in 28% of the attacks, with the suicide bomber responsible for 54% of those. Attacks by VBIEDs, IEDs, and grenades made up the remaining explosive-based attacks. In the final two attacks, one was a kidnapping while one employed an edged weapon.

Success Rate

Attacks staged at these locations had an overall 66% success rate. Four attacks targeted mobile victims (in the process of arriving to or departing from the event), of which only one was successful. Pedestrian targets, which made up the bulk of the attack targets at a public event, resulted in a 70% rate of success.

Global and Regional Perspective

The United States suffered the most attacks at a public event, having documented seven. Sri Lanka and India followed, each having recorded four attacks. The remaining were spread out over twenty-five countries from every region on the planet. Each of these countries suffered between one and two attacks at public events. Regionally, South Asia, with twelve such attacks, suffered the most. North America followed closely with nine public event targeted attacks. The remaining regions of Europe, Asia and the Pacific Islands, Central/South America, and Africa were each witness to four or more attacks.

Most Likely Employed By

Islamic extremists (groups that were not identified) were found to be behind eight of the attacks against targets at public events. Following closely behind was the Tamil Tigers of Sri Lanka, which was found to be responsible for five such attacks. The remaining attacks were dispersed over eleven different groups. Eleven attacks came at the hands of terrorist or extremist groups. Criminals or criminal organizations were known or believed to be behind five of the attacks, while government agents are strongly suspected in three of the attacks. Responsibility for the remaining ambushes could not be determined.

Most Likely Employed Against

Perhaps lending credence to the threats and security nightmare that public events represent, world leaders fell victim most often to attacks staged at these events, accounting for 45%. Following a distant second, but still of note, were candidates for office, who were targeted 13% of the time. Wrapping up the top three were lawmakers—another targeted class that often attends public events—with 9% of the documented attacks. The remaining ambushes at these events were spread out over nine different targeted classes of individual.

RESIDENCES

There were a total of 272 attacks that are known to have occurred at the target's residence. Residences can be an attractive locale to spring an ambush. They tend to have less vehicle and pedestrian traffic, which means less chance of witnesses. While the Internet has made it easier to determine a potential target's residence, it still requires some form of on-site surveillance/reconnaissance to confirm.

Timing the attack shortly after the target departs from or arrives to his or her home, the adversary takes advantage of human nature. Depending upon the hours the victim works, as well as the time of the year, it is quite possible that the level of ambient light will be low, if not outright dark. While traveling to work, most people are thinking about the day ahead, perhaps drinking their coffee, taking kids to school, maybe not even fully awake. While traveling home from work, the target can be tired after a long day, upset about what occurred during the workday, thinking about what to prepare for dinner, family issues, etc. Regardless, his or her focus is not on what is going on around him or her, making him or her very susceptible to attack.

Timing of Ambush

In 155 of the attacks at a residence, the approximate time they occurred is known. As could be expected, the majority of those attacks were staged during the traditional departure/ arrival times. The morning hours between 0601 and 0900 accounted for 27% of the attack activity. The evening hours between 1801 and 2100 accounted for 28% of the attack activity. The nighttime hours between 2101 and 2400 accounted for 15% of the attacks, while the later morning hours of 0901 to 1200 and the afternoon hours of 1201 to 1500 each recorded 10% of the attacks. The remaining 10% of the attacks were dispersed over the hours of between 1501 and 1800 and between 0001 and 0600.

Type of Attack

The shooting attack reigns supreme at the residence, accounting for 185 of the ambushes. Of those, 24% of attacks were at the hand of a lone gunman. Attacks by the three- to five-gunmen hit team were the next most prevalent method of shooting attack, accounting for 14%. The two-person hit team was responsible for 13% of the shooting attacks. Five percent of the attacks were conducted by a motorcycle attack team, as well as by snipers. Drive-by attacks were used in only of 3% of the ambushes. The remaining shooting attacks came from an unknown number of shooters or unknown method of shooting attack.

There were fifty explosive-based ambushes known to have been conducted at the target's residence. The IED placed at or near the residence was the most preferred method of explosive attack, accounting for 46% of documented ambushes. The VBIED and booby-trap device were each deployed 24% of the time. The remaining explosive attacks came from suicide bombers, a grenade, and a firebomb. The last thirty attacks staged at the victim's residence took the form of nineteen kidnappings, ten stabbings, and one case of poisoning.

Success Rate

Overall, attacks staged at the victim's residence had an 82% rate of success. The vast majority of those attacks targeted pedestrian-based victims. In fact, the attacks perpetrated solely against pedestrian targets had an 84% rate of success. The attacks staged against vehicle-borne targets had a 74% rate of success.

Global and Regional Perspective

The United States recorded the most attacks occurring at the residence, but with only 12% of the total, remained relatively low. Italy, with 8% of the total, suffered the next highest number of attacks, and France rounded out the top three with 7%. Sixty-two other countries witnessed targeted attacks conducted at the victim's residence. The vast majority of countries experienced only between one and three attacks. Eight countries had between four and ten attacks, while only four countries had between eleven and eighteen attacks.

Regionally, with 39% of the attacks, Europe had the greatest number of ambushes staged at the victim's residence. North America was next in line, with 18% of the attacks. Following somewhat distantly was Russia and the republics, which recorded 10% of the attacks. Central/South America had 6% of the attacks, followed by the Middle East with 5%.

Most Likely Employed Against

While there were twenty-four classes of targeted victims ambushed at the residence, nine recorded the most attacks. Of those nine, all of which documented in excess of sixteen attacks each, corporate executives had the greatest number, with twenty-eight. Judges, with twenty-three, and law enforcement officials, with twenty-two, rounded out the top three. Government ministers and diplomats each suffered nineteen attacks, while law-makers, world leaders, and activists/dissidents accounted for eighteen each. Prosecutors rounded out the top nine, with seventeen recorded attacks occurring at the residence.

Most Likely Employed By

Attacks at the residence were conducted by forty-seven separate terrorist organizations, which were responsible for 45% of the total. Of these groups, Spain's ETA had the most, with seventeen attacks. Ireland's Irish Republican Army had the second most attacks, with fifteen. Eight different organized criminal groups were found to be responsible for 8% of the attacks. Of the criminal organizations, the drug cartels of Mexico and Colombia accounted for twelve attacks. Eleven percent of the attacks were known to be or strongly believed to be at the hand of government agents. The remaining ambushes at the residence came from rivals, former defendants, or could not be determined.

5

Methods of Operation

The use of targeted violence, while perhaps a more common occurrence than society at large may be aware of, is still a rarely employed act. This is then one of, if not the most predominant reasons targeted violence can be so difficult to predict, detect, deter, and even survive. The most vehement user of targeted violence in the modern era, Spain's ETA (Euskadi ta Askatasuna), has only been known to have employed it on average once a year. Further, the ETA, as with other groups worldwide, has generally not focused these attacks on a specific type of individual, such as a judge or diplomat, but rather targeted a variety of victims.

While many a conspiracy theorist will point to the "government" as being behind targeted violence, it is difficult to determine with any sort of certainty. Unlike criminal organizations or terrorist groups, governments do not traditionally make claims of responsibility. They can employ a variety of methods, and even outsource the contract to other groups. They have also been known or suspected of using the tactics and weapons of known terrorist groups to conduct a hit. This effectively serves to conceal a government's involvement and causes further confusion during the investigation into determining and locating those responsible.

It is therefore important to be aware of and examine those attacks that are known or strongly believed to have been conducted by government agents. Whether the reasons behind these believed government attacks are for the good of humankind is not the topic or concern of this work. What is of concern is that in the vast majority of these attacks, the actual men on the ground are never known or identified. These men will eventually move on to other careers, retire, etc., and may then decide to train others. There has been an explosion in organizations, many with former military special forces or intelligence officers, providing training for a price. While many of these companies are very professional and generally target military and law enforcement professionals, there are those that will work for the highest bidder, such as the initial members of Mexico's Los Zetas.

As with the previous sections, the goal here is to provide the protective detail member or member of one of the targeted classes of individuals a total perspective. By reviewing and understanding the methods of operation of past and current groups, the reader is provided the insight as to how a particular group went about its mission. Knowing who is in your backyard that might decide to target individuals, and understanding their methods, you can dramatically increase your chances of survival. By understanding the information obtained from open-source material, the reader now knows what a potential adversary knows. Learn from the past, develop your tactics and strategies, be alert, and survive.

Note: Terrorist organizations have been known to make claims of responsibility for attacks they did not perpetrate, as well as not claiming others. Attacks listed in the following pages are those that the author, to the best of his ability, could confirm as being the work of the specified group.

ABU NIDAL ORGANIZATION

This Palestinian group under the leadership of Sabri al-Banna, known globally as the Abu Nidal Organization (ANO), was a true international terrorist outfit. While some of their most high-profile attacks included attempting to hijack aircraft, and shooting attacks on synagogues and airports, they were known/suspected to be responsible for ten targeted attacks in nine countries (occurring in the European, Middle Eastern, and South Asian regions). Only the country of France documented more than a single targeted attack. Between May 1981, the date of their first known targeted hit (the majority of which occurred during the 1980s) and June 1993, they managed to obtain a 70% success rate (target killed or kidnapped) (Figure 5.1).

Preferred Target of Attack

The Abu Nidal killers preferred to ambush pedestrian-based targets, which accounted for 67% of their attacks. Strikes against vehicle-borne targets made up the remaining 33% of their ambushes. Accounting for 40% of the victims, the Abu Nidal Organization ambushed diplomats the most often over a twelve-year period. Embassy staffers accounted for the second most often targeted class of victim, being hit 20% of the time. The remaining attacks were carried out against four other classes of target.

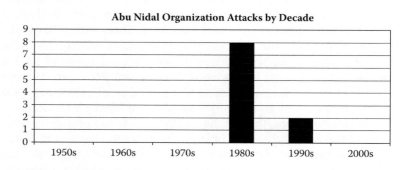

FIGURE 5.1 Abu Nidal Organization attacks by decade.

Timing of Attacks

Unfortunately, in only two of the ambushes were the exact times of attack able to be determined. However, in those two cases, ANO followed the general times of targeted attacks carried out by adversaries from around the world. One attack was found to have occurred between the morning hours of 0901 and 1200, and the second between 2101 and 2400. Members of the ANO showed a clear preference for staging their hits on Wednesdays, accounting for 60% of their attacks. The remaining strikes occurred, in order of occurrence, on Thursdays, Tuesdays, and Fridays.

Given the low total number of targeted attacks, it is difficult to know with any degree of certainty if the Abu Nidal Organization preferred a specific month in which to strike. That being said, the month of June recorded three attacks, while October had two. These were the only months documenting more than a single attack by ANO killers. The remaining ambushes were spread out over the entire year, with no clear preference for season.

Preferred Locations of Attacks

In two of the attacks by the Abu Nidal Organization the exact location could not be determined. Of the remaining eight that are known, two were carried out at the victim's residence, as well as two at the victim's office. The final four attacks occurred at hotels and while the victim was in transit.

Preferred Method of Attack

Use of the gun was the method of attack most often selected by the ANO in its strikes, accounting for eight of the nine ambushes in which the method was able to be determined. Four of these attacks came at the hand of a lone gunman. Two others were staged by hit teams of two gunmen. There was also a single kidnapping case attributed to the ANO. Finally, in one attack the method used was not known.

ASALA

The Armenian Secret Army for the Liberation of Armenia (ASALA) was known to have been responsible for thirteen targeted attacks. This group was a global assassination outfit that, interestingly enough, traces its origins to a targeted attack that occurred at the Biltmore Hotel (now the Four Seasons Biltmore) in Santa Barbara, California. It is also perhaps one of the least well-known (in the United States) active terrorist groups of the 1980s.

On January 27, 1973, Armenian Kurken (Gourgen) Yanikian contacted Turkish consular diplomats Mehmet Baydar and Bahadir Demir using the ruse of wanting to return Turkish antiquities. The invitation was for lunch at the Santa Barbara Biltmore, a beautiful hotel situated along the scenic Pacific coastline, offering an outdoor lunch patio overlooking the beach. Upon the arrival of the two diplomats, Yanikian took them to a room and at some point pulled out a Luger pistol and shot both Baydar and Demir to death. Mr. Yanikian then calmly sat down in the patio area and notified law enforcement of the crime. The motive for the killings was apparently to bring world attention to the Armenian genocide at the hands of the Turkish government. In July 1973, Mr. Yanikian was found guilty of the two murders and sentenced to life in prison. On October 22, 1975, the Prisoner Kurken Yanikian Group, which later changed its name to the Armenian Secret Army for the Liberation of Armenia, carried out its first targeted killing.

The ASALA is unique among the groups examined within this section, as it focused exclusively on conducting targeted killings of its identified "enemy," the Turkish government. It also represents a truly international organization in that its attacks took place in eleven separate countries. Only France, with three targeted attacks, registered more than one ambush by the ASALA. While the majority of the strikes took place in Europe, ASALA is known to have conducted one hit in Canada and one in Iran. While conducting a relatively limited number of operations, its attacks focused on the diplomats and staffers of Turkish embassies. Between October 1975, the date of the first known attack, and April 1984, ASALA was responsible for or claimed responsibility for thirteen targeted attacks. It also managed to obtain a 77% success rate (target killed).

As Figure 5.2 indicates, the majority of the targeted attacks occurred during the 1980s. Considering its first attack was staged in the autumn of 1975, ASALA averaged less than one attack per year during the remainder of that decade. During the 1980s ASALA increased this average to more than two attacks a year, with the last known hit occurring in 1984.

Preferred Target of Attack

ASALA showed only a slight preference for ambushing pedestrian-based targets, accounting for 58%, which represented only a small percentage above attacks against vehicle-borne targets. A single attack was conducted against a target whose exact positioning could not be determined. Accounting for 69% of the victims, ASALA ambushed Turkish embassy staffers the most often over the fifteen-year period. Turkish diplomats accounted for the second most often targeted class of victim (half of those being family members of the diplomats) being hit 31% of the time.

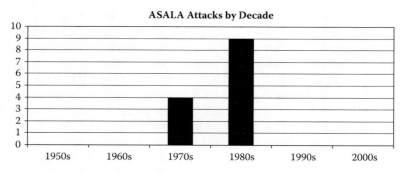

FIGURE 5.2 ASALA attacks by decade.

Timing of Attacks

Unfortunately, the timing of only one attack was able to be determined. This occurred during the evening hours between 2101 and 2400. ASALA did show clear preference for striking its targets on Fridays, 38% of the time. Thursdays followed closely with 31%. The remaining attacks were staged on Wednesdays, Tuesdays, and Saturdays.

There was no clear preferred month of the year, or season, in which ASALA chose to ambush its victims, although it was never known to strike during the winter months. April and October were found to have recorded the most attacks by ASALA, each with three. June, July, and September each accounted for two attacks, while March documented one.

Preferred Locations of Attacks

ASALA staged five ambushes at its victims' residence. Another five were carried out while the victim was in transit, one of which was known to have occurred at a traffic intersection. Two attacks were carried out at the victim's office, while the final one occurred at an unknown location.

Preferred Method of Attack

ASALA employed firearms in all of its targeted attacks. In ten of these ambushes, the exact makeup of the hit was not known. Of the remaining three that were known, one attack employed a motorcycle hit team, another involved a two-gunmen team, while the final attack used at hit team of between three and five gunmen.

CONTRACT KILLERS

Professional contract killers or hitmen, if there really is such a profession, are difficult to quantify given the complexity in determining which attacks can be attributed to which professional. How does one obtain such a title? Does getting paid for one or more targeted killings over the course of a year or more make a person a hitman? Oftentimes, especially of late with the continual federal prosecutions of the various mafia families within the United States, the media has referred to a defendant as a "mob hitman." Only during the course of the trial does it come out that the subject is in his fifties and is known or suspected of carrying out five to ten hits over the course of his mob career. In some of these cases, that career spanned decades (not including time spent in prison). Many of those killings ultimately are the result of internal conflicts within the mob. The hitman would kill one of his own for whatever reason, or kill a rival in an attempt to take over a region or product.

The point is that in many cases, the victim of the hit is known to the hitman or more likely to the hitman's organization or family. This therefore creates a direct link between the two. It also negates some of the steps involved on the part of the killer in order to get close to his target. If the hitman's employer is going to arrange a meeting at a specific time and location, such as what occurred during the targeted killing of Gambino crime family boss Paul Castellano, then the hitman just needs to be in the area, ready to go. This negates the need to conduct reconnaissance or surveillance of the target in order to determine routes, habits, weak points, etc.

Occasionally, however, the hitman may be tasked to kill a subject outside of the organization's span of control. This then requires the killer to conduct a more specialized course of duties prior to the hit. Another difficulty in examining the nature of contract killers is that society only really knows what these men tell us of their operations (usually after they have been captured). Even that, as any law enforcement professional knows, can only be taken with a grain of salt, as these men can claim credit for hits they didn't commit as well as not claiming ones they did. The point is that we will never know with any certainty if an individual is truly a professional killer for hire.

Perhaps the most well known of these assassins was Richard Kuklinsky, a white male adult of Polish dissent. He claimed that he was a contract killer primarily for the Italian mafia families of New York. It is believed that he was involved in the killing of Paul Costellano, the boss of bosses, as well as the Gambino crime family, and Carmine Galante, the boss of the Bonanno crime family. He laid claim to killing a lot of men, most of whom were involved in some fashion with organized crime. In many of his claims, he described how he would surveil his target, recon the residence, and even make use of ruses in order to close this initial distance with his victim.

His preferred killing weapons were .38 caliber derringers and .22 caliber pistols, as well as cut-down .22 magnum rifles, all of which employed suppressors (it is not known if these were professionally made or makeshift devices). He never used the same weapon for more than one killing, always preferring to rid himself of the weapon after completing his contract. He stated the reason for this was that if he were ever caught, it would be nearly impossible to connect him to other murders (such as happened with a certain .45 caliber pistol found to be used by the Greek November 17 organization in several killings). He also occasionally shot the same victim with two weapons of different calibers to make it appear as though there had been more than one killer.

Generally, when he wasn't killing for his own needs (he said he started out dealing with people he had a problem with), the mafia member hiring him would provide him with a name, photo, and address of the target. This would be followed with instructions of whether the target needed to suffer prior to death, or disappear completely after death or be left out in the open. With this information, Kuklinski would then recon/surveil the target's home, business, or location frequented. This would last for a day or two, up to ten days on occasion, allowing him to determine the routine as well as identify the location to make the ambush. While he would occasionally hit the victim in the open, generally speaking, he would kidnap the victim and make the kill at another location. If the target had a protective detail, he would take up to ten days to meticulously plan out the hit.

Where possible, he would make use of foul weather to strike. The reason being that under those conditions, most people hurry in and out without paying much attention to their surroundings, as well as there being generally less people out and about. He made frequent use of a ruse to approach the target. One of his favorites would be to flatten a tire on the victim's car, then position his van next to the victim's car, allowing for a quick snatch. Most times he knocked the victim unconscious with some sort of sap, bound and gagged the victim, and placed the victim in his trunk or van. This would allow him to kill the target at another location with more privacy.

Kuklinski laid claim to killing at least one law enforcement officer, whom he alleged was involved with the Gambino crime family. He was later arrested for his killings as he was in the process of targeting the detective that had been hunting him for a considerable period of time. Fortunately, he was arrested and died in prison, as there is no telling how many more people would have been targeted by this man.

COLOMBIAN DRUG CARTELS

The Colombian drug cartels, specifically the Cali and Medellin cartels, are known to have been responsible for seventeen targeted attacks. As would be expected, all but one of the attacks occurred in Colombia. The last attack, which took place in Hungary, is of note because at the time the country sat behind the Iron Curtain, and thus the attack revealed a considerable amount of dedication.

The drug cartels differ greatly from terrorist organizations in that they generally have no political statement/goal behind their targeted attacks. They are driven by the massive amounts of wealth generated by the drug trade. Their targeted hits are therefore focused upon those individuals they deem as interfering with their generation of wealth and power. Another major difference over terrorist organizations is, given the funds they have access to, the cartels have the ability to afford more sophisticated weaponry and expertise.

The first known targeted strike by the Colombian cartels occurred in April 1984 (Figure 5.3). While the majority of their ambushes were staged during the latter half of the 1980s, the attacks continued into March 1997. Over the thirteen-year period in which the Colombian drug cartels waged their war with law and order, they averaged more than one targeted attack a year. Out of their seventeen targeted hits, the cartels managed to obtain a 94% success rate (target killed).

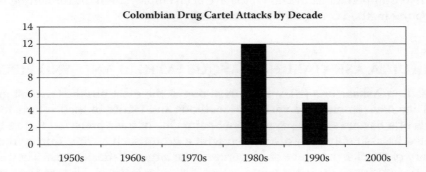

FIGURE 5.3 Colombian drug cartel attacks by decade.

Preferred Target of Attack

The Colombian drug cartels ambushed vehicle-borne targets the most often, accounting for 59% of all the attacks. The remaining 41% were carried out against pedestrian targets. Accounting for 35% of the victims, the Colombian cartels ambushed Colombian judges the most often over the thirteen years. Presidential candidates, local government officials, and law enforcement officials each fell victim to attack 12% of the time. The remaining ambushes were focused upon five other targeted classes of victim.

Timing of Attacks

The timing could be determined in only three ambushes, all of which were found to have been staged between the hours of 0601 and 0900. The cartels, however, were found to prefer striking on Tuesdays, which accounted for 35% of all attacks. Mondays and Fridays followed, each having accounted for 18% of the attacks. When analyzed by the calendar year, Colombian hitmen struck their victims throughout the year with the exception of only February, May, and June. April and August documented the most attacks, each with three, followed by January, March, July, and September, each with two.

Preferred Locations of Attacks

Victims in transit were targeted 47% of the time by the drug cartels of Colombia. The cartels, however, did not shy away from conducting targeted strikes at a variety of locales, to include residence, office, airports and aircraft, as well as public events. In only one attack was the exact location not able to be determined.

Preferred Method of Attack

Their preferred methods of attack were shootings, as they are known to have used explosives in only one targeted hit. Of the shootings, the cartel hitmen employed the motorcycle-bound hit team in six of the sixteen shootings. Another four came at the hand of a lone gunman, while the drive-by tactic was used in two. In only one case was the use of a three- to five-gunmen hit team known to have been employed. In the remaining three, the exact shooting method could not be determined.

EUSKADI TA ASKATASUNA (BASQUE FATHERLAND AND LIBERTY)

The Euskadi ta Askatasuna (ETA) have been one of the most prolific terrorist groups in history. They have employed a variety of methods and tactics in their efforts to achieve their goals of a Basque state separate from Spain. One of their preferred tactics has been the targeted assassination. However, even with a group such as this, during their forty-year history of attacks, they have only averaged one targeted attack a year. They also have an interesting position within the world of terrorist organizations. They can be considered primarily a domestic terror organization, as the vast majority of their operations have

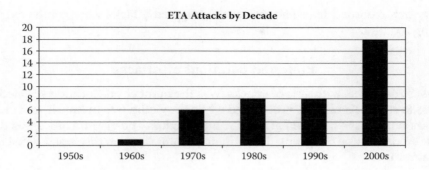

ETA Attacks by Decade

FIGURE 5.4 ETA attacks by decade.

targeted Spanish nationals and have occurred within the boundaries of Spain. The interesting difference is that they are known to operate in parts of France, specifically keeping weapon caches as well as maintaining cells tasked solely with running intelligence collecting operations, giving them an international area of operation.

While the ETA has conducted a large number of operations, the information within this section deals only with its attacks targeting a specific individual or class of individual. Between August 1968, the date of the ETA's first known attack, and December 2008, the ETA was or claimed to be responsible for forty-one targeted attacks (Figure 5.4). They have also managed to obtain a 93% success rate (target killed or kidnapped). The majority of the ambushes have occurred between 2000 and 2008. Of those eighteen attacks, eight occurred in 2000 and another six occurred in 2001. With only one attack in 2002, ETA waited six years before carrying out another targeted attack.

Preferred Target of Attack

The ETA preferred to ambush pedestrian-based targets, which accounted for 59% of attacks. Strikes against vehicle-borne victims were second at 34%, and five attacks occurred at unknown locations. Accounting for 27% of the victims, the ETA ambushed Spanish military officers the most often over its forty-year period of operation. Local government officials accounted for the second most often targeted class of victim, being hit 24% of the time. Federal government officials rounded out the top three with 15%.

Timing of Attacks

While the exact timing of over half of the attacks could not be determined, those that were known revealed that the ETA preferred striking in the morning hours 52% of the time. Hits occurring in the afternoon and evening stood even, each at 24% of the total. ETA did not show any clear preference for a day of the week to attack, beyond the global norm of striking predominantly during the workweek. That being said, there was a slight spike on Thursdays, representing 22% of the attacks, and Wednesdays, at 17%. There was also no clear preferred month of the year in which the ETA chose to ambush its victims; however, June had the most at six attacks, and the months of January, February, and May each recorded five. The rest of the targeted attacks were conducted over the remaining months.

Preferred Locations of Attacks

The target's residence, with 44% of attacks, was the number one location selected by ETA operatives to strike. Another 27% occurred while the victim was in transit, and only one of those is known to have occurred at a traffic intersection. The victim's office was the site of an attack on only three occasions. The remaining attacks were dispersed between hotels and restaurants.

Preferred Method of Attack

The ETA's preferred method of attack was shootings, accounting for 59% of all hits. Explosives were used in another 34% of ambushes. Unfortunately, the majority of the shooting attacks came from an unknown number of gunmen. In those that were known, the use of teams of two gunmen occurred 25% of the time. A lone gunman was used in another 17% of the attacks. The ETA is known to have only made a single use of the motor-cycle hit team tactic.

When employing explosives against the target, the ETA used booby-trap devices, placed either on or inside of the victim's vehicle, three times. With these types of devices, the ETA generally used only 1 to 2 kilos of explosive material. Given the low amount of explosive, they often positioned the device where they knew with reasonable certainty the target would be seated. As a result, they often placed the device under or near the driver's seat or in the back seat.

With vehicle-borne improvised explosive device (VBIED) attacks, which accounted for 40% of all explosive-based attacks, ETA traditionally placed the device at or near intersections. This has a major benefit in that the intersection forces the targeted car to slow down without raising unnecessary suspicion. At the same time, it makes timing the triggering of the device far easier, with a greater chance of success. With the VBIEDs, ETA generally made use of between 20 and 25 kilos of explosive material.

The ETA was also one of the only organizations known to employ buried explosives in a targeted attack. This attack, which occurred early in its history (and is examined in detail in the case studies section of this book), revealed that the ETA is willing to think outside of the box when developing ambush plans. It also showed that ETA had an exceptional level of patience when carrying out its ambushes.

FUERZAS ARMADAS REVOLUCIONARIOS DE COLOMBIA

Colombia's Revolutionary Armed Forces of Colombia (FARC) have carried out a number of operations during their twenty-year conflict with the Colombian government. During those years, beginning in November 1988, with their first known strike, through December 2005, FARC was responsible or claimed responsibility for nineteen targeted attacks over

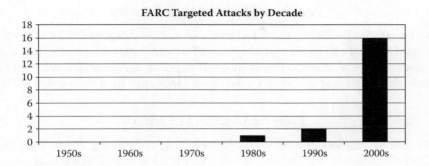

FIGURE 5.5 FARC targeted attacks by decade.

the seventeen years. They have also managed to obtain an 89% success rate (target killed or kidnapped).

The vast majority of the targeted attacks perpetrated by FARC have occurred between 2000 and 2008 (Figure 5.5). While the first targeted ambush occurred in November 1988, they waited almost four years before carrying out another strike. In August 1994, FARC operatives carried out their second and last targeted hit for that decade. They would wait six years, until February 2000, before they killed a specific victim again.

Preferred Target of Attack

While for five of the attacks the exact positioning of the target could not be determined, FARC preferred striking vehicle-borne victims, which accounted for 64% of the total. The remaining 36% of attacks were conducted against pedestrians. Accounting for 26% of the victims, FARC ambushed lawmakers the most often over the seventeen-year period. Corporate executives were targeted by FARC 16% of the time. They were followed by judges, prosecutors, government ministers, and mayors, each accounting for 11% of attacks. Governors/prefects, military officials, and members of clergy were also attacked by FARC killers.

Timing of Attacks

While the exact timing of over half of the attacks could not be determined, those that were known revealed that FARC preferred striking equally in the morning and evening hours. The exact timing was found to be between 0601 and 0900 44% of the time, as well as between 1801 and 2100. Only one attack was found to have been staged between the hours of 0301 and 0600. When examined by the day of the week, 26% of the attacks took place on a Tuesday. This was followed by Sundays, with 21% of the attacks. Thursdays and Saturdays rounded out the top three, with 16% of the ambushes.

When analyzed by the calendar year, FARC conducted their ambushes throughout the year with no clear preference for a season or month. Only July did not record any attack activity by FARC. That being said, February and December registered the most attack activity with 16%. March, April, August, and November each suffered 11% of the attacks.

Preferred Locations of Attacks

In five of the attacks by FARC, the location could not be determined. In those that were, attacks staged against victims in transit occurred 60% of the time (one of which was known to have taken place at a common traffic congestion point). Another 20% were carried out at the victim's office. The rest of the ambushes took place at or near the victim's residence.

Preferred Method of Attack

FARC's preferred method of attack was kidnapping, accounting for 47% of the known attacks. Shootings accounted for another 41% of the hits, with 12% making use of explosives. In two of the attacks, the exact methods used were not able to be determined. When carrying out their assassinations by way of firearms, FARC operatives are known to have employed the motorcycle hit team twice. Attacks by a hit team consisting of two gunmen occurred on two occasions, while one attack was staged by a three- to five-gunmen hit team. In the final two attacks, the makeup of the attacking force could not be determined. With the two explosive-based attacks, the devices consisted of IEDs staged along the victim's route.

GOVERNMENT HITS

Government agents are known or suspected to have been responsible for carrying out a number of targeted attacks during the research period. While the point of this is not to pass judgment on whether governments should carry out such attacks on their perceived enemies, it is important to be familiar with their methods of attack. There are many individuals around the world that have spent their careers assigned to special operations, be it in military, police, or intelligence organizations. When these people move on, they often go into training military and law enforcement personnel, and for the more unscrupulous, members of criminal or terrorist organizations. It is for this reason that it is important to examine attacks believed or known to have come at the hand of government agents, if for nothing else, to understand how potential adversaries may be trained.

In forty-four of the attacks, the following countries are believed to have been responsible:

- South Africa—eleven attacks
- Israel—ten attacks
- Russia—seven attacks
- Syria—six attacks
- Libya—four attacks
- Iran—three attacks
- Bulgaria—two attacks
- Indonesia—one attack

Between October 1957, the date of the first known attack, and August 2008, government agents as a whole are known or strongly believed to be responsible for seventy-nine targeted hits. They have also managed to obtain an 89% success rate (target killed or

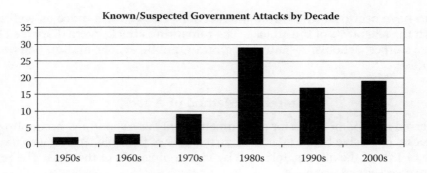

Known/Suspected Government Attacks by Decade

FIGURE 5.6 Known/suspected attacks by decade.

kidnapped). As Figure 5.6 indicates, the majority of the urban ambushes occurred during the 1980s. Overall, there has been a gradual increase in targeted attacks believed to be by the hand of government agents since the 1950s.

Preferred Target of Attack

Government agents preferred to ambush pedestrian-based targets, which accounted for 63% of attacks. Strikes against vehicle-borne targets were second at 32%, and four attacks occurred at unknown locations. Government agents targeted the activist/dissident 29% of the time. Terrorists were the target in another 16% of the attacks. Rounding out the top three, world leaders were targeted 13% of the time. The remaining strikes were conducted against individuals falling within fifteen separate categories of victim.

Timing of Attacks

In only fifty-one of the attacks conducted by government agents was the timing able to be determined. Of those, the majority, at 24%, were conducted in the evening hours between 1801 and 2100. This was followed by another 15% of ambushes staged between 0601 and 0900. The remaining attacks were dispersed almost evenly throughout the remainder of the day. However, only three attacks were known to have been conducted between the hours of 0001 and 0600.

While attacks were carried out almost without regard to a particular day of the week, Tuesdays, with 22%, had the most. This was followed by Thursdays and Fridays, each of which accounted for 18% of the total. This trend on a lack of preference held true when examining the calendar year. While every month documented between four and five attacks, April, with 14%, had the most targeted attacks. September accounted for 11% of the total, followed by February and March, which each had 10% of attacks.

Preferred Locations of Attacks

The target's residence was the number one selected location, with 43% of the attacks. Another 26% occurred while the victim was in transit, and only one of those was known to have occurred at a traffic intersection. The victim's office as well as hotels were each the site of 7% of the attacks. The remaining attacks were dispersed between the victim's office, schools, restaurants, aircraft, public events, and on one occasion, a dentist office.

Preferred Method of Attack

The preferred method of attack for government agents was shootings, accounting for 56% of all attacks. Explosive-based attacks occurred 23% of the time. Poison was the weapon of choice in 13% of the attacks, followed by kidnappings 5% of the time. The remaining attacks involved edged weapons.

In only thirty-one of the shooting attacks were the number of gunmen or tactics used known. The lone gunman was responsible 29% of the time, followed by two gunmen hit teams in 26% of the attacks. Snipers conducted another 13% of the total targeted hits. The motorcycle-based hit team, as well as drive-bys, were each involved in 10% of the attacks. Use of a hit team of between three and five gunmen was responsible for another 10% of the ambushes. The remaining came by way of teams of six or more gunmen.

In their use of explosives, the VBIED reigned supreme, accounting for 44% of the attacks. The booby-trap device was employed in 33% of the attacks, with the remaining coming from IEDs. Government agents were the only ones known to employ poison, which accounted for 13% of the attacks. In these poisonings, a variety of methods were used to deliver the toxic substance—everything from a specially constructed gun that deployed a toxic mist to a custom-made umbrella that injected the poison. Poison was also known to have been employed in a drink consumed shortly afterwards by the target.

HIZBOLLAH

The Shiite extremist group Hizbollah (aka the "Islamic Jihad," among others) is an organization well known for carrying out terrorist attacks, to include the use of targeted violence. As with all of its operations, its targeted attacks have taken place around the world, although most were restricted to the Middle East region. Lebanon, long its home base of operations, recorded the most attacks with seven. Perhaps its most high-profile targeted attack was its successful kidnapping of the CIA station chief in Lebanon, William Buckley. Ultimately Mr. Buckley was killed by Hizbollah operatives, but given his training and background, it provides graphic insight into the level of professionalism this organization utilizes in carrying out its objectives.

While Hizbollah has conducted a large number of operations, the information within this section deals only with its attacks targeting a specific individual or class of individual. Between March 1984, the date of their first known targeted hit, and August 1993, Hizbollah was responsible or claimed responsibility for eleven targeted attacks. It has also managed to obtain an 82% success rate (target killed or kidnapped). As Figure 5.7 indicates, the majority of the targeted attacks were staged during the 1980s. During the nine years in which Hizbollah/Islamic Jihad was active (or rather claimed responsibly for its targeted killings or kidnappings), it averaged just over one attack per year.

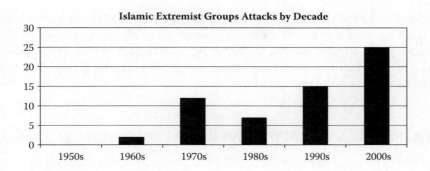

Islamic Extremist Groups Attacks by Decade

FIGURE 5.7　Hizbollah attacks by decade.

Preferred Target of Attack

Hizbollah operatives struck vehicle-borne targets in six of their attacks, and pedestrian targets on four occasions. One attack occurred while the positioning of the victim could not be determined. There were seven different targeted classes victimized by Hizbollah. Military officials, embassy staffers, diplomats, and corporate executives were the only classes of victims to document more than a single attack.

Timing of Attacks

In only four of the targeted attacks by Hizbollah were the exact times able to be determined. Three of those took place between the hours of 0601 and 1500, and one between 2101 and 2400. Hizbollah operatives appear to prefer the first part of the workweek in which to stage their ambushes. Eight out of the eleven were found to have occurred between Monday and Wednesday, with the latter recording the most. Three attacks were carried out between Friday and Saturday.

While there was no particular month found to be favored above others by Hizbollah, there was a clear concentration of attacks during the late autumn and winter months. Between October and March, ten of eleven attacks were found to have been staged by Hizbollah, although there were none documented during the month of December. The remaining ambush occurred in August.

Preferred Locations of Attacks

With four attacks, Hizbollah targeted victims while in transit, followed by two at the victim's residence. One attack was found to have been staged at a hotel and one at the victim's office. In three attacks, the positioning of the victim could not be determined.

Preferred Method of Attack

Hizbollah's preferred method of attack was to kidnap its victims, which occurred in five, or 45% of their attacks. This was followed by three shooting attacks and three explosive-based ambushes. In the shooting attacks, each came using a different methodology, such as drive-by, a team of three to five gunmen, or could not be determined. In the case of the explosive-based attacks, the suicide bombing, a tactic with which Hizbollah is largely identified, was used in the last attack directly attributed to the group. The booby-trap device was deployed on the previous two occasions.

IRISH REPUBLICAN ARMY/PROVISIONAL IRISH REPUBLICAN ARMY

More commonly referred to as the IRA and PIRA, they are known to have been responsible for twenty-one targeted attacks. One of the most infamous and feared terrorist organizations in history, they employed a variety of methods and tactics in their efforts to achieve their goals of independence from Great Britain. One of their tactics was targeted assassination. While the majority of their attacks took place in England, Ireland, and Northern Ireland, they also struck on occasion in the Netherlands.

Perhaps one of their most well-thought-out attacks was one in which they attempted to assassinate then prime minister Margaret Thatcher. The attack occurred at the Grand Hotel in Brighton, England, and involved an improvised explosive device. The device had been cached inside of a wall some three and half weeks prior to her occupying the room (and is covered in more detail in Chapter 8). Ultimately the attack was not successful in obtaining their goal of killing Mrs. Thatcher, but the blast did kill a member of Parliament.

While the IRA/PIRA conducted a large number of operations, this section deals exclusively with their attacks targeting specific individuals. From the date of their first targeted attack in December 1971 through February 1991, the IRA/PIRA were responsible or claimed responsibility for twenty-one targeted attacks. They have also managed to obtain a 71% success rate (target killed or kidnapped). As Figure 5.8 indicates, of the twenty years, the vast majority of targeted attacks occurred during the 1970s. After that time there was a drastic decrease in attacks during the 1980s. The 1990s saw the continued lessening of targeted attacks, albeit by only one, and no attacks have been known to have occurred during the 2000s.

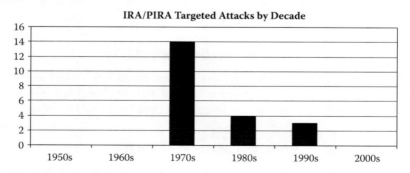

FIGURE 5.8 IRA/PIRA targeted attacks by decade.

Preferred Target of Attack

The IRA/PIRA showed no clear preference for striking pedestrian or vehicle-borne targets. While one ambush was staged against a victim whose position was not known, eleven targeted pedestrians, and nine were against vehicle-borne victims. While certainly preferring to strike at those individuals that represented the British government, the IRA/PIRA did not show any clear preference for one class of target over another. That being said, members of the royal family and prime ministers, as well as corporate executives, were each targeted by the IRA/PIRA 24% of the time. Rounding out the top three, members of Parliament were the targeted subject 19% of the time. The remaining attacks were focused upon five other targeted classes of victim. In a single case, the victim was believed to have been a mistake, but the attack occurred in a residential location where several of the targeted classes lived.

Timing of Attacks

The IRA/PIRA preferred to strike their targets 50% of the time between the hours of 1801 and 2100. They attacked 25% of the time between 0601 and 0900, and 17% of the time between 0901 and 1200. While one attack was known to have occurred after midnight, the timing of nine other attacks could not be determined. When examined by the day of the week, the IRA/PIRA preferred to strike on Mondays 33% of the time, followed by another 24% on Thursdays. They struck evenly over the remaining workweek days as well as Saturday. There was only one attack found to have taken place on a Sunday.

While there was no clear preferred month in which to attack, the IRA/PIRA concentrated their targeted attacks during the autumn and winter months. December, with 19%, recorded the most attack activity. This was followed by October, November, and March, each of which accounted for 14% of the attacks. The remaining ambushes by the IRA/PIRA were spread out over the rest of the year, with the exception of January and May, which recorded none.

Preferred Locations of Attacks

The target's residence was selected by the IRA/PIRA for a targeted ambush 71% of the time. Another 24% of attacks occurred while the victim was in transit, and only one of those is known to have occurred at a traffic intersection. Finally, a single attack was staged at a hotel and one occurred at an unknown location.

Preferred Method of Attack

The preferred method of attack by IRA/PIRA operatives was through the use of explosives, accounting for 48% of all attacks. This was followed by firearms-based attacks 38% of the time. The remaining attacks took the form of kidnappings. When employing explosives against their target, the IRA/PIRA used the booby-trap device 50% of the time. This was followed by IEDs in 40% of the attacks and VBIEDs in another 10%. The majority of the shooting attacks were carried out by an unknown number of gunmen. The use of teams of two gunmen occurred twice, and one attack was perpetrated by a three-gunman hit team.

ISLAMIC EXTREMISTS

The number of Islamic extremist organizations active in the world today are almost too numerous to count. While many may only be active in name only, or have a membership of only one or two individuals, there are plenty of others that carry out terrorist attacks. Many of these Islamic extremist individuals or groups conducting targeted attacks have never claimed responsibility or were never discovered. The amount of crossover or name changes of these individuals and groups further complicates the ability to track (at least at the open-source level) those responsible for such attacks.

It is for this reason that it is important to monitor the methods employed in the attacks, especially with the Internet and the availability of videos and training in carrying out targeted attacks available to would-be assassins. Of the sixty-one attacks by Islamic extremists (that have not been covered in their own sections), twenty-seven are believe to have come from the following groups:

- Al Qaida was responsible for five attacks.
- Armed Islamic Group (GIA) was responsible for four attacks.
- Abu Sayyaf was responsible for three attacks.
- Popular Front for the Liberation of Palestine (PFLP) was responsible for three attacks.
- Al-Gama Al-Islamiya was responsible for three attacks.
- Black September was responsible for three attacks.
- Palestinian Liberation Organization (PLO) was responsible for two attacks.
- Chechens were responsible for two attacks.
- Al Aqsa Martyr's Brigade was responsible for one attack.
- Jemaah Islamiya was responsible for one attack.

From September 1964, the date of the first known attack directly attributed to an Islamic extremist, through November 2008, Islamic extremists were responsible or claimed responsibility for sixty-one targeted attacks. They have also managed to obtain a 64% success rate (target killed or kidnapped). As Figure 5.9 indicates, with of the exception of the 1970s, when there was a dramatic increase in attacks, the majority of targeted violence began in the early 1980s. The first eight years of the 2000s saw a dramatic increase in such attacks and is on course for doubling the total amount experienced in the 1990s.

Preferred Target of Attack

Islamic extremists showed no clear preference in striking pedestrians, which accounted for 49%, or vehicle-borne targets, which occurred 51% of the time. Accounting for 20% of the victims, world leaders found themselves the most frequent target of Islamic extremists. Diplomats were the second most often targeted victim, having documented 13% of the

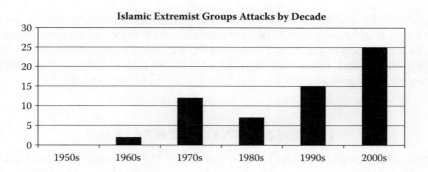

Islamic Extremist Groups Attacks by Decade

FIGURE 5.9   Islamic extremist group attacks by decade.

attacks. With 10% of the attacks, government ministers rounded out the top three classes of victims. The remaining attacks were dispersed over another fourteen target classes.

Timing of Attacks

While the exact timing of only thirty-seven attacks was able to be determined, those that were known revealed that the attacks in the morning hours of 0601 to 0900 occurred 24% of the time. With 19% of the total, the hours of 1201 to 1500 accounted for the second most frequent time frame selected by Islamic extremists to strike. Strikes between the hours of 1501 and 1800, 1801 and 2100, and 2101 and 2400 each accounted for 14% of the total.

Islamic extremists appeared to prefer to ambush their victims on Wednesdays, which recorded 25% of the attacks. This was followed by Mondays, which recorded 20% of the strikes. Tuesdays and Sundays rounded out the top four days in which Islamic extremists carried out attacks, each having documented 15% of the total. When reviewed by the calendar year, October had the most attacks, accounting for 15% of the total. November, with 13%, had the second most attacks, followed by March and December, each with 11%. The greatest concentration of ambushes by Islamic extremists was found to occur during the late autumn through winter months, accounting for 64% of the total.

Preferred Locations of Attacks

Attacks targeting victims in transit accounted for the most ambushes, representing 38% of the total (four of these were found to have occurred at traffic intersections). The victim's residence was the site selected for another 28% of the ambushes. Those attacks occurring at public events rounded out the top three locations at 13%.

Preferred Method of Attack

The preferred methods of attack perpetrated by Islamic extremists were shootings, accounting for 64% of all ambushes. This was followed by explosive-based attacks 28% of the time. The remaining attacks were either kidnappings or edged-weapon assaults. The majority of the shooting attacks came from an unknown number of gunmen. A lone gunman was found to be responsible for 28% of the targeted hits. Teams of two gunmen conducted another 13% of the shooting attacks. Another 10% were carried out by teams of between three and five gunmen. When employing explosives against their target, the suicide bomber was responsible for 59% of the total. The remaining explosive-based attacks included two VBIEDs, two IEDs, two attacks by grenades, and a single instance of a booby-trap device.

ITALIAN MAFIA ORGANIZATIONS

The Italian mafia groups, the Cosa Nostra from Sicily, the N'drangheta from the Calabrian region, and the Camorra from the Naples region, are known to have been responsible for numerous targeted attacks (documented as being committed by only the Cosa Nostra and N'drangheta). Like the drug cartels of the Americas, the Italian mafia groups are focused on maintaining their way of life and their criminal enterprises. When they do conduct a targeted killing outside of their own groups, the individual is generally a person who has been deemed a threat to their business.

While the Italian criminal groups have conducted a large number of killings, generally among themselves, the information within this section deals only with their attacks targeting a specific individual. Between May 1971, the date of their first known attack, and February 2008, the Italian mafias were found have been responsible for twenty-five targeted attacks (although they were known to have killed thousands during internal wars). They have also managed to obtain a 96% success rate (target killed).

As Figure 5.10 indicates, the vast majority of the targeted attacks occurred during the 1980s, all of which came at the hands of the Sicilian mafia. The 1990s also witnessed a significant amount of attacks, and again, all but one was perpetrated by the Sicilians, the other by the N'drangheta. The two attacks during the 2000s were carried out by members of the N'drangheta.

Preferred Target of Attack

In six of the cases analyzed, the positioning of the target at the time of the attack could not be determined. Of the nineteen that were known, pedestrian victims were found to

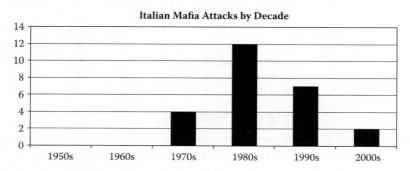

FIGURE 5.10   Italian mafia attacks by decade.

be attacked 58% of the time. Ambushes staged against vehicle-borne victims made up the rest of the attacks. Given the nature of the Italian mafias, it is not surprising that the most often attacked victims fell within the criminal justice community. Judges suffered 24% of the attacks, followed closely by law enforcement officials 20% of the time. Prosecutors rounded out the top three victims, recording 16% of attacks. The remaining assassinations by Italian mafias targeted individuals within eight other targeted classes.

Timing of Attacks

While the exact timing of over half of the attacks could not be determined, those that are known revealed that the mafias preferred striking in the evening hours 40% of the time. Two hits occurred in the morning hours of between 0601 and 0900, with another two during the afternoon hours of 1201 to 1500. Two more were perpetrated between 1501 and 1800. Members of the mafias attacked throughout the workweek, but tended to concentrate their attacks between Friday and Sunday. Sundays accounted for 24% of the attacks, followed by Friday with 20%. Wednesdays and Saturdays each documented 16% of the total attacks.

The mafias appeared to prefer the month of September in which to strike, recording 24% of the total attacks. August followed closely, with 16% of the ambushes, while January and May each recorded another 12%. The remaining attacks occurred over the other months, with only June, November, and December not reporting a single attack.

Preferred Locations of Attacks

Striking the target while in transit was the number one location for 42% of the ambushes. The office of the victim was the site of another 26% of all attacks (one of the few groups to select such a site over a residence). The victim's residence was used 16% of the time, while the remaining hits were staged at locations frequented by the victim as well as a bar.

Preferred Method of Attack

The Italian mafias overwhelmingly preferred to ambush their victims using firearms, representing 81% of all the attacks. The remaining 19% of targeted attacks employed explosives to accomplish their mission. Four of the attacks involved an unknown method of operation. The methods of shooting attacks carried out by these mafia hitmen ran the gamut from motorcycle hit teams to a lone gunman, as well as hit teams of two. A hit team of between three and eight gunmen was also found to have been used on one occasion (in several of these targeted killings, the same AK-47 rifle was used).

Of the explosive-based attacks, the mafia deployed a VBIED on three occasions and used an IED once. However, it was this single IED attack that was perhaps their most infamous assassination. This attack, which is detailed in depth in the coming case studies, involved a buried explosive that killed Prosecutor Giovanni Falcone and his wife, a sitting judge. The attack, which also employed a ruse, demonstrated the level of professionalism employed by the Sicilians in carrying out their objectives.

TAMIL TIGERS

The Tamil Tigers (more commonly referred to as the LTTE) is certainly one of the most prolific terrorist groups within the last twenty years, carrying out a large number and variety of operations. As part of that repertoire, the targeted assassination has played a part. In the majority of these attacks, the target employed a protective detail, which the Tigers were able to successfully overwhelm. The Tigers are known primarily for their use of the suicide bomber, one of which was so extreme and shocking that the entire world took notice. This attack was, of course, the suicide bombing assassination of Rajiv Gandhi. This attack, which is covered in-depth in the case studies, graphically revealed how the ruse has been used with great effect by the Tigers.

Beginning March 1991, the date of their first known targeted attack, through October 2008, the Tigers were known to have been responsible or claimed responsibility for thirteen targeted attacks. During that time they managed to obtain a 92% success rate in their targeted killings. As Figure 5.11 indicates, the majority of the targeted ambushes occurred during the 1990s. During the seventeen years in which they have been active, the Tigers have averaged less than one targeted attack a year against their declared enemies, the Sri Lankan and Indian governments.

Preferred Target of Attack

The Tigers attacked almost equally vehicle-borne targets (six attacks) and pedestrian-based victims (seven attacks). World leaders and military officials found themselves under attack by Tamil Tiger assassins the most often, each documenting three ambushes. Government ministers and political leaders each suffered two targeted attacks by the Tigers. The remaining ambushes were focused upon federal government officials, judges, and a world leader candidate.

Timing of Attacks

The Tigers focused their attacks during the morning and evening hours when their target was moving within his or her routine. Three attacks were staged between 0601 and 0900,

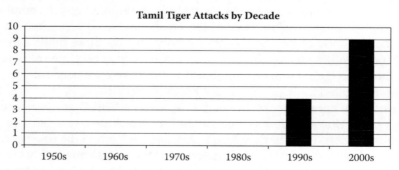

FIGURE 5.11 Tamil Tiger attacks by decade.

152

and three occurred between 2101 and 2400. There were two attacks documented between 0901 and 1200, and one between 1201 and 1500. The Tigers struck most often on Fridays, which recorded four attacks. This was followed by Mondays and Thursdays, each of which recorded three attacks. Only one attack was found to have taken place on a Tuesday. There were no attacks found to have occurred on a Wednesday or Sunday.

There was also no clear preference for a specific month in which the Tigers ambushed their victims. May had the most, with three attacks. The remaining ambushes were dispersed fairly evenly throughout the year, with only January, February, and September having no recorded targeted attacks. Seasonally, the Tigers conducted the majority of their assassination strikes during the spring and summer months.

Preferred Locations of Attacks

The Tigers carried out their ambushes on five occasions while the victim was attending a public event. Another five were staged while the victim was in transit. These were followed by two attacks at the victim's residence and another one at the office.

Preferred Method of Attack

The Tigers overwhelmingly preferred using explosives in their targeted attacks, with the suicide bomber employed in nine out of the ten. Three attacks used firearms, each consisting of a different makeup of hit team. Ultimately, regardless of the method of attack employed by the Tigers, they made extremely effective use of the ruse in order to get within striking distance of their target, and recorded some of the most dramatic assassinations in history.

MEXICAN DRUG CARTELS

The five Mexican drug cartels—Gulf Cartel, Sinaloa, Juarez, Tijuana, and Familia Michoacana—are known to have been responsible for thousands of murders. Given the focus on their profits in the illegal drug trade, they have carried out an enormous amount of killings among themselves and the civilian population. As with the Colombian cartels, those in Mexico often use assassination to remove those individuals identified as a threat to their operations.

Beginning in February 1985, the date of their first known attack, to December 2008, the Mexican drug cartels were responsible or claimed responsibility for thirty-four targeted attacks. For their efforts, they managed to obtain a 79% success rate (target killed or kidnapped). As Figure 5.12 indicates, the majority of the targeted attacks have occurred between 2000 and 2008. Of those, twenty-one attacks were perpetrated in 2008, and only four during 2007.

Preferred Target of Attack

The cartels preferred to ambush vehicle-borne targets, which accounted for 56% of attacks. Strikes against pedestrian targets occurred 44% of the time. Accounting for 62% of the

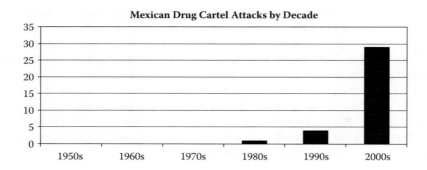

FIGURE 5.12 Mexican drug cartel attacks by decade.

victims, the cartels ambushed law enforcement officials the most often over the twenty-three-year period. Prosecutors accounted for the second most often targeted class of victim, being hit 15% of the time. The remaining attacks targeted seven other classes of victim.

Timing of Attacks

Of the twenty-five targeted attacks in which the timing was able to be determined, most occurred during the hours of darkness. The hours between 1801 and 2100 experienced 32% of attacks, while another 20% were documented between 2101 and 2400. The morning hours of 0601 to 0900 witnessed 24% of the attacks. The remaining 24% were staged between 1201 and 1800 (with one occurring after midnight).

The cartels of Mexico did not show any clear preference for a day of the week to carry out their attacks. There was, however, a concentration conducted during the beginning of the week. Monday experienced 24% of the ambushes, the most of any single day of the week. This was followed by Tuesday and Wednesday, which each documented 18% of attacks. Thursday rounded out the top four with 15% of ambushes. Mexican cartels also failed to show any clear preference for a month of the year in which to ambush their victims. The month of May, however, recorded the most ambush activity of any single month, with seven attacks. This was followed by February, with four attacks. January, March, September, November, and December each recorded three attacks. The remaining attacks were dispersed over the rest of the year.

Preferred Locations of Attacks

Given the preference of attacks against vehicle-borne targets, ambushes staged while the victim was in transit occurred the most often, accounting for 35% (three were known to have been staged at traffic intersections). The victim's residence was the site of another 29% of the targeted attacks. The office was selected by the cartels in another 12% of attacks. The remaining ambushes were staged at hotels, restaurants, frequented locations, and even an airport.

Preferred Method of Attack

The Mexican drug cartels' preferred method of attack was shootings, used in 88% of all ambushes. The use of explosives in targeted attacks, as well as kidnappings, each accounted for only 6% of the total. In fourteen of the attacks, the exact makeup of the shootings could not be determined. The most popular known firearm methodology used by the cartels was the drive-by. This method was documented in eleven of the attacks. The lone gunman and the two-gunmen hit team were each known to have been used in two attacks. There was also one case in which a three- to five-gunmen hit team was employed. With the explosive attacks, one took the form of a grenade attack, while the other involved a booby trap that detonated during installation.

NOVEMBER 17 ORGANIZATION

The Greek terrorist organization known as November 17 carried out a number of violent attacks during the twenty-five years it was active. However, it made the greatest use of the targeted killing, all of which occurred within the territorial boundaries of Greece. Beginning in December 1975, when it carried out its first known attack, through June 2000, November 17 was found to be responsible or claimed responsibility for twenty-one targeted ambushes. Of those, the organization managed to obtain a 76% success rate (target killed or kidnapped). As Figure 5.13 indicates, the majority of the targeted attacks occurred during the 1980s and 1990s. Still, over the twenty-five-year period, November 17 averaged less than one targeted attack each year.

Preferred Target of Attack

November 17 operatives appeared to show a preference for ambushing vehicle-borne targets, who accounted for 52% of their victims. Another 38% of the attacks targeted pedestrian victims, while the remaining occurred against victims at unknown locations. Accounting for 29% of the victims, November 17 ambushed corporate executives the most often over the twenty-five years. Military officials were the second most often targeted class of victim,

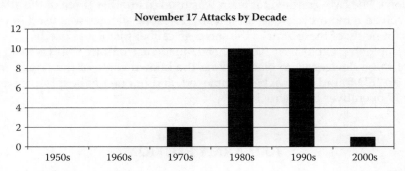

FIGURE 5.13 November 17 attacks by decade.

155

being hit 19% of the time. Embassy staffers rounded out the top three, suffering 14% of the attacks. The remaining ambushes were staged against seven different target classes.

Timing of Attacks

In only six of the attacks was the exact timing able to be determined. Of those, three were found to have occurred between the hours of 0601 and 0900. Another three were staged between the evening hours of 1801 and 2100. When examined by the day of the week selected for the ambush, November 17 showed a clear preference for striking its targets 52% of the time on a Tuesday. This was followed somewhat distantly by Mondays, accounting for 19% of the attacks. The remaining hits were perpetrated on Wednesdays, Thursdays, and one on Sunday. No attacks were found to have been staged on a Friday or Saturday.

Unlike the day of week which November 17 operatives selected for their attack, they did not show any preference for a particular month in which to strike. January, however, recorded four attacks, the most of any single month. July and November each documented three attacks, while the remaining were spread out over the rest of the year. Only August did not have any known attacks by the November 17 terrorist organization. Seasonally, November 17 operatives chose to strike most often during the late autumn and winter months.

Preferred Locations of Attacks

While three attacks took place at unknown locations, November 17 attacked its targets 50% of time while they were in transit (two of these attacks were known to have occurred at a traffic intersection or traffic congestion points). The residence was the site of another 33% of the ambushes, while the office registered 17% of attacks.

Preferred Method of Attack

The preferred method of attack of November 17 operatives was shootings, used in 71% of the ambushes. Explosives were used in another 29% of the targeted attacks. The majority of the shooting attacks came from an unknown number of gunmen. In those in which the method was known, the use of teams of between three and five gunmen occurred on four occasions. The two-gunmen hit team was used in another three of the attacks, while another involved a motorcycle-based hit team. The lone shooter was used in only two of the attacks (in many of these attacks the same .45 caliber pistol was used).

When employing explosives, November 17 made use of four VBIEDs to attack its victims. All of these devices were placed along the known route of the target. In only one attack was an IED found to have been deployed, and in one final explosive-based attack, November 17 operatives fired a rocket.

RED ARMY FACTION

Germany's Red Army Faction (RAF), also known as the Baader-Meinhof gang, carried out a number of violent attacks during its heyday. All but one of these attacks was staged

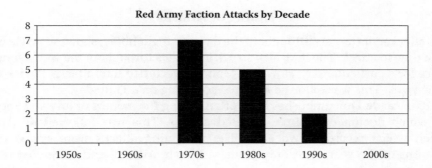

Red Army Faction Attacks by Decade

FIGURE 5.14 RAF attacks by decade.

in Germany, with a single attack taking place in Belgium. While not its first targeted attack, the RAF's strike against German federal prosecutor Siegfried Buback brought the group to the attention of the world. This attack, which is covered more in-depth in the case studies section, involved two assassins on a motorcycle that patiently went about the killing of their target. This represented the first documented assassination employing this methodology.

Perhaps the RAF's most infamous attack occurred later in its history. This concerned the IED-based killing of corporate executive Alfred Herrhausen (although there has been considerable debate over whether the attack was really the work of the RAF). In this attack, which is covered in detail in Chapter 7, an infrared mechanism was used to trigger the device at the precise time. The RAF operatives made use of a ruse, which successfully allowed them to stage the ambush.

Beginning in May 1972, when RAF carried out its first known attack, through April 1991, the RAF was responsible or claimed responsibility for fourteen targeted attacks. Over the course of its terror, the RAF managed to obtain a 64% success rate (target killed or kidnapped). As Figure 5.14 illustrates, the majority of the targeted attacks occurred during the 1970s and 1980s. Over half of the total number occurred during the last eight years of the 1970s. Overall, during the nineteen years the RAF was active, it averaged considerably less than one targeted attack a year.

Preferred Target of Attack

The RAF preferred to ambush vehicle-borne targets, which accounted for ten out of the fourteen attacks. Strikes against pedestrian targets only occurred in four instances. As with other European terrorist organizations, the RAF tended to focus its attacks upon government representatives. However, corporate executives suffered the most attacks by the RAF, with a total of four. Government ministers, with three attacks, recorded the second highest number of ambushes. Judges and military officials, with two each, tied for the top three targeted classes of victims. The other attacks targeted a political leader, a prosecutor, and a federal government official.

157

Timing of Attacks

The RAF attacked its targets throughout the day and night hours, showing no clear preference for a time to attack. The RAF also struck its targets throughout the week, showing no preference for a particular day. However, Mondays recorded four attacks, the most of any day of the week. This was followed by three occurring on a Thursday.

The RAF carried out ambushes most often during the months of July and September, each of which documented three targeted attacks. This was followed by April and November, which recorded two each. The remaining attacks were staged over the other months of the year, with only January, March, August, and December recording no attacks. Seasonally, the majority of attacks by the RAF were carried out during the autumn months.

Preferred Locations of Attacks

Red Army Faction operatives struck their targets at only one of two locations during their history: while in transit or the victim's residence. Striking the target at preidentified sites while in transit was the number one location for RAF attacks, documenting a total of eight. This was followed by hits at the victim's residence, making up the remaining six attacks.

Preferred Method of Attack

The preferred method of attack for the RAF was shootings, accounting for seven of the fourteen hits. This was followed by six employing explosives, with a single kidnapping ambush. Of the shootings, the RAF made use of the sniper, the lone gunman, and the motorcycle hit team, on one occasion each. The RAF employed a hit team of between three and five gunmen on two occasions. The remaining shooting attacks employed an unknown method.

When using explosives against its targets, the RAF used the improvised explosive device on three occasions. The booby-trap device was used in a single attack, as was the VBIED. A rocket-propelled grenade was recorded as being used in an assassination attempt on the then commander of NATO.

RED BRIGADES

Italy's Red Brigades, or "Brigade Rosa," was second only to Spain's ETA in the use of targeted violence by a single organization. The Red Brigades are known to have conducted a considerable number of attacks during the decades of the 1970s and 1980s, of which the targeted attack featured prominently. All of their targeted attacks took place within the boarders of Italy.

The Red Brigades made effective use of the ruse in order to carry out some of the most spectacular and brazen kidnappings in history. Their successful operations against Aldo Moro and James Dozier brought them to the attention of the world stage. The sophistication

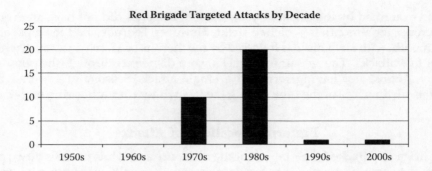

FIGURE 5.15   Red Brigade targeted attacks by decade.

that the Red Brigades brought to their targeted attacks revealed a substantial amount of planning and professionalism, the likes of which has rarely been seen.

Of the thirty-two targeted attacks occurring between March 1972 and March 2002, they managed to obtain a 94% success rate (target killed or kidnapped). As Figure 5.15 indicates, the majority of the targeted attacks occurred during the 1970s and 1980s. Only one attack was attributed to the Red Brigades during the 1990s, and one during the first eight years of the 2000s.

Preferred Target of Attack

The Brigades showed no clear preference on ambushing pedestrian-based targets over mobile targets. Unfortunately, in eleven of the attacks, it was not able to be determined whether the victim was a pedestrian or traveling in a vehicle at the time of the ambush. Of the twenty-one attacks where the victim's position was known, 52% were vehicle borne, while 48% were pedestrians.

Accounting for 22% of the victims, the Red Brigades ambushed law enforcement officials the most often. Judges accounted for the second most often targeted class of victim, attacked 16% of the time. Corporate executives rounded out the top three, with 13% of the attacks. The remaining 49% of attacks occurred against individuals within twelve targeted classes of victim.

Timing of Attacks

The exact timing of well over half of the attacks could not be determined. In the eight that were known, the Brigades showed no clear preference. Four attacks were found to have taken place between the hours of 0601 and 0900, two occurred between 1801 and 2100, and the last two during the afternoon hours of 1201 to 1800. The Red Brigades also did not show a preference for a day of the week to attack, although their ambushes were concentrated in the middle of the week. Attacks between the days of Tuesday and Thursday accounted for 59% of the total. The remaining attacks were dispersed evenly on Mondays, Fridays, and Saturdays. Only one attack was known to have occurred on Sunday, and three occurred on an unknown day.

When examined by the calendar year, the Red Brigades did not have an overwhelming preference for a month in which to strike. However, February had the most attacks of any one month, with six. This was followed by the months of March and April, which each recorded five attacks. The remaining attacks were dispersed through the other months, with only August not having recorded a single attack. Seasonally, the Red Brigades attacked its victims 81% of the time during the late winter through spring months.

Preferred Locations of Attacks

The Red Brigades attacked their targets at the residence and while in transit (two of which were known to have been staged at a traffic intersection) equally, accounting for ten attacks each. One attack was known to have been staged at a university in which the victim had been giving a speech. In eleven of the attacks, the exact location of the victim at the time could not be determined.

Preferred Method of Attack

The Red Brigades chose to ambush their victims most often using firearms, which accounted for 65% of the total attacks where the method was known. Of these shootings, there was no overwhelmingly preferred technique. The Brigades employed a lone gunman, motorcycle hit teams, and shooting teams of between three and seven gunmen almost evenly. In nine of the shootings, the exact method of attack was not known. Interestingly enough, there were no documented ambushes perpetrated by Red Brigade terrorists involving explosives.

While only accounting for 28% of their targeted attacks, the kidnapping became the real claim to fame for the Red Brigades. These nine kidnappings were conducted with such brazenness that it bought the group to the forefront of terrorist organizations.

6

Victimology

INTRODUCTION

In order to obtain a more thorough understanding of targeted violence, it is important to also examine the victimology of the attacks. While similar to other forms of investigation into violent acts, this section will look at the commonalities of a class of victim rather than the individual. The coming pages will review the timing of attacks, tactics employed, and groups involved in the ambushing of the major classes of target. Figure 6.1 provides a breakdown of the eighteen groups experiencing the greatest number of attacks (accounting for 91%) during the research period.

As any military professional would advise, it is critical that one be familiar with the tactics, techniques, strategies, weapons, etc., of their potential adversaries. One major difference is that in targeted violence it is also important to gain a historical understanding of how victims have been attacked. This allows for more focus upon the most often employed tactics. This research then leads to the opportunity for the development of responses to

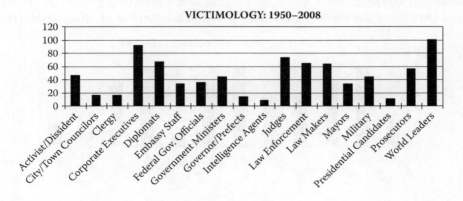

FIGURE 6.1 Victimology of top eighteen victim groups.

such attacks. However, this is not to suggest in any way that because a particular attack method has not been employed against a target, it can be discounted, but rather where the focus should lie initially. For those assigned a protective role, this section will provide the information on which attack methods to train for and develop immediate action drills. Used in conjunction with the knowledge of the region to be worked, and coupled with the types of groups operating in the area, it will provide the best information needed to begin preparation of protective operations.

ACTIVISTS/DISSIDENTS

There have been a total of forty-seven attacks known to have been perpetrated against activists/dissidents worldwide, resulting in forty successful assassinations and one successful kidnapping. These ambushes on activists/dissidents had a steady beginning in the 1950s and hit a plateau in the 1980s, which recorded 38% of all such attacks. Since the 1980s, a continual decline in attacks against activists/dissidents has been recorded. The 1990s recorded 28% of the attacks, followed by the first eight years of the 2000s, at 13%.

Of all of the attacks against the activist/dissident, 68% were conducted against a pedestrian-based target. Activists traveling in a motorized vehicle accounted for another 30% of the attacks. The remaining attacks on an activist/dissident occurred at an unknown location and time. As could be expected, the vast majority of activists/dissidents did not have a protective detail at the time of the attack. In fact, only two are known to have employed one at the time the ambush was staged.

The greatest number of attacks against the activist/dissident during the research period occurred in the months of February, June, and September (Figure 6.2). However, there were enough attacks over the remaining months to make predicting a particular month of year in which an attack is more likely to occur difficult at best. There was a distinct reduction in attacks during the winter months of November through January. Seasonally, the activist/dissident victims suffered the greatest number of attacks during the spring/early summer months, accounting for 46% of the total number of ambushes.

Activists/dissidents were found to be attacked, interestingly enough, during two different periods of the week (Figure 6.3). The greatest number of attacks occurred on a

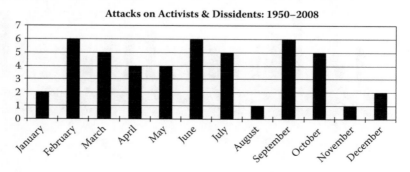

Attacks on Activists & Dissidents: 1950–2008

FIGURE 6.2 Attacks on activists/dissidents by month of the year.

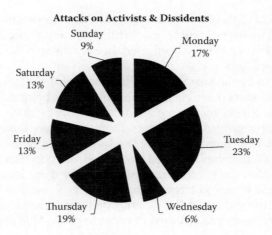

Attacks on Activists & Dissidents

Sunday 9%
Monday 17%
Saturday 13%
Friday 13%
Tuesday 23%
Thursday 19%
Wednesday 6%

FIGURE 6.3 Attacks on activists/dissidents by day of the week.

Monday or Tuesday, which in total accounted for 40% of the ambushes. This was followed by ambushes occurring between the three-day period of Thursday through Saturday, which accounted for another 45% of the attacks.

Timing of Attacks

Of the thirty attacks in which the time they occurred is known, five were between the hours of 0601 and 0900. Another seven ambushes were staged between the hours of 0901 and 1200 (representing a full 40%). Only three attacks occurred between the hours of 1801 and 2100. The afternoon hours of between 1201 and 1800 recorded another five attacks. Additionally, there were six attacks occurring between the hours of 2101 and 0300.

Location of Attacks

Representing the majority, the residence of the activist/dissident was the location of attack 38% of the time. In one of the attacks occurring at the residence, the killers employed a ruse of a prearranged meeting with the victim in order to get close enough to strike. The next most often selected location used to strike the activists/dissidents was while in transit, accounting for 19% of attacks. Another 13% of attacks occurred at the victim's office. The remaining ambushes were staged at a hotel/restaurant 9% of the time, at a public event 6% of the time, or could not be determined.

Type of Attacks

In the types of ambushes encountered by activists/dissidents, 68% took the form of shooting attacks. Of these attacks, 31% were carried out by an unknown number of gunmen. Teams of two gunmen accounted for 19% of the shooting-based ambushes. Attacks by teams of three or more shooters accounted for another 16% of the total. Lone gunmen struck activists/dissidents 13% of the time. The final 21% of the shooting attacks came from snipers, drive-bys, and motorcycle hit teams. While fully automatic submachine guns and assault weapons were known to have been used, in only three of the attacks were suppressors known to have employed.

Poison was found to be the weapon of choice in six of the attacks against activist/dissident targets. This represents the highest number of victims being targeted by this method of attack. Additionally, all six of these poison-based attacks came at or are believed to have come at the hands of government agents. Explosives were employed in only a single instance against an activist/dissident taking the form of an improvised explosive device. The remaining types of ambushes included two edged-weapon attacks and a kidnapping.

In three of the attacks, the killers employed a ruse or disguise in order to get within striking distance of their intended target. One of the ruses consisted of several men seeking an interview with the victim. In the others, one man dressed as a mail deliveryman, while the other assassin wore a false beard in order to protect his identity.

Groups Conducting Attacks

Unfortunately, in only fifteen of the cases of activists/dissidents being ambushed were the groups or individuals responsible identified, either by their own doing or through investigation. Thirteen of these ambushes came at the hands of terrorist organizations, both national and international. Only one attack was found to have been staged by an organized crime group. One attack was also believed to have come at the hands of a rival. As has already been mentioned, government agents were believed to have been responsible for all of the poison attacks, but in total are believed to be behind twenty-two attacks.

Region/Countries Attacks Occurred

Regionally, Europe accounted for the most activists/dissidents being attacked at 49%, spread out over eleven countries. This was followed by the African region, which experienced 17% of all attacks spread out over six countries. The remaining attacks occurred in countries encompassing North and Central/South America and parts of the Middle East and Asia.

When examined by individual countries, the United States had 19% of the attacks, the greatest number targeting the activist/dissident. France was second with 13% of all of the attacks worldwide. The United Kingdom accounted for another 11%, while Germany and Austria tied, each with 6%. The remaining attacks were spread out over twenty separate countries, each experiencing only one or two attacks over the fifty-eight-year period.

CITY/TOWN COUNCILORS

A total of sixteen attacks are known to have been perpetrated against city/town councilors worldwide, resulting in twelve successful assassinations and two successful kidnappings. Seven of these attacks have occurred within the first eight years of the 2000s. The 1990s recorded four ambushes, followed closely by the 1980s with three. The decade of the 1970s documented two attacks.

Of all of these attacks, ten targeted the pedestrian victim. City/town councilors traveling in a motorized vehicle accounted for another four of the attacks. The remaining attacks staged against city/town councilors occurred at unknown locations and times. Of all the attacks, only five of the city/town councilors had protective details at the time.

While the total number of attacks was relatively low when compared to the other victims, the greatest number of attacks during the research period occurred in the months of May and July (Figure 6.4). This was followed closely by September and November. The months of March and August suffered no attacks at all.

City/town councilors were found to be attacked predominantly on a Monday, at 31% of the time (Figure 6.5). This was followed by Thursdays, with another 25% of attacks. Wednesdays with 19% and Fridays with 13% of the attacks rounded out the top four days in which a councilor was targeted. Interestingly enough, there were no attacks occurring on Tuesday.

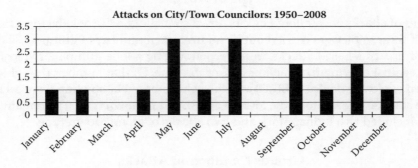

FIGURE 6.4   Attacks on city/town councilor by month of the year.

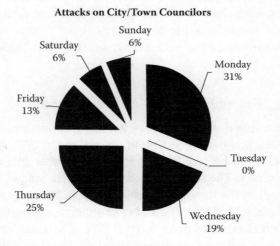

FIGURE 6.5   Attacks on city/town councilors.

165

Timing of Attacks

Of the five attacks in which the time of day was able to be determined, two occurred between the hours of 0901 and 1200. Only one was staged between the hours of 1801 and 2100. The remaining two attacks occurred during the nine-hour period between 1201 and 1800.

Location of Attacks

The councilor's residence was the scene of the majority of attacks, accounting for 38% of the total number. This was followed closely by another 25% of ambushes conducted against city/town councilors while they were in transit. The remaining attacks occurred at the victim's office, a hotel, a frequented location, or could not be determined.

Type of Attacks

In the types of attacks encountered by city/town councilors, 44% took the form of shooting attacks. Of these, 43% were carried out by an unknown number of gunmen. The remaining 57% of firearms-based attacks were perpetrated by a lone gunman. Explosives were deployed against city/town councilors 31% of the time. Of that number, the vehicle-borne improvised explosive device (VBIED) and the vehicle-based booby trap were each used in two of the attacks. The last took the form of an IED of unknown type. The remaining types of attacks included two kidnappings and two attacks of an unknown type.

Groups Conducting Attacks

With responsibility for a full 50% of the attacks, Spain's ETA (Euskadi ta Askatasuna) was the most dominant group in targeting city/town councilors. Two attacks came at the hands of Italy's Red Brigades, with the Palestinian terrorist group of Abu Nidal claiming one. A Colombia drug cartel was believed to be responsible for a single attack. Political rivals were behind two other targeted attacks. Unknown groups or individuals were behind the final two ambushes.

Region/Countries Attacks Occurred

Regionally, Europe accounted for the most city/town councilors being attacked (due mainly to Spain's ETA's aggressive targeting of councilors) at 69%, spread out over three countries. This was followed by North America with another 19% of all attacks, which occurred in a single country. The remaining ambushes were staged in the Central/South American region, as well as the Russian/republic's region. When examined by individual countries, Spain stood out with the most number of attacks, accounting for 50% (again due to the ETA). The United States was second, with 19% of attacks. The remaining attacks were spread out over four separate countries, each experiencing only one or two attacks during the fifty-eight-year period.

CLERGY

There have been a total of sixteen attacks known to have been perpetrated against clergy worldwide, resulting in twelve successful assassinations and one successful kidnapping. With 50% of the attacks, the decade of the 1990s witnessed far and away the most attacks against clergy around the world. This was followed by the 1980s, which recorded 31%, and the 2000s, with 13%. While the 1970s accounted for 6% of attacks, there were no known attacks found to have occurred against clergy during the 1960s or 1950s.

Of all of these attacks, nine were carried out against clergy traveling on foot. Clergy traveling in a motorized vehicle accounted for another five of the ambushes. The remaining attacks on clergy occurred at unknown locations and times. Of the sixteen attacks, twelve of these clergy members had protective details at the time.

The greatest number of attacks against members of the clergy occurred equally during the months of January, March, and May (Figure 6.6). However, of note is the total lack of activity occurring during the months of June, July, and December, but this could just be a result of the low total number of attacks. Seasonally, the spring documented the majority of attacks targeting clergy members.

Clergy were found to be attacked almost equally on the days of Sunday (which only had a slightly higher percentage than the other two days), Monday, and Wednesday (Figure 6.7). However, with the slight decrease of activity occurring on Thursdays, attacks against clergy were relatively steady throughout the seven-day week.

Timing of Attacks

Of the nine attacks in which the time of day was known, five occurred between the hours of 1801 and 2100. Only one was found to have been staged between the hours of 0901 and 1200. One occurred during the six-hour period between 1201 and 1800. Additionally, there were two attacks carried out between the hours of 2101 and 0300.

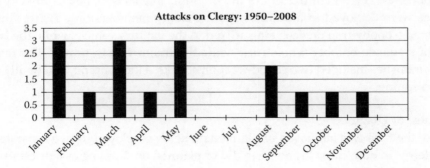

FIGURE 6.6 Attacks on clergy.

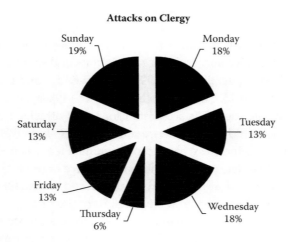

FIGURE 6.7   Attacks on clergy by day of the week.

Location of Attacks

The house of worship (office) was the location most often used to strike the clergy member, accounting for 38% of all attacks. Interestingly enough, this was followed 19% of the time by attacks against clergy while at an airport. The remaining attacks were staged while the victim was in transit, attending a public event, at a residence, or could not be determined.

Type of Attacks

In the types of ambushes suffered by members of the clergy, 63% took the form of shooting attacks. In these attacks, 50% were carried out by an unknown number of gunmen. Teams of two gunmen and a lone gunman were each responsible for 20% of the shooting-based ambushes. The remaining 10% of the shooting attacks were perpetrated by snipers. Explosives were deployed in ambushes against clergy members only twice. One attack documented a booby-trap device being affixed to the victim's vehicle, while the last came by way of a suicide bomber who struck while the Imam was in prayer. The remaining types of ambushes included two edged-weapon attacks, a kidnapping, and finally, a single case of poisoning.

Use of Ruse or Disguise

The use of the ruse was employed or planned on being employed in two separate attacks against clergy. In both cases the assassin did or planned on dressing as a priest in order to close the initial striking distance. Only one of these attacks, one that was never able to be carried out, was the work of a terrorist organization.

Groups Conducting Attacks

The groups or individuals responsible for ambushes were identified, either through their own doing or through the subsequent investigations, in thirteen of the cases of victimizing a clergy member. Of those, five came at the hands of four different terrorist organizations. Only the Abu Sayyaf Organization laid claim to having struck more than once, having targeted clergy on two occasions.

Organized criminal groups were determined to have been responsible in three targeted attacks against clergy. One of these attacks was the work of a Mexican drug cartel, while the other two were from Italian mafia families. Three other attacks were believed to have been the work of government agents. The remaining attacks were perpetrated by a criminal, a rival religious extremist, or could not be determined.

Region/Countries Attacks Occurred

Regionally, Europe and North America each accounted for 25% of attacks perpetrated against clergy members. In Europe, those attacks were spread out over three countries. In North America, the attacks were carried out in two countries. The remaining attacks occurred in countries encompassing every region except South Asia and Russia and its republics. When examined by individual countries, the Philippines, with 25%, stood out with the highest number of attacks. The United States had the second greatest number of attacks on clergy members, with 19%. The remaining ambushes were dispersed over eight separate countries, each experiencing only one or two attacks over the fifty-eight-year period.

CORPORATE EXECUTIVES

A total of ninety-two attacks were perpetrated against corporate executives worldwide, resulting in fifty-three successful assassinations and thirty-nine successful kidnappings. With 34%, the decade of the 1990s witnessed far and away the most attacks against corporate executives around the planet. This was followed by the first eight years of the 2000s, which recorded another 23%. The 1970s and 1980s each witnessed 21% of all known attacks targeting corporate executives. Finally, there was a single known attack during the 1960s, and none found to have occurred in the 1950s.

Of these attacks, forty-nine targeted a pedestrian-based corporate executive. Corporate executives traveling in a motorized vehicle accounted for another thirty-two of the attacks. The remaining attacks on corporate executives occurred at unknown locations and times. Of all the attacks, in only twenty-three was a protective detail known to have been present at the time.

The greatest number of attacks against a corporate executive during the research period occurred in the month of March, in which thirteen attacks were documented (Figure 6.8). This was followed closely by November, with twelve attacks. The month of August, with only four attacks, recorded the fewest. While the concentration of attacks occurred during the late autumn through early spring, there was significant activity throughout the calendar year.

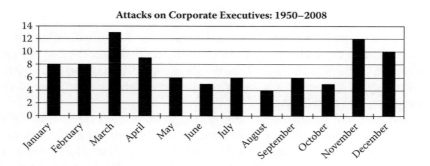

FIGURE 6.8 Attacks on corporate executives by month of the year.

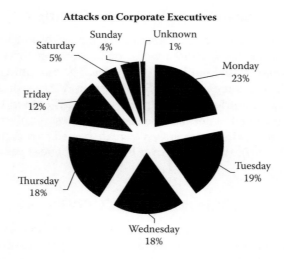

FIGURE 6.9 Attacks on corporate executives by day of the week.

Monday recorded 23% of the attacks perpetrated against corporate executives, the most of any single day (Figure 6.9). There was a significant concentration of attacks staged between Monday and Thursday, accounting for 78% of the total. There was a slight decrease of attacks on Friday, followed by a marked decline over the weekend.

Timing of Attacks

Of the fifty-one attacks in which the time of day was able to be determined, 37% occurred between the hours of 0601 and 0900. Only 14% occurred between the nine-hour period of 0901 to 1800. The hours between 1801 and 2100 accounted for the most attacks conducted against corporate executives, with 41% of the total number. Lastly, another 6% of attacks occurred between the 2101 and 2400.

170

Location of Attacks

The residence of the corporate executive was found to be the site of the majority of attacks, recording 30% of the total. This was followed closely by another 26% of attacks staged against a corporate executive while in transit. The office rounded out the top three locations, with 16% of the attacks. While unfortunately 15% of the ambush locations could not be determined, the remaining known attacks occurred at (in order of frequency) frequented locations, restaurants, hotels, a public function, a sports complex, and a courthouse.

Type of Attacks

In the types of urban ambushes encountered by corporate executives, 45% took the form of shooting attacks. Of these attacks, 44% were at the hands of an unknown number of gunmen. Lone gunmen were the most active and accounted for 22% of the shooting attacks. Snipers struck corporate executives another 10% of the time. Teams of two gunmen as well as motorcycle-based hit teams were each responsible for 7% of the ambushes. The remaining shooting attacks came in the form of drive-bys and teams of three or more shooters. In one of the shooting attacks, believed to have come at the hands of government agents, suppressed pistols were known to have been employed.

Explosives were employed in ambushes against corporate executives in only ten instances. The VBIED was the device of choice in five of those attacks. IEDs of various configurations were used in a further five attacks. Of note was the deployment method used in one of these IED-based attacks. In this attack, the device was concealed inside of an attaché case that had been rapidly placed on the roof of the targeted vehicle by a motorcycle rider. The device was then quickly detonated, possibly by remote, which resulted in the target and the assassin being killed.

Kidnappings accounted for the other most often employed tactic against a corporate executive, which were 42% of all attacks. The majority of these kidnappings were for financial gain. The remaining attack was the case of a savage beating upon the corporate executive perpetrated by animal rights activists. While it isn't known if the goal was to kill, given the use of clubs and the number of men involved, the victim was lucky to have survived.

Use of Ruse or Disguise

In five of the ambushes carried out against a corporate executive, a ruse or disguise was implemented to allow the assassins to close the initial distance with their target without raising suspicions. These ruses included a man posing as a door-to-door flower salesman, men disguised as police officers conducting a traffic stop on the target (committed on two separate occasions), and a kidnapper acting as though he was having car trouble on an isolated road near the target's residence. The use of disguises included the donning of wigs, false mustaches, and sunglasses.

Groups Conducting Attacks

In sixty-six of the cases of a corporate executive being ambushed, the groups or individuals were identified, either by their own doing or through the subsequent investigation. Of those, forty-four were found to have been perpetrated by twenty-one separate terrorist organizations. The Greek November 17 organization claimed responsibility for six of the attacks, the most of any single group. The Irish Republican Army was behind five of the attacks, followed by the Italian Red Brigades, the German Red Army Faction, and Argentina's People's Revolutionary Army (ERP), each of which carried out four attacks. Spain's ETA and Colombia's FARC (Revolutionary Armed Forces of Colombia) each laid claim to another three ambushes against corporate executives.

Six of the attacks against corporate executives were found to be at the hands of organized criminal groups. This included Mexican and Colombian drug cartels, the Sicilian mafia, and others. Twelve of these attacks stemmed from criminals seeking profit through ransom. Finally, four of the attacks were believed to have been conducted by government agents.

Region/Countries Attacks Occurred

Regionally, Europe accounted for 45% of all corporate executives being ambushed. These attacks were spread out over thirteen countries. Europe was followed by the North American region, which documented 18% of all attacks spread out over three countries. With 14% of ambushes, Central/South America wrapped up the top three regions recording attacks against corporate executives. The attacks in the Central/South American region were dispersed over four separate countries. The remaining attacks occurred in seven countries, encompassing every region on the planet but Africa. (Note: While there have been numerous attacks against employees of corporations in Africa, primarily oil exploration, they could not be confirmed as falling within the parameters of this research.)

When examined by individual countries, the United States and Russia stood out with the greatest number of attacks on corporate executives, each documenting 12% of the total. Greece and Germany each accounted for 8% of attacks, followed by Colombia and Italy, with another 7% each. The United Kingdom, Argentina, and Mexico were also tied, each recording 5% of attacks. The remaining ambushes were spread out over eighteen separate countries, each experiencing between one to three attacks over the fifty-eight-year period.

DIPLOMATS

A total of sixty-seven attacks were found to have been committed against diplomats worldwide, resulting in thirty-six successful assassinations and thirteen successful kidnappings. Documenting 42% of the ambushes, the decade of the 1970s witnessed far and away the most attacks against diplomats worldwide. This was followed by the 1980s, which witnessed 37% of the known attacks. The remaining decades had significant decreases in diplomats being targeted, with the 1990s at 12% and the first eight years of the 2000s at only

3%. The 1960s recorded 6% of the attacks, while there were no known documented attacks carried out against diplomats during the 1950s.

Of all those attacks, twenty-seven targeted the pedestrian-based victim. Diplomats traveling in a motorized vehicle accounted for another thirty-five of the attacks. The remaining ambushes occurred at locations and times that could not be determined. In all the attacks, only twenty-one of these diplomats were known to have had protective details at the time. The greatest number of ambushes carried out against diplomats during the research period occurred in the month of March, which recorded 12% of the attacks (Figure 6.10). Seasonally, the majority of targeted attacks occurred during winter to early spring. There were enough attacks, however, over the remaining months to make predicting a particular time of year difficult at best. However, there were marked reductions noted in April and September.

When the attacks were analyzed by the day of the week in which the attack against diplomats occurred, it was found to follow the statistical norm (Figure 6.11). The majority of the attacks were staged between Monday and Friday, when diplomats were moving

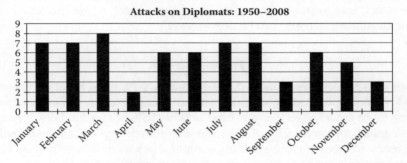

FIGURE 6.10 Attacks on diplomats by month of the year.

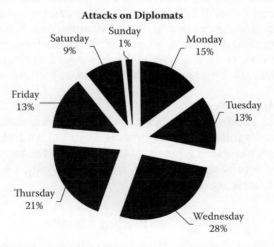

FIGURE 6.11 Attacks on diplomats by day of the week.

173

within their normal work-related routines. However, the middle days of Wednesday and Thursday recorded almost 50% of the total number of attacks.

Timing of Attacks

Of the eighteen attacks in which the time of day could be determined, eight occurred between the hours of 0601 and 0900. Another seven attacks occurred during the six-hour period between 0901 and 1500. Finally, there were three attacks occurring between the hours of 2101 and 0300.

Location of Attacks

Attacks on diplomats while in transit witnessed the majority, accounting for 46% of the total. This was followed by attacks staged at or near the target's residence, which recorded another 28%. Only 10% of the attacks were found to have occurred at or near the victim's office. One attack was found to have been staged at a hotel, while the remaining attacks occurred at locations that could not be determined.

Type of Attacks

In the types of ambushes encountered by diplomats, 64% were firearms based. Of these attacks, 30% were perpetrated by an unknown number of gunmen. Hit teams consisting of two gunmen were recorded as being behind another 33% of attacks. Lone gunmen carried out attacks against diplomats 21% of the time. The remaining 16% of the shooting attacks came from teams of three or more gunmen, a sniper attack as well as a drive-by. In two of the attacks, suppressed weapons were known to have been used by the assassins.

Explosives were deployed in ambushes targeting diplomats on only eight occasions. Of those eight, the VBIED was used in two of the attacks. IEDs of unknown types and configurations accounted for another three attacks. A booby-trap device was deployed in a single attack, while grenades were used in two other ambushes. Kidnappings were a popular attack method targeting diplomats, occurring 19% of the time, the bulk of which happened in the early decades. The remaining ambushes staged against diplomats involved a chemical-weapon-based attack and one in which the exact method was unknown.

Use of Ruse or Disguise

The use of the ruse was known to have been employed in four attacks on diplomats. The methods included men disguised as police officers conducting a traffic stop on the victim. In another attack, a man requested a lunch/discussion with the targets. Two men entered an embassy requesting new passports prior to attacking. Finally, a female assassin wore a wig and glasses prior to striking her target.

Groups Conducting Attacks

In fifty-two of the attacks on diplomats, the groups or individuals responsible are known, either through their own doing or through investigation. Of that number, forty-six were perpetrated by thirty-three separate terrorist or extremist groups. Criminals or organized criminal organizations accounted for only three of the attacks, while government agents were suspected of an additional three.

Of those attacks in which the responsible party was known, the Justice Commandos for the Armenian Genocide (JCAG) struck the most often, accounting for 12% of attacks. They were followed by the Armenian Secret Army for the Liberation of Armenia (ASALA) and the Abu Nidal Organization, each of which was responsible for 6% of attacks. Other targeted terrorist attacks were attributed to many of the better known groups, including South America's Shining Path and Montonerros; the Middle East's Hizbollah, Palestine's Popular Front for the Liberation of Palestine (PFLP), the Palestine Liberation Organization (PLO), and Black September; and Europe's Irish Republican Army (IRA), Action Directe, and the ETA.

Region/Countries Attacks Occurred

Regionally, Europe had the greatest number of diplomats being ambushed, documenting 52% of the attacks, spread out over seventeen countries. This was followed by the Middle East, with 16% of all attacks occurring in over five countries. The Central/South American region rounded out the top three, accounting for 13% of all attacks occurring within six countries. The remaining attacks were carried out in countries encompassing every region on the planet.

When examined by individual countries, Lebanon witnessed the most attacks, recording 10% of the total number. France followed closely behind, with another 9% of attacks. The United Kingdom, Spain, Austria, the Netherlands, Brazil, and the United States each accounted for 5% of all ambushes targeting diplomats. The remaining attacks were spread out over twenty-nine separate countries, each experiencing only one or two attacks over the fifty-eight-year period.

EMBASSY STAFFERS

A total of thirty-three attacks were found to have been perpetrated against embassy staffers worldwide. Of those attacks, there were twenty-three successful assassinations and three successful kidnappings. With 73% of the total, the decade of the 1980s witnessed far and away the most attacks against employees of embassies around the world. This was followed by the 1970s and 1990s, each of which documented 12% of all known attacks. There was only one case of a targeted attack against embassy staffers perpetrated between 2000 and 2008.

Out of the thirty-three attacks, sixteen were perpetrated against pedestrian-based victims. Embassy staffers traveling in a motorized vehicle accounted for fourteen of the attacks. The remaining attacks on embassy staffers occurred at unknown locations and times. Of all the attacks, only one of these embassy staffers was known to have had a protective detail at the time.

The greatest number of attacks during the research period against embassy staffers occurred during the month of April, which recorded 21% of the total number (Figure 6.12). There was significant activity against embassy staffers during the months of March and September, followed closely by June and July. Also of interest was the relatively low

175

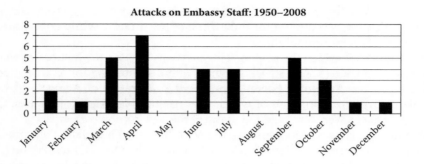

FIGURE 6.12   Attacks against embassy staff by month of the year.

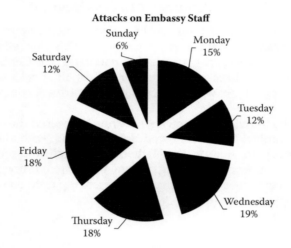

FIGURE 6.13   Attacks against embassy staff by day of the week.

attack activity during the winter months. Only May and August were without any known attacks. Seasonally, spring had the greatest number of attacks perpetrated against the staff of embassies.

Embassy staffers were found to be attacked on Wednesdays 19% of the time (Figure 6.13). This day was followed closely by Thursdays and Fridays, each of which documented another 18% of attacks. Monday followed as the fourth most popular day to strike at embassy staff, recording 15% of the attacks. Of interest was the 12% of attacks perpetrated on a Saturday, the same amount as occurred on a Tuesday.

Timing of Attacks

Of the eight attacks in which the time of day was able to be determined, three occurred between the hours of 0601 and 0900. The remaining five known attacks were staged at times dispersed evenly over the other time periods.

Location of Attacks

The residence was the site of 42% of the ambushes on embassy staffers. This was followed closely by attacks staged while in transit, accounting for 30%. Only 12% of the attacks are known to have occurred at or near the target's office. The remaining attacks on embassy staff occurred at locations that could not be determined.

Type of Attacks

In the types of ambushes encountered by embassy staffers, 76% took the form of shooting attacks. In these attacks, 52% were perpetrated by an unknown number of gunmen. Lone gunmen as well as teams of two gunmen were each responsible for 12% of the shooting attacks. The remaining 24% of ambushes employing firearms came from teams of three or more gunmen, drive-bys, and motorcycle-based attacks.

Explosives were employed in ambushes against embassy staffers on only five occasions. In those attacks, the VBIED was documented as being used twice. A booby-trap device was attached to the victim's vehicle in three other explosive-based attacks. Kidnappings only occurred in three of the known attacks.

Groups Conducting Attacks

In thirty of the cases of embassy staffers being ambushed, the groups or individuals were able to be determined, either through their own doing or through subsequent investigation. Of those, twenty-seven were perpetrated by fifteen different terrorist organizations. Accounting for 21% of all attacks against embassy staffers, the ASALA terrorist organization was the most active. Islamic-based terrorist organizations as a whole targeted embassy staffers the majority of the time, accounting for 43% of attacks.

In two of the cases of embassy staffers being targeted, it was found to have been at the hands of government agents. Specifically, Libyan intelligence agents linked with members of local groups struck twice after the bombing of Libya by the United States. These attacks were staged in separate countries, but within several days of each other.

Region/Countries Attacks Occurred

Regionally, Europe accounted for the most embassy staffers being attacked, with 61% spread out over ten countries. This was followed by the Middle East, which recorded 15% of all attacks, spread out over four countries. The remaining attacks occurred in countries in North America and Southern Asia regions. When examined by individual countries, France, with 18%, experienced the greatest number of ambushes. Greece followed closely behind, with 15% of all of the attacks worldwide. The remaining ambushes upon embassy staffers were spread out over nineteen separate countries, each experiencing only one or two attacks over the entire fifty-eight-year period.

FEDERAL GOVERNMENT OFFICIALS

There were thirty-six documented ambushes orchestrated against federal government officials (those working in positions of authority within a country's government, but not holding the top position) worldwide. These attacks resulted in twenty-nine successful assassinations. The decade of 1990s, as well as the first eight years of the 2000s, each recorded 36% of the known attacks against federal government officials. This was followed by the decade of the 1980s, which witnessed 22% of all attacks. The final 6% of attacks occurred during the 1970s, with no ambushes against federal government officials known to have happened during the 1950s and 1960s.

Of the thirty-six attacks, nineteen targeted a pedestrian-based victim. Federal government officials traveling in a motorized vehicle accounted for fifteen attacks. The remaining two ambushes on federal government officials occurred at unknown locations and times. Of all the attacks, only fourteen of these federal government officials had a protective detail at the time.

The greatest number of attacks targeting federal government officials was found to have occurred during the month of September, accounting for 25% of the total (Figure 6.14). The month of May documented the second highest amount of activity, with 17% of the attacks. The months of January and June were the only two months that did not have any recorded attacks. Seasonally, autumn had the majority of attacks against federal government officials.

Federal government officials were found to be ambushed most often on a Wednesday, which recorded 23% of the attacks (Figure 6.15). This was followed, interestingly enough, by Saturday, which had 22% of the attacks. There was, however, fairly consistent attack activity over the remaining days of the week. Of note is the sustained activity through the weekend, unlike what many of the other victims experienced.

Timing of Attacks

Of the fifteen attacks in which the time of day was known, two were found to have occurred between the hours of 0601 and 0900. A further five were documented between the hours of 1801 and 2100. Only five attacks occurred during the nine-hour period between 0901 and 1800. Additionally, there were two attacks occurring between the hours of 2101 and 0300.

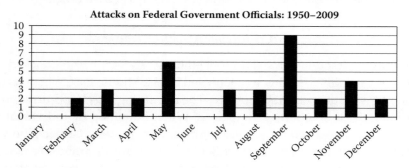

FIGURE 6.14 Attacks on federal government officials by month of the year.

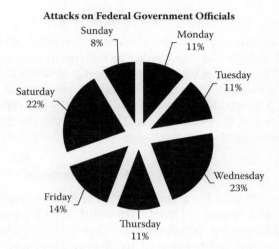

Attacks on Federal Government Officials

FIGURE 6.15 Attacks on federal government officials by day of the week.

Finally, there was one attack that occurred during the daylight hours, but the exact time could not be determined.

Location of Attacks

The residence of the federal government official was far and away the scene of the majority of ambushes, documented in 44% of the attacks. This was followed by attacks perpetrated while the victim was in transit, accounting for another 28%. Only 8% of the ambush sites were at or near the official's office. The remaining attacks occurred at a hotel, a store, a university, an airport, a public event, or could not be determined.

Type of Attacks

In the types of ambushes encountered by federal government officials, 75% took the form of shooting-based attacks. Of these attacks, 33% were at the hands of an unknown number of gunmen. Teams of two gunmen were responsible for 15% of the attacks, as were hit teams consisting of three gunmen. A lone gunman struck federal government officials 11% of the time. The remaining shooting ambushes were perpetrated by snipers, drive-bys, four or more gunmen hit teams, and motorcycle hit teams. Of all of the attacks, there were only two known instances of suppressed weapons being used in the attacks on federal government officials.

In the remaining ambushes, explosives were employed against federal government officials on seven occasions. In those attacks, the VBIED was used in three of them, while IEDs of unknown construction accounted for two further attacks. The booby trapping of an official's car and a thrown grenade accounted for the final two attacks using explosives. The remaining attacks were two incidents in which the official was stabbed by an assassin armed with an edged weapon.

Groups Conducting Attacks

Unfortunately, in only nineteen of the cases of federal government officials being ambushed were the groups or individuals identified, either by their own doing or through subsequent investigation. Of those nineteen, eight came at the hands of seven different terrorist organizations. Interestingly enough, five attacks on federal government officials were or are believed to have been perpetrated by government agents. In two other attacks, organized criminal groups were found to be responsible. The remaining attacks came from political rivals, lone criminals, and right-wing extremists.

Region/Countries Attacks Occurred

Regionally, Europe accounted for the greatest number of federal government officials being ambushed, recording 36%, spread out over eight countries. This was followed by Russia and the Russian republics, which documented another 17% of all attacks spread out over five countries. The remaining ambushes occurred in countries encompassing every region on the planet. When examined by individual countries, Italy stood out with the greatest number of attacks, accounting for 17%. Colombia witnessed the second most ambushes targeting federal government officials, with 8% of attacks. The remaining attacks were spread out over twenty-three separate countries, each experiencing only one or two attacks over the fifty-eight-year period.

GOVERNMENT MINISTERS

Forty-four ambushes were documented as having targeted government ministers (those in charge of federal and state agencies) worldwide. These attacks resulted in twenty-three successful assassinations and three successful kidnappings. Recording 43% of all of the known attacks, the first eight years of the 2000s were the deadliest for government ministers around the globe. This was followed by the decade of the 1990s, which witnessed another 32% of all known attacks. During the 1980s, government ministers were the victims in 18% of the documented attacks. The last 7% took place during the 1970s.

Of these forty-four attacks, they were split evenly in that twenty-two were targeted against pedestrian-based victims and twenty-two were perpetrated against government ministers traveling in a motorized vehicle. Of all the cases, only nineteen of these government ministers are known to have had protective details of any form at the time of the hit.

The greatest number of attacks orchestrated against government ministers occurred during the month of October, which recorded 16% of the total (Figure 6.16). November followed closely behind, with another 14% of the targeted attacks. There was a significant decrease in ambushes against government ministers during the months of December, January, April, and May. Seasonally, the majority of attacks were carried out in the late summer to early autumn months.

Government ministers were found to be ambushed far and away more often on a Tuesday, which recorded 27% of all of the attacks (Figure 6.17). Friday followed somewhat

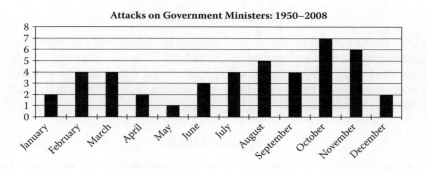

FIGURE 6.16 Attacks on government ministers by month of the year.

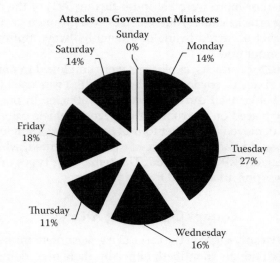

FIGURE 6.17 Attacks on government ministers by the day of the week.

closely behind, accounting for 18% of all attacks. While there were no attacks documented as occurring on a Sunday, Saturdays were found to have a fairly substantial number of ambushes. In fact, Saturdays, with 14% of attacks, had the same of number as was documented as occurring on Mondays.

Timing of Attacks

Of the twenty-four attacks in which the time of day was able to be determined, eight occurred between the hours of 0601 and 0900. A further seven occurred between the hours of 1801 and 2100. Seven attacks were perpetrated during the nine-hour period between 0901 and 1800, with 57% of those occurring between 0901 and 1200. Finally, there were two attacks recorded between the hours of 2101 and 0300.

Location of Attacks

The area in and around the residence was witness to the majority of ambushes targeting government ministers, accounting for 43% of the total. This was followed closely by attacks staged while the victim was in transit, accounting for another 39%. The remaining attacks occurred at such venues as hotels, public events, a mosque, a restaurant, the victim's office, and even university grounds.

Type of Attacks

In the types of ambushes encountered by government ministers, 48% took the form of shooting attacks. Of these attacks, 43% were at the hands of an unknown number of gunmen. Lone gunmen carried out targeted hits on government ministers 29% of the time. Teams of three gunmen or more were behind a further 19% of the attacks. The remaining 9% of the shooting attacks came from teams of two gunmen or motorcycle hit teams. In one of the attacks that occurred inside of a hotel hallway, suppressed weapons were believed to have been employed.

In the remaining 52% of attacks, explosives were employed in ambushes against government ministers on sixteen occasions. Of those, an IED was used in seven attacks, followed by the VBIED being used during three other attacks. In one of the IED attacks, the device was rapidly placed on the roof of the target's vehicle prior to being detonated. Suicide bombers were deployed in another four of the attacks. A single instance of a booby-trap device being affixed to one minister's car was documented, while in another attack a rocket-propelled grenade (RPG) was fired. The remaining types of ambushes included three cases of edged-weapon attacks and four kidnappings.

Groups Conducting Attacks

Unfortunately, in only twenty-eight of the cases of a government minister being ambushed were the groups or individuals identified, either by their own doing or through subsequent investigation. Of those, twenty-four were the work of sixteen different terrorist organizations. Germany's Red Army Faction was documented as perpetrating three ambushes, the most targeting a government minister. With the remaining known attacks, two were believed to have been conducted by government agents, while another two stemmed from lone criminals.

Region/Countries Attacks Occurred

Regionally, Europe accounted for the most government ministers being attacked, with 34%, spread out over eight countries. This was followed by the Middle East, which recorded 18% of all attacks occurring in four countries. Russia and its republics witnessed 14% of the attacks against government ministers, staged in two countries. Finally, the region of South Asia documented another 14% of attacks spread out among three countries. The remaining attacks occurred in countries encompassing every region on the planet.

When examined by individual countries, Germany, Dagestan, and Lebanon each had four documented attacks, the most for any single country. India suffered the next highest number of attacks on government ministers, with three. The remaining attacks were spread out over nineteen separate countries, each experiencing only one or two attacks over the fifty-eight-year period.

GOVERNORS/PREFECTS

A total of fourteen ambushes were found to have been perpetrated against governors/prefects (individuals with state and regional areas of responsibility) worldwide, resulting in ten successful assassinations. With 50% of the ambushes, the decade of the 1990s witnessed far and away the greatest number of attacks against governors/prefects around the globe. This was followed by the first eight years of the 2000s, which documented 29% of the attacks. The decade of the 1980s accounted for 14% of all known attacks. Finally, the 1970s recorded the first known documented attack against a governor/prefect.

Of these attacks, seven targeted governors/prefects while they are on foot. Another six ambushes were carried out against governors/prefects traveling in a motorized vehicle. The remaining attack occurred at an unknown location. Of all the attacks, only three of the victims had protective details at the time.

While August recorded the greatest number of ambushes targeting governors/prefects, it still only accounted for three, or 21% of the total (Figure 6.18). Following with two attacks each were January, March, and September. There were no attacks found to have occurred during the months of May, June, and November. Seasonally, the summer months recorded the majority of attacks targeting governors/prefects.

Documented in 37% of all ambushes targeting a governor/prefect, Friday was the most often selected day in which to strike (Figure 6.19). This was followed interestingly enough by Tuesdays, Saturdays, and Sundays, each of which recorded 14% of the attacks. In fact, the 28% of attacks perpetrated against a governor/prefect occurring on a weekend day represented one of the highest concentrations for any class of victim.

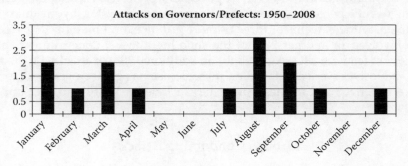

FIGURE 6.18 Attacks on governors/prefects by month of the year.

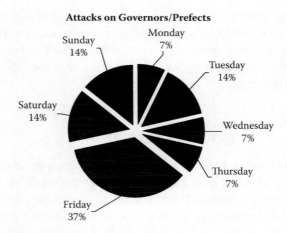

FIGURE 6.19   Attacks on governors/prefects by day of the week.

Timing of Attacks

Of the eight attacks in which the time of day was known, three occurred between 0601 and 0900. The remaining five occurred between 1501 hours and 2400.

Location of Attacks

Ambushes staged while a governor/prefect was in transit occurred the most often and accounted for 43% of the attacks. This was followed closely by another 21% of attacks staged while a governor/prefect was at or within close proximity (100 meters or less) of his or her residence. The remaining ambushes occurred at the victim's office, a bar, at public events, or could not be determined.

Type of Attacks

In the types of ambushes encountered by governors/prefects, 71% took the form of shooting attacks. Twenty percent of these shootings were committed by an unknown number of gunmen. Snipers, teams of three or more gunmen, and motorcycle-based gunmen were each involved in another 20% of the shooting attacks. Lone gunmen, along with two-gunmen hit teams, each accounted for an additional 10% of attacks. Of the remaining ambushes, explosives were employed on three occasions against a governor/prefect. The explosive techniques used in these ambushes included a VBIED, an IED, and a suicide bomber attack.

Groups Conducting Attacks

Unfortunately, in only seven of the cases of a governor/prefect being ambushed were the groups or individuals identified, either by their own doing or through subsequent investigation. Of that seven, five were found to have come at the hands of five different terrorist organizations. Members of the Sicilian mafia were behind the remaining two.

Region/Countries Attacks Occurred

Regionally, Europe accounted for the most governors/prefects being attacked, documenting 36%, spread out over four countries. Russia and the republics followed suit, with 29% of attacks, which occurred in a single country. The remaining attacks occurred in countries encompassing the regions of Central and South America, the Middle East, and South Asia.

When examined by individual countries, Russia, with 29%, stood out with the majority of targeted attacks against governors/prefects. Italy and Turkey each accounted for another 14% of all of the ambushes worldwide. The remaining attacks were spread out over six separate countries, each of which experienced only one attack over the fifty-eight-year period.

INTELLIGENCE AGENTS

There were nine documented attacks found to have been committed against intelligence agents (current and former) worldwide, resulting in seven successful assassinations and one successful kidnapping. The first eight years of the 2000s recorded four such attacks, the most of any of the previous five decades. The 1970s and 1990s each documented two attacks against intelligence agents, followed by the 1980s with one. No attacks were found to have occurred during the 1950s or 1960s. (Note: Given the nature of intelligence work, there is little doubt that these numbers should be higher, but these numbers represent those incidents that could be confirmed via open-source material.)

Of these nine attacks, six were committed against pedestrian-based victims. Agents traveling in a motorized vehicle accounted for the remaining three attacks. As would be expected, none of these agents were known to have had protective details at the time of the attacks.

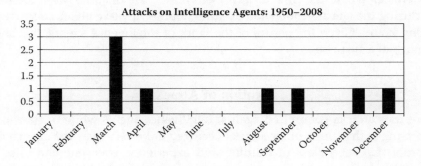

FIGURE 6.20 Attacks on intelligence agents by month of the year.

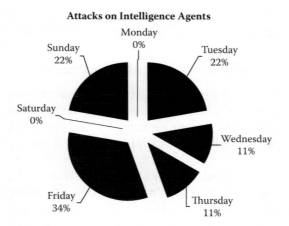

FIGURE 6.21 Attacks on intelligence agents by day of the week.

The greatest number of attacks during the research period targeting intelligence agents occurred in the month of March, which recorded three (Figure 6.20). The remaining attacks took place in January, April, August, September, November, and December, each of which had one attack only. There were no attacks known to have occurred during the months of February, May, June, July, or October. With the few known attacks, coupled with their disbursement over the calendar year, it is impossible to determine a season in which the chance of attack was more likely.

Intelligence agents were found to be attacked 34% of the time on a Friday (Figure 6.21). Attacks staged on a Tuesday or a Sunday were each recorded 22% of the time. While the concentration of targeted attacks against intelligence agents occurred during the work-week, it is of note that there none were documented on a Monday or Saturday.

Timing of Attacks

In the six attacks where the time of day was known, the majority were found to have occurred during the late afternoon and evening hours. Only two attacks occurred during the morning hours. Given the nature of the work of intelligence agents, this should not come as much of a surprise.

Location of Attacks

There were four attacks committed against intelligence agents while in transit. Perhaps most surprising is that three other attacks occurred at or very near the agent's residence (further proof that regardless of training and experience, everyone can miss clues of potential hostile surveillance). Two more attacks were documented as occurring at bars or restaurants.

Type of Attacks

In the types of attacks encountered by intelligence agents, six took the form of shootings. Of these attacks, two were committed by an unknown number of gunmen. A team of two gunmen was documented in a single targeted attack. A lone gunman struck an intelligence agent on one occasion, followed by a single incident of a sniper attack. Finally, there was one instance of a drive-by-style shooting attack.

Explosives were documented as being employed in only a single attack against an intelligence agent, taking the form of a VBIED. Poison, in the form of a radioactive isotope, was employed in the last and most recent attack against an intelligence agent. This attack was conducted when the poison was slipped into a beverage consumed by the victim. There was also one known case of a kidnapping, during which the agent was later killed.

Groups Conducting Attacks

In only six of the cases of intelligence agents being ambushed were the groups or individuals ultimately identified, either by their own doing or through subsequent investigation. Of those that are known, three are believed to have come at the hands of government agents. The remaining three were each perpetrated by three separate terrorist organizations.

Region/Countries Attacks Occurred

Regionally, Europe accounted for the most intelligence agents being ambushed, with three, spread out over three countries. The remaining attacks occurred in the Middle East, South Asia, Russia/republics, and North American regions. When examined by individual countries, Lebanon documented two attacks, the most of any single country. The remaining attacks were spread out over seven other countries.

JUDGES

There were seventy-four attacks documented as having been carried out against judges worldwide, resulting in sixty-eight successful assassinations. Additionally, there was a single attack against the family of a sitting judge, which resulted in the deaths of two family members. With 34% of the attacks, the decade of the 1980s witnessed far and away the most judges being targeted around the globe. This was followed by the first eight years of the 2000s, during which 27% of the attacks were recorded. The decade of the 1970s had 19% of known attacks, while the 1990s recorded another 18% of attacks against judges. The decade of the 1950s witnessed just 2% of the attacks. There were no documented attacks during the 1960s.

Of all of these ambushes on judges, 53% targeted the pedestrian-based victim. Judges traveling in a motorized vehicle accounted for 31% of attacks. The remaining attacks occurred at unknown locations and times. Of all the attacks, only one-quarter of these judges are known to have had protective details at the time.

While targeted violence against judges occurred consistently throughout the year, the greatest number of ambushes targeting judges were staged in March, which accounted for 14% of the total (Figure 6.22). November was the next most often selected month to strike, with 12% of the attacks. February followed close behind, with 11% of attacks. Seasonally, the spring months recorded the majority of attacks, having documented 32% of the total.

Judges were found to be attacked most often on Tuesdays, 28% of the time, and Wednesdays, 20% of the time (Figure 6.23). While the exact reason for this is difficult to determine with absolute certainty, a reasonable explanation could be as simple as allowing time for an adversary to confirm the targeted judge would be following his or her normal weekly routine. Overall, the vast majority of ambushes occurred during the workweek; however, with 17% of the total attacks, the weekends were anything but neglected.

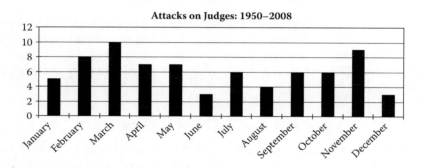

FIGURE 6.22 Attacks on judges by month of the year.

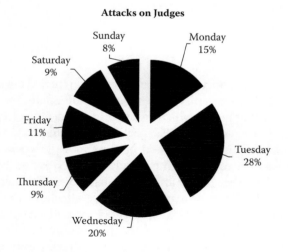

FIGURE 6.23 Attacks on judges by day of the week.

188

Timing of Attacks

Of the thirty attacks in which the time of day was able to be determined accurately, ten occurred between the hours of 0601 and 0900. A further four occurred between the hours of 0901 and 1200, while another four hit between 1201 and 1500. Six attacks occurred between the hours of 1801 and 2100. Three attacks are known to have occurred during daylight hours, but the exact time could not be pinpointed. The last three attacks occurred during the hours of 2101 and 0300.

Location of Attacks

The residence was the most common location for judges to be attacked, documenting 32% of the total number. This was followed closely by attacks conducted against judges while they were in transit, 27% of the time. Attacks occurring inside of a courtroom or judge's chambers accounted for only 18% of all attacks. Approximately 15% of the attacks occurred at unknown locations. The remaining known attack locations included a restaurant, a frequented location, and a university.

Type of Attacks

Of the types of ambushes encountered by judges, 77% took the form of shooting attacks. The lone gunman was the most active, responsible for 28% of the shootings. The motorcycle hit team was the next most often employed type of attack, conducting another 18% of the shootings. In all of the shooting attacks, 33% involved more than one adversary engaging the judge or protective detail. In several of the attacks, automatic weapons were documented as having been used. There was only one case of a suppressor known to have been used. In two of the shooting attacks, the killers wore masks in order to conceal their identities.

Explosive-based attacks accounted for only 12% of all ambushes against judges. However, a targeted ambush using explosives accounts for one of the more dramatic attacks in Europe. This attack (which is covered in more detail within the chapters on case studies) occurred when the Spanish Supreme Court judge Jose Lombardero was assassinated by a VBIED attack near his residence. The remaining 11% of attacks were either kidnappings or not able to be determined.

Use of Ruse or Disguise

The use of a ruse was employed against a judge on at least one occasion. In this case, the assassins used the disguise of selling flowers, allowing them to approach the residence front door without raising suspicions.

Groups Conducting Attacks

While there was a wide spectrum of adversaries specifically targeting judges, there was no clear group that tended to dominate or specialize in them. That said, 32% of all of the attacks upon judges came from terrorist organizations, such as Spain's ETA, Italy's Red Brigades, Sri Lanka's Tamil Tigers, and Colombia's FARC. Organized crime or drug cartels, such as the Sicilian mafia and the Colombian drug cartels, accounted for another 24% of attacks. Only 8% of the attacks against judges came from current or former defendants. The remaining attacks came at the hands of unknown groups or individuals.

Region/Countries Attacks Occurred

Regionally, Europe witnessed the greatest number of judges falling victim to targeted violence, accounting for 37% of the attacks over the fifty-eight years. North America was second, with 26%, followed by Central/South America, with 22% of the attacks.

When examined by individual countries, the United States accounted for the most ambushes perpetrated against judges, accounting for 23% of the attacks. Italy had the second highest number of judges being attacked, with 20% of the total, most occurring on the island of Sicily. Colombia, with 15% of the attacks, had the third highest number of attacks against judges. Spain was a distant fourth, with 7% of the attacks. This is interesting in that Spain's ETA is perhaps the most prolific employer of assassinations in the last three decades and accounted for one of the most dramatic attacks ever perpetrated against a judicial official (covered in detail in Chapter 7). The remaining ambushes against judges were spread out over twenty-one separate countries.

LAW ENFORCEMENT

Sixty-five ambushes were found to have been perpetrated against law enforcement officers (primarily command officers) worldwide, resulting in fifty-four successful assassinations and two successful kidnappings. With 42% of the attacks occurring during the first eight years of the 2000s, this decade by far recorded the most attacks of any decade against law enforcement officials around the world. This was followed by the 1980s, which experienced 29% of all known attacks. The 1990s accounted for an additional 15% of attacks, followed by the 1970s, with 12%. Only one targeted attack is known to have occurred in the 1960s, and none during the 1950s.

Of all of the attacks, twenty-six were targeted upon a pedestrian-based law enforcement officer. Officers traveling in a motorized vehicle accounted for an additional thirty-two attacks. The remaining targeted ambushes on officers occurred at unknown locations or times. Only thirteen of these officers are known to have had protective details of some fashion at the time.

The month of January with 18%, recorded the majority of attacks targeted upon law enforcement officers (Figure 6.24). This was followed by May, which had 15%, and July, with 14% of the attacks. The remaining ambushes were staged almost uniformly through the remaining calendar months. Seasonally, the summer and winter months recorded the greatest concentration of attacks on law enforcement officers.

Law enforcement officers were found to be attacked most often on a Thursday, accounting for 22% of the total (Figure 6.25). Attacks on a Friday or a Monday occurred 18% of the time. Saturday and Sunday were witness to the fewest number of attacks; the vast majority were concentrated during the traditional Western world workweek.

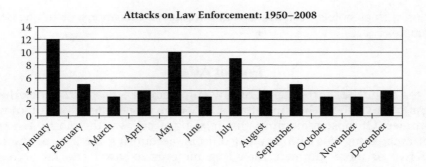

FIGURE 6.24 Attacks on law enforcement by month of the year.

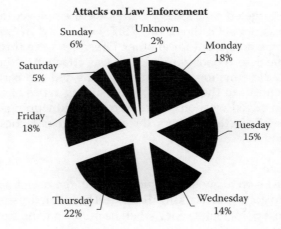

FIGURE 6.25 Attacks on law enforcement by day of the week.

Timing of Attacks

Of the thirty-three attacks in which the time of day was known, five occurred between the hours of 0601 and 0900. A further eleven attacks were perpetrated between the hours of 1801 and 2100. Only nine attacks were documented during the nine-hour period between 0901 and 1800. Additionally, there were five attacks that occurred between the hours of 2101 and 0300. Finally, three attacks occurred during the daylight hours (the exact time could not be confirmed).

Location of Attacks

Ambushes targeted against law enforcement officers while in transit occurred 40% of the time. The residence was witness to the second greatest number of attacks, with 32% of the total. Not surprisingly, only 5% of the attacks occurred at the officer's office. While 11% of the attacks occurred at unknown areas, those remaining that were known occurred

191

at locations such as hotels, restaurants/bars, frequented locations, or in one occasion, a sports complex.

Type of Attacks

Of all of the ambushes encountered by law enforcement officers, 82% took the form of shooting attacks. Of these shooting attacks, 47% were perpetrated by an unknown number of gunmen. Of those remaining, the drive-by attack was the most often employed means of ambushing law enforcement officers, accounting for 25% of the total. Hit teams of two or more gunmen, including motorcycle-based attacks, accounted for another 19%. Lone gunmen struck officers only 9% of the time. In three of the attacks, suppressed pistols were known to have been used, two of which occurred at the target's residence.

In the remaining targeted attacks, explosives were employed against law enforcement officers on six occasions. Of those, the VBIED was used in two of the attacks. An IED of an unknown type accounted for another. Grenades were thrown in two separate attacks, and in only one case, a booby-trap device was attached to the officer's car. While the booby-trap device did function, it fortunately activated too early, resulting in only non-life-threatening injuries to the officer. The remaining types of attacks included one involving the use of an edged weapon. There were two kidnappings of law enforcement officers documented, while in three others, the exact nature of tactics or techniques used could not be determined.

Use of Ruse or Disguise

During one of the attacks on a law enforcement official, the use of a ruse was employed, allowing the assassin to get within striking distance. The killer, dressed as a mailman, was able to get within almost point blank range when he pulled a handgun out and fired three rounds into the head of the victim.

Groups Conducting Attacks

In fifty-two of the cases of law enforcement officers being ambushed the groups or individuals were identified, either through their own doing or through investigation. Of those, sixteen came at the hands of nine separate terrorist organizations. The remaining thirty-five attacks were staged by organized crime groups, ranging from the Mexican drug cartels to the Hell's Angels to the Sicilian and Serbian mafias. The last attack in which the perpetrator was known was the unusual case of a political rival. In this attack it was the incumbent county sheriff who arranged for the killing of the newly elected sheriff.

Region/Countries Attacks Occurred

Regionally, North America accounted for the most number of law enforcement officers being attacked, with 43%, spread out over three countries. This was followed by Europe, which had 38% of all attacks, spread out over seven countries. The remaining attacks occurred in countries in the regions of the Middle East and South America.

When examined by individual countries, Mexico recorded 35% of the attacks, standing out far and away from all other countries. Of course, the vast majority of these attacks on law enforcement officers occurred at the hands of the drug cartels between 2007 and 2008. Italy was next in line, with 26% of attacks, the bulk of which occurred during the conflict with the Sicilian mafia in the late 1980s. Colombia rounded out the top three with 11% of attacks, many by the drug cartels.

LAWMAKERS

A total of sixty-four targeted ambushes are known to have been orchestrated against lawmakers (members of Congress or Parliament) worldwide, resulting in fifty-three successful assassinations and two successful kidnappings. With 45% of the attacks, the first eight years of the 2000s witnessed far and away the most committed against lawmakers around the world. This was followed by the 1990s, which experienced 38% of all known attacks. The attacks decreased with each decade, with the 1980s accounting for 9%, while the 1970s recorded 6%, and the 1960s 2%. There were no documented attacks found to have occurred during the 1950s.

Of the attacks, thirty-two targeted pedestrian-based lawmakers. Lawmakers traveling in a motorized vehicle accounted for another twenty-eight of the attacks. The remaining attacks on lawmakers occurred at unknown locations and times. Of all the attacks, only fourteen of these lawmakers were known to have had protective details at the time.

Lawmakers were the target of violence 16% of the time in October, the most of any single month (Figure 6.26). March followed close behind, with another 14% of the recorded attacks. Seasonally, the greatest concentration of attacks occurred during the autumn and winter months. There was a slight reduction in attack activity noted during the late spring and summer months.

Lawmakers were found to be ambushed predominantly on Mondays and Fridays, which recorded 21% and 20% of the attacks, respectively (Figure 6.27). While there was activity during the traditional workweek, as would be expected, there was a slight decrease noted on Thursdays. Interestingly, though, was the increase in attack activity on Saturdays, equal to or greater than that occurring on Wednesday and Thursdays.

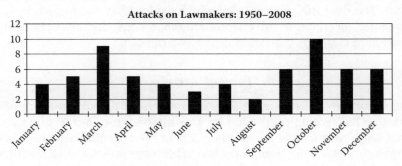

Attacks on Lawmakers: 1950–2008

FIGURE 6.26 Attacks on lawmakers by month of the year.

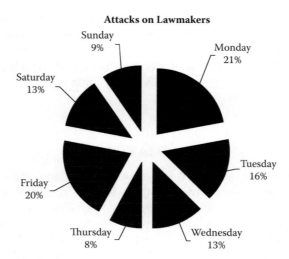

Attacks on Lawmakers

FIGURE 6.27   Attacks on lawmakers by day of the week.

Timing of Attacks

Of the thirty-two attacks in which the time of day was known, eight occurred during the hours of 0601 to 0900. Another ten occurred between the hours of 1801 and 2100. Only eight attacks were recorded during the nine-hour period of 0901 to 1800. Additionally, there were two attacks occurring between the hours of 2101 and 0300. Finally, only one attack was found to have been staged between the hours of 0301 and 0600, and three during daylight hours, in which the exact time could not be determined.

Location of Attacks

Accounting for 34% of the ambushes, lawmakers were targeted the majority of the time while in transit. This was followed closely by the residence, which was documented being used in 28% of the attacks. Another 14% were staged at or within close proximity to the victim's office. The final 16% of attacks for which the location was known included public events, frequented locations, a university, a church, a hotel, and airports. The remaining attacks occurred at locations that could not be determined.

Type of Attacks

In the types of ambushes encountered by lawmakers, 78% took the form of shootings. Of these attacks, 26% were perpetrated by an unknown number of gunmen. Teams of two gunmen were responsible for another 16% of the shooting attacks. Lone gunmen struck lawmakers 22% of the time. Motorcycle hit team attacks were conducted 12% of the time. Attacks from hit teams of three or more shooters accounted for an additional 10%. The final 14% included attacks from snipers and drive-by-style shootings. In at

194

least one case, a suppressed pistol was employed in the attack and left near the body of the target.

In the remaining targeted attacks, lawmakers suffered twelve by way of explosive devices. The booby-trap device was used the most often, accounting for a quarter of all explosive-based attacks targeting lawmakers. The VBIED attack was used in another three instances, as were IEDs. In one of the IED attacks, the device was rapidly placed on the roof of the target's vehicle prior to being detonated. There was one recorded attack wherein a grenade was thrown at the victim, while in another the lawmaker was attacked by a suicide bomber. The two remaining types of attacks consisted of kidnappings.

Use of Ruse or Disguise
In two of the attacks committed against lawmakers, a disguise or ruse was employed. In one of these attacks, the assassins dressed as sports enthusiasts attending a local event. As they came within striking distance, they open fired. In another case, the assassin feigned a flat tire in front of the target's residence, attacking when the victim came out to provide assistance.

Groups Conducting Attacks

Unfortunately, in only twenty-nine of the cases of a lawmaker being ambushed were the groups or individuals identified, either through their own doing or through investigation. Of those twenty-nine, nineteen came at the hands of twelve terrorist organizations. Another four of the attacks were carried out by organized criminal groups, including the Colombian drug cartels and the Italian N'drangheta. Of the remaining six, two attacks are believed to have been at the hands of government agents, two from political rivals, and another two from street criminals.

Region/Countries Attacks Occurred

Regionally, Central/South America accounted for the most lawmakers being attacked, with 25%, spread out over six countries. This was followed by Europe recording 19% of all attacks, disbursed over seven countries. The remaining attacks occurred in seventeen countries, encompassing every region on the planet. When examined by individual countries, Colombia stood at number one, documenting 16% of all attacks committed against lawmakers. Russia and the Philippines were tied for second, each with 8% of the attacks.

MAYORS

Thirty-three ambushes were documented to have been targeted against mayors (including deputy mayors) worldwide, resulting in twenty-four successful assassinations and one successful kidnapping. With 67% of the attacks, the first eight years of the 2000s were devastating for mayors around the planet. This was followed distantly by the decade of the 1990s, which experienced 24% of all known attacks. The 1980s recorded another 6% of attacks, followed by the 1970s, with 3%. No attacks were found to have occurred during the 1950s or 1960s.

In these thirty-three attacks, twenty-two were pedestrian based, in which the mayors were not traveling in a vehicle. Eight attacks were committed against mayors traveling in a motorized vehicle. The remaining attacks on mayors occurred at unknown locations and times. Of all the attacks, only eight of these mayors had protective details at the time.

With 21% of all attacks targeted against mayors, January recorded the greatest number over any other month (Figure 6.28). March and November each documented another 12% of the attacks. Seasonally, the concentration of attacks against mayors and deputy mayors was found to be in the late autumn and winter months. There was a noticeable decrease in ambushes against mayors during the late spring and summer months.

With a full 22% of the recorded ambushes, Thursday was found to have the most attack activity perpetrated against mayors (Figure 6.29). This was followed by attacks on a Tuesday, with 18%; however, there was found to be a significant amount of targeted attacks against mayors occurring during the rest of the workweek. Also of note was that while

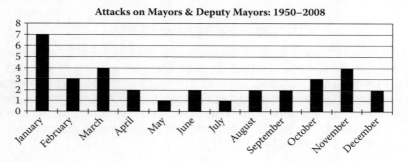

FIGURE 6.28 Attacks on mayors and deputy mayors by month of the year.

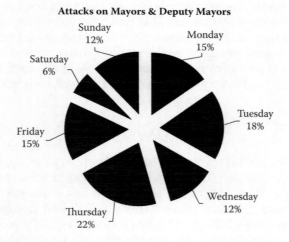

FIGURE 6.29 Attacks on mayors and deputy mayors by day of the week.

196

there was the normal decrease in attack activity during the weekend, attacks on a Sunday were double those occurring on a Saturday.

Timing of Attacks

Of the twenty-three attacks in which the time of day was known, nine occurred between the hours of 0601 and 0900. A further five occurred between the hours of 1801 and 2100. Only six attacks were documented during the nine-hour period of 0901 to 1800. Additionally, there were three attacks occurring between the hours of 2101 and 0300.

Location of Attacks

The residence of the mayor was the most often selected ambush location, accounting for 30% of attacks. This was followed by attacks occurring at the office, accounting for an additional 24%. Another 18% of attacks were sprung while the targeted mayor or deputy mayor was in transit. The remaining attacks occurred at public events, frequented locations, a bar, a bus terminal, and a church, or could not be determined.

Type of Attacks

In the types of ambushes encountered by mayors or deputy mayors, 73% took the form of shooting attacks. Of these shootings, 38% were perpetrated by an unknown number of gunmen. Teams of two gunmen accounted for 25% of the shooting attacks, representing the most often employed tactic. Lone gunmen were responsible for another 17% of the attacks targeting mayors. The remaining 20% of the shootings came by way of snipers, drive-bys, motorcycle-based hit teams, and teams of four or more gunmen. In one of the attacks by a sniper, a suppressor was known to have been employed.

In the remaining attacks carried out against mayors, explosives were employed in ambushes on only five occasions. Of those, the VBIED was used in four of the attacks, while an IED accounted for the fifth. The other attacks included a single case of the use of an edged weapon, a kidnapping, and finally, two attacks in which the exact nature of tactics or techniques could not be determined.

Groups Conducting Attacks

Unfortunately, in only twelve of the cases of a mayor being ambushed were the groups or individuals identified, either by their own doing or through subsequent investigation. Of those twelve, eight came at the hands of seven different terrorist organizations, with only FARC laying claim to having twice attacked a mayor. With the remaining four, two were staged by organized crime groups, one from the Japanese Yakuza and one from the Italian N'drangheta. The last two attacks came from a political rival and one was later determined to be by a criminal.

Region/Countries Attacks Occurred

Regionally, Central and South America accounted for the greatest number of mayors or deputy mayors being attacked, with 21% spread out over three countries. This was followed by Europe, which recorded 18% of all attacks disbursed over four countries. The remaining attacks occurred in countries encompassing every region but Africa.

When examined by individual countries, Russia stood out with the majority of attacks, having 24% of the total. The Philippines followed, having documented another 18% of all of the attacks worldwide. Colombia rounded out the top three countries with 12%. The remaining attacks were spread out over ten separate countries, each experiencing only one or two attacks (with the exception of Italy having three) over the fifty-eight-year period.

MILITARY

A total of forty-four documented attacks were perpetrated against military officials worldwide, resulting in thirty-four successful assassinations and two successful kidnappings. With 43%, the decade of the 1980s witnessed far and away the most attacks against military officials. This was followed by another 27% of attacks carried out during the first eight years of the 2000s. The 1990s accounted for 14% of all known attacks. Another 9% took place in the 1970s. Finally, there were two known attacks during the 1960s, and none found to have occurred in the 1950s.

Of all of these attacks, eleven targeted a pedestrian-based military official. Military officials traveling in a motorized vehicle accounted for another thirty of the attacks. The remaining attacks on military officials occurred at unknown locations and times. Of all the attacks, only fourteen of the military officials are known to have had protective details at the time.

August recorded 14% of the attacks targeting military officials, the most for any single month (Figure 6.30). This was followed by February and November, each of which accounted for another 11% of the attacks. Seasonally, the greatest concentration of ambushes on military officials was found to be during the winter months; however, there was fairly consistent attack activity throughout the calendar year.

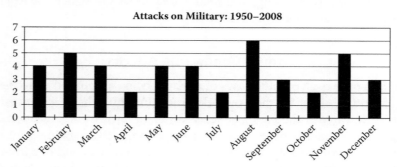

FIGURE 6.30 Attacks on military officials by month of the year.

Attacks on Military Personnel

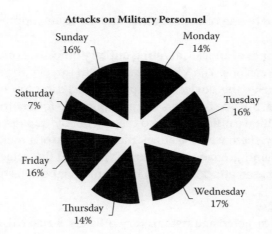

FIGURE 6.31   Attacks on military personnel by day of the week.

Military members found themselves being attacked almost equally Sunday through Friday, with Saturday showing the only noticeable decrease (Figure 6.31). Wednesday documented the greatest number of attacks, with 17% of the total. However, this was only 1% above that which was recorded on a Tuesday, Friday, or Sunday.

Timing of Attacks

Of the seventeen attacks in which the time of day was known, eight occurred between the hours of 0601 and 0900. Only three were between the hours of 1801 and 2100. Two attacks were documented as having occurred during the nine-hour period from 0901 to 1800. Additionally, there were three attacks occurring between the hours of 2101 and 0300. Finally, one attack was recorded to have occurred during the daylight hours, but the exact time could not be determined.

Location of Attacks

The vast majority of ambushes perpetrated against military officials occurred while they were in transit, accounting for a full 59%. This was followed by attacks at or near the residence, accounting for another 20%. The remaining attacks were staged at the victim's office, university grounds, or could not be determined.

Type of Attacks

In the types of ambushes encountered by military officials, 57% took the form of shooting attacks. Of these, 44% were the work of an unknown number of gunmen. Ambushes employing motorcycle hit teams accounted for 20% of the shooting attacks. Drive-bys, as well as those coming from teams of two gunmen, each accounted for 12% of the attacks. The remaining 12% of the shooting attacks came by way of snipers, and teams of three

199

or more gunmen. In only one of the shooting attacks were suppressors known to have been used.

In the remaining types of attacks targeting military officials, explosives were employed on fourteen separate occasions. The VBIED was used in three of the attacks, as were IEDs. In one of the IED attacks, the device was quickly placed on top of the target's vehicle before being detonated. Suicide bombers were responsible for another four of the attacks perpetrated against military officials. In two cases, a booby-trap device was affixed to the victim's vehicle. Finally, there was one attack that made use of a rocket-propelled grenade and another where a hand grenade was thrown. The final five attacks included two kidnappings, one poison-based attack, and two that could not be determined.

Use of Ruse or Disguise
In three of the attacks targeted against military officials, a ruse/disguise was employed, thus allowing the assassins to get close to their intended target before striking. One type implemented involved men disguised as plumbers who went up to the front door and were able to get partially inside before attacking. In another, men disguised as reporters seeking an interview were able to strike. In the last, the adversaries posed as telephone repairmen.

Groups Conducting Attacks

In thirty-nine of the cases of a military official being ambushed the groups or individuals were identified, either through their own doing or through investigation. Of those, thirty-three were carried out by sixteen different terrorist/extremist organizations. Spain's ETA was by far the most aggressive toward military officials, accounting for eleven of the attacks. It was followed by Greece's November 17 terrorist organization, which carried out four targeted attacks on military officials. Of the remaining six attacks, four were believed to have been conducted by government agents, while the last two came from organized criminal groups.

Region/Countries Attacks Occurred

Regionally, Europe accounted for the majority of military officials being attacked, with 52%, spread out over seven countries. This was followed by the Middle East, which had 11% of the attacks, spread out over three countries. The remaining attacks occurred in countries encompassing every region but Africa.

When examined by individual countries, Spain, with 25%, stood out with the greatest number of attacks. Greece and Italy both accounted for another 9% of all of the attacks worldwide. Sri Lanka and Pakistan rounded out the top five with 7% each. The remaining attacks were spread out over seventeen separate countries, each experiencing only one or two attacks over the fifty-eight-year period.

CANDIDATES FOR PRESIDENT/PRIME MINISTER

Eleven attacks were documented to have been committed against presidential or prime minister candidates worldwide, resulting in seven successful assassinations. With six, the decade of the 1990s witnessed far and away the most attacks against candidates. This was followed by the first eight years of the 2000s with two. The three decades of the 1980s, 1970s, and 1960s each experienced a single documented attack. No attacks could be found as having occurred during the 1950s.

Of these attacks, five targeted candidates while they were on foot. Candidates traveling in a motorized vehicle accounted for the remaining six attacks. Of all the attacks, nine of these candidates are known to have had protective details at the time.

While the greatest number of attacks during the research period occurred in the month of October, given the low overall numbers, this is of little value. However, seasonally, the concentration of attacks against candidates occurred during the spring and early summer (Figure 6.32).

Candidates were found to be attacked most often on Thursday, with 40% of all the ambushes (Figure 6.33). This was followed by Monday and Wednesday, each of which

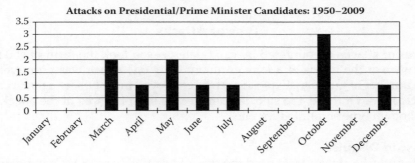

FIGURE 6.32 Attacks on presidential/prime minister candidates by month of the year.

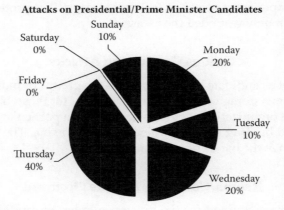

FIGURE 6.33 Attacks on presidential/prime minister candidates by day of the week.

accounted for 20% of the attacks. There were no documented attacks found to have occurred on a Friday or a Saturday.

Timing of Attacks

Of the six attacks in which the time of day was known, none occurred during the morning or afternoon hours. All were concentrated during the late afternoon to late nighttime hours between 1500 and 2400. The greatest number of attacks occurred at night after 2101. These statistics, given the type of victim, coupled with the location for the majority of the attacks, are not a surprise.

Location of Attacks

As could be expected considering the type of target, the location most often employed for the hit was a public event, accounting for six of the attacks. Two attacks are known to have occurred while the candidate was in transit, with another two occurring at an airport or onboard an aircraft. The last attack was documented as having occurred at the candidate's residence.

Type of Attacks

In the types of attacks encountered by candidates, seven took the form of shootings. Of these, six were at the hands of a lone gunman. Only one attack was perpetrated by an unknown number of gunmen. Explosives were employed in ambushes against candidates on four occasions. Of those, the suicide bomber was used in three of the attacks, and an IED of unknown type accounted for one.

Use of Ruse or Disguise

In one of the attacks, the assassin used the ruse of wanting to meet the candidate while in the airport. This caused the candidate to lower his guard, while allowing the killer to get within striking distance. At some point the assassin pulled a small submachine gun out from a folded newspaper and open fired, killing his target. The protective detail immediately returned fire but only wounded the assassin.

Groups Conducting Attacks

In nine of the cases of a candidate being ambushed the groups or individuals were identified, either by their own doing or through investigation. Of those, six came at the hands of terrorist/extremist organizations, with no one group in particular claiming more than one. Two were staged by drug cartels of Mexico and Colombia. The last known attack is believed to have been at the hands of government agents.

Region/Countries Attacks Occurred

Regionally, South Asia accounted for the greatest number of candidates being attacked, with four occurring in two countries. This was followed by North America, with three attacks over two countries, and Central/South America, with three attacks in one country. The remaining attack occurred in a country in Africa.

When examined by individual countries, Colombia and Pakistan each experienced three attacks on candidates. The United States was next, with two attacks over the fifty-eight-year period. The remaining ambushes were spread out over three separate countries, each documenting only one attack over the fifty-eight-year period.

PROSECUTORS

A total of fifty-six attacks were found to have been conducted against prosecutors worldwide, resulting in forty-nine successful assassinations and three successful kidnappings. With 41% of the attacks, the first eight years of the 2000s were witness to the vast majority perpetrated against prosecutors. This was followed by the decade of the 1980s, with 21% of attacks. The 1990s had 20% of attacks, followed closely by the 1970s with 14%. The 1960s and 1950s were each found to have had a single attack.

Of these attacks, twenty-four targeted a pedestrian-based prosecutor. Prosecutors traveling in a motorized vehicle accounted for seventeen attacks. The remaining attacks on prosecutors occurred at unknown locations and times. Of all the cases, only nine of these prosecutors were known to have had protective details at the time the hit went down.

January recorded 14% of the attacks targeting prosecutors, the most of any single month (Figure 6.34). Following closely were the months of April, August, and November, each of which documented another 13% of the attacks. Seasonally, the ambushes on prosecutors were concentrated during the winters months; however, the spring and summer months were also very active.

Prosecutors were found to be attacked predominantly on Wednesdays, accounting for 25% of the total (Figure 6.35). Mondays followed, with another 21% of the attacks, and Tuesdays, which recorded 18%. As has been seen in other victims, there was a notable reduction in attacks during the weekend days of Saturday and Sunday.

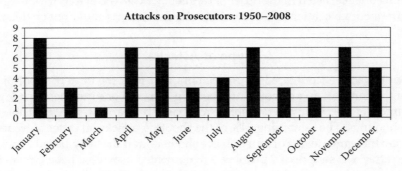

Attacks on Prosecutors: 1950–2008

FIGURE 6.34 Attacks on prosecutors by month of the year.

Attacks on Prosecutors

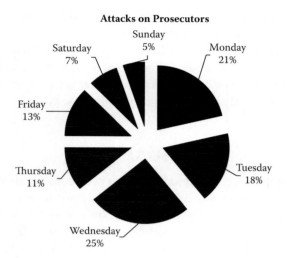

FIGURE 6.35   Attacks on prosecutors by day of the week.

Timing of Attacks

Of the twenty-seven attacks in which the time of day was known, eight occurred between the hours of 0601 and 0900. Another three occurred between the hours of 1801 and 2100. Five attacks were found to have been sprung between 1201 and 1500, with another four occurring between 1501 and 1800. Additionally, there were four attacks occurring between the hours of 2101 and 0300. Of the final three attacks, two were known to have occurred during the daylight hours, while the last one was staged between 0901 and 1200 hours.

Location of Attacks

The area of the residence witnessed 32% of the attacks against a prosecutor. This was followed closely by attacks conducted while a prosecutor was in transit, accounting for another 29%. The remaining attacks, listed in the order of frequency, occurred at a courthouse, the victim's office, and frequented locations. Sixteen of the attack locations could not be determined.

Type of Attacks

In the types of attacks encountered by prosecutors, 68% took the form of shootings. Of these, 37% were at the hands of an unknown number of gunmen. Lone gunmen struck prosecutors 26% of the time, the most of any tactic. Motorcycle-based hit teams were responsible for another 13% of the shootings. The remaining 24% of the shooting attacks, in order of frequency, came from two-man hit teams, teams of four or more shooters, and drive-by-based attacks. In one of the shooting attacks, a suppressed pistol was documented as having been employed.

Explosives were employed in ambushes against prosecutors eight times. Of those, the VBIED was used in two of the attacks, and IEDs of various types accounted for three. One of these IED attacks employed the use of a roof bomb, in which the assassin ran up to the vehicle and placed the device on the roof of the vehicle near the victim. As the assassin fled, the device was detonated. The final three explosive-based attacks came in the form of a booby-trap device affixed to the prosecutor's vehicle.

The remaining types of attacks included three kidnappings and a single stabbing. One unusual attack method that was employed by a lone gunman was the tipping of hollow-point bullets with cyanide poison.

Use of Ruse or Disguise

In only one instance was the use of a disguise or ruse known to have been implemented by assassins in order to get close to their target. In this case, the killers dressed as police officers conducting a traffic enforcement stop.

Groups Conducting Attacks

In forty of the cases of a prosecutor being ambushed, the groups or individuals were identified either by their own doing or through investigation. Of those, seventeen came at the hands of thirteen terrorist organizations, with no particular group laying claim to having attacked more than twice. Sixteen of the attacks stemmed from organized crime groups, three from the Italian Sicilian mafia, six from the drug cartels of Mexico and Colombia, and five from other organized crime groups. The remaining attacks came from criminals/defendants and in one case another attorney.

Region/Countries Attacks Occurred

Regionally, North America accounted for the most prosecutors being attacked, with 39% of the total number, spread out over two countries. This was followed by Europe, with 30% of all attacks spread out over five countries. Another 25% of attacks occurred in the region of Central/South America, spread out over six countries. The remaining attacks occurred in countries encompassing the regions of Russia and the republics as well as Asia.

When examined by individual countries, the United States, with 25%, stood out with a majority of attacks. Colombia and Italy each accounted for 16% of all of the attacks worldwide. Mexico rounded out the top four countries with 14%. The remaining attacks were spread out over twelve separate countries, each experiencing only one or two attacks (the exception being Greece with four) over the fifty-eight-year period.

WORLD LEADERS

One hundred and one attacks are known to have been perpetrated against world leaders (current and former, as well as leading members of royal families) worldwide, resulting in forty-six successful assassinations and five successful kidnappings. With 22%, the 1990s documented the greatest number of attacks of any decade against leaders around the world. This was followed by the 1980s, which experienced 21% of all known attacks. The

1970s and the first eight years of the 2000s each accounted for 18%. The 1960s had 13% of attacks and the 1950s had the final 8%.

Of those attacks, fifty-one were pedestrian based, in which the world leaders were not traveling in a vehicle. World leaders traveling in a motorized vehicle accounted for forty-seven of the attacks. The remaining attacks on world leaders occurred at unknown locations and times. Of all the attacks, only sixty-five of these world leaders are known to have had protective details at the time.

With 13%, the majority of attacks on a world leader occurred in September (Figure 6.36). This was followed by another 12% staged during the month of July. The months of June and August each recorded another 10% of the targeted ambushes against a world leader. Seasonally, the attacks were concentrated during the summer and autumn months, accounting for 53%.

World leaders were found to be attacked most often on Mondays, recording 18% of the total (Figure 6.37). This was followed by Tuesdays and Fridays, both of which had 17% of

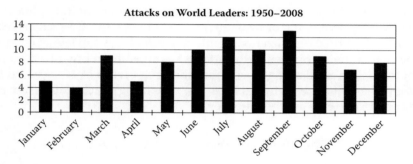

FIGURE 6.36   Attacks on world leaders by month of the year.

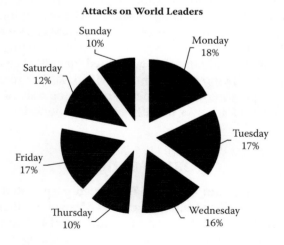

FIGURE 6.37   Attacks on world leaders by day of the week.

the attacks. While most of the attacks were concentrated during the traditional workweek of Monday through Friday, there were a considerable number of attacks staged during the weekends.

Timing of Attacks

Of the fifty-three attacks in which the time of day was known, ten occurred between the hours of 0601 and 0900. Fourteen attacks were found to have been staged between 0901 and 1200. Thirteen attacks were recorded to have taken place between the hours of 1201 and 1500. Only three attacks were staged between the hours of 1501 and 1800. Seven occurred between the 1801 and 2100. Additionally, there were four attacks documented between the hours of 2101 and 0600. Finally, two attacks are known only to have occurred during the daylight hours.

Location of Attacks

World leaders were attacked 37% of the time while in transit. This was followed by attacks occurring at public events another 22% of the time. Ambushes staged at or within close proximity of the victim's residence accounted for another 18% of the attacks. At or near the victim's office accounted for only 7% of the attacks, while another 8% occurred at hotels. The remaining attacks occurred at frequented locations, a mosque, or could not be determined.

Type of Attacks

In the types of attacks encountered by world leaders, 50% took the form of shootings. Of these, 30% were at the hands of an unknown number of gunmen. Lone gunmen struck world leaders 47% of the time. The remaining 23% of the shooting attacks came from snipers, teams of two gunmen, or teams of three or more gunmen.

Explosives were employed in ambushes against world leaders 39% of time. Of those, the VBIED was used in 31% of the attacks, and an IED of unknown type accounted for 33%. The suicide bomber was deployed 23% of the time. The remaining 13% of explosive-based attacks came in the form of a rocket-propelled grenade, a grenade attack, and a booby-trapped device. The remaining types of attacks included three stabbings, five kidnappings, and a single poison-based attack.

Use of Ruse or Disguise

Ruses/disguises were found to have been implemented on several occasions when attacking world leaders. The ruses/disguises known to have been employed include a VBIED painted to resemble a United Nations vehicle, killers dressed in military uniform, or posing as a reporter seeking an interview (used on at least three occasions), and an innocent female seeking to hand out a flower garland.

Groups Conducting Attacks

Unfortunately, in only fifty-four of the cases of world leaders being ambushed were the groups or individuals identified, either by their own doing or through investigation. Of those, thirty-six came at the hands of eighteen terrorist/extremist organizations, with Islamic extremists groups having attacked the most. Government agents were found to be or suspected to be behind eleven of the attacks. Organized criminal groups were only known to have been responsible for one attack. General criminals accounted for four attacks while rivals were behind three.

Region/Countries Attacks Occurred

Regionally, the Middle East, at 24%, accounted for the most world leaders being attacked, spread out over twelve countries. Europe accounted for world leaders being attacked at 21%, spread out over ten countries. This was followed by Central/South America, with 11% of attacks spread out over ten countries. With 10% of attacks, South Asia rounded out the top four regions with attacks perpetrated against world leaders over four countries. The remaining attacks occurred in countries encompassing every region on the planet.

When examined by individual countries, Lebanon, the United States, and France, each with 7% of attacks, stood out with the most worldwide. They were followed by Russia and Pakistan, each with 5% of attacks. The remaining attacks were spread out over fifty-two separate countries, each experiencing only one or two attacks over the fifty-eight-year period.

PROTECTIVE DETAILS

For 269 of the ambushes researched, a protective detail (any individual listed as having either a chauffeur or a bodyguard, or both, was deemed as having a protective detail) was present, accounting for 30% of all attacks. Of those attacks, the protective detail was successful in preventing the kidnapping or killing of their principal only 34% of the time. Unfortunately, the level of training of the individual protective detail and whether they were armed at the time of attack could not be determined.

The most prevalent method employed in ambushes against those targets having a protective detail was shootings, with 57% of attacks. This was followed by the use of explosives, accounting for 32%. In 5% of the attacks, kidnapping was the objective of adversaries. The last 6% of attacks came in the form of edged-weapon attacks, or could not be determined.

Unfortunately, with the shooting-based attacks, in 36% of the cases the exact number of gunmen could not be determined. A lone gunman, however, was responsible for 22% of the shooting attacks. This was followed closely by attacks from teams of two gunmen, accounting for 20%. Attacks by teams of four or more gunmen were behind 12% of the attacks. The final 10% stemmed from attacks from teams of three gunmen, snipers, and drive-bys.

In attacks employing explosives, the VBIED was used 40% of the time. This was followed by improvised explosive devices at 30%. The suicide bomber struck protected details

22% of the time. The remaining 8% of attacks came in the form of booby-trap devices being attached to the victim's vehicle, rocket-propelled grenades, a mortar attack, and grenades.

When examined by location of the ambush, attacks occurring while the detail was in transit accounted for 54%. This was followed by attacks at or near the residence at 15%. The public event was the third most common location for ambushes at 12%. This was followed distantly by the office with 5% and hotels with 4%.

7

Case Studies of Attacks on Motorcades

PIERRE GEMAYEL: NOVEMBER 21, 2006, TUESDAY, BEIRUT, LEBANON

Pierre Gemayel, a leading anti-Syrian Lebanese minister, was assassinated while in transit on the streets of Beirut. He had been driving his vehicle with a bodyguard seated in the front passenger seat, and a second bodyguard in the back seat armed with at least one semiautomatic rifle. The vehicle had dark tinted windows all around. There was no known follow or lead car.

Gemayel had reportedly just left a church when the car in front of Gemayel's, possibly a Honda CRV, slammed on the brakes, causing Gemayel's vehicle to rear end the Honda. The impact caused the hood of Gemayel's car to buckle slightly. A second vehicle, believed to be a type of Jeep, then cut off any rearward escape. Three men rapidly exited the Jeep and open fired with suppressed 9mm caliber weapons into the driver's side and front passenger windows. It is also possible, albeit unknown, that one or more men exited the front vehicle, also armed with 9mm automatic weapons. In excess of twenty rounds were fired through the driver's window, six of which appear to have impacted or exited through the front passenger door. At some point during the attack, it was reported that the bodyguard in the back seat fled the scene, apparently unharmed.

Unknowns

1. If vehicle was equipped with airbags and whether they deployed
2. Protective detail level of training or experience
3. Whether any site/route preplanning was conducted
4. Whether any indicators of preattack surveillance had been noted
5. Whether there had been any current or recent threat assessments conducted

Analysis

This attack revealed in dramatic fashion the dangers involved with protection work conducted over an extended period of time. Eventually the routines and routes are identified for the protectee. Regardless of how careful a person or team is, everyone has a home, an office, and certain locations they frequent. A careful hit team (and there is wide speculation that this was conducted by Syrian intelligence agents) that is patient can, over a period of time, identify these target-specific locations. Then, regardless of where the protectee is traveling from, by analysis of direction of travel, time and day of the week, it is relatively easy to extrapolate the ultimate destination. Once this is known, a hit team can quickly get into place, previously identified as the location to strike.

Gemayel had been known for varying his routes and changing up vehicles he traveled in. However, it appears that enough preattack intelligence had been obtained that the hit team knew that the cars were not armored (being that armored cars are an expensive commodity, and most people do not have multiples, it is fair to assume Gemayel had access to some sort of fleet allowing multiple changes)—hence the 9mm caliber weapons. Unfortunately it appears as though the bodyguards did not immediately go on the offensive or the outcome might have been different. Even in a scenario where the front two individuals were incapacitated, a trained man in the back seat with a large-caliber automatic rifle would have been able to put down a considerable rate of fire, especially given the fact that the windows were tinted: the guard would have been able to deliberately aim at most suspects prior to firing.

Offensive Point of View

The tactic used in this operation provides the aggressor with a large amount of flexibility in where the attack can take place. Further, the safety features of modern vehicles, such as airbags that deploy at approximately 175 to 200 mph in the event of a crash, would at best severely delay any immediate response and at worst incapacitate the driver and front passenger (jaws and arms have been broken, skin on the inner forearms has been removed, sunglasses have been forced into the face and eyes from airbag deployment), both of which provide ample time for the aggressor to move into a position for a killing strike. A major problem with this technique, however, is getting two vehicles into position. The goal of the aggressor would be to position a vehicle in front of the motorcade without alarming the motorcade operators, at the same time allowing a follow vehicle to get into position. At anytime during this maneuvering, the motorcade could make a turn or alert to a possible attack and conduct an immediate action drill. In this case, it appears that enough was known about Gemayel's route to allow the second assaulting vehicle to be prepositioned on a side street, or near an intersection where the attack ultimately went down.

Defensive Point of View

In order for this tactic to be effectively used, the attackers must position a vehicle in front of the protectee's car in order to slam on the brakes and force the collision. This need to get into position, not only in the same lane but also close enough to cause a rear-end collision, potentially provides the protective detail the time and opportunity to recognize the preattack indicators. Once detected, immediate action could be taken.

RAFIK HARIRI: FEBRUARY 14, 2005, MONDAY, 1255, BEIRUT, LEBANON

Former Lebanese Prime Minister Rafik Hariri and member of parliament Bassel Fleyhan were assassinated by a suicide bomber vehicle-borne improvised explosive device (SBVBIED). After finishing at the Lebanese parliament, Hariri was returning to his home, taking a route along the ocean front. Unbeknownst to Hariri and his protective detail, a large explosive device (estimates have been put at over 1,000 kilograms of explosive material), cached inside of a truck and driven by a suicide bomber, was positioned alongside the route being traveled by the motorcade.

The motorcade consisting of six heavily armored vehicles was traveling on Corniche Road by the derelict St. George Hotel when they pulled alongside of the device as it was triggered. One of the cars was blown up into the third floor of the annex of the hotel. Another car was blown over a wall of the hotel. The blast, which left a thirty-foot-wide by fifteen-feet-deep crater, destroyed Hariri's armored car, killed sixteen members of Hariri's protective detail, and wounded over one hundred others.

Unknowns

1. Was this a route he often took going home?
2. Were there other routes available?
3. Had there been any recent threats to indicate he was being targeted?

Analysis

In this case, an explosive device in the form of an SBVBIED was prepositioned along Hariri's route back to his residence. The location selected for the placement was ideal in that it provided the attackers with effective concealment as this one-way roadway had vehicles routinely parked along both sides. Further, by placing the device between two large buildings, in this case the St. George Hotel and St. George Yacht Club building, the destructive force would have been increased by means of reflective pressure. By the placement and size of the device, it is clear that the attackers were aware of Hariri's route and that he traveled in armored vehicles.

This ambush also provides insight into the benefits from an adversarial point of view, in striking a target when the starting and ending points are known, in this case, his work and residence. What isn't known is how often he took this particular route home. There again, given an understanding of human psychology, it is easy to imagine that a drive along the coast would have been a popular one, especially during difficult and trying times. Regardless, there are only so many ways of travel between locations, and therefore it is only a matter of time before routes are traveled more than once.

Defensive Point of View

This type of attack is difficult to defeat as a suicide bomber can properly time the device for maximum effect. This also defeats any type of radio frequency (RF) jamming equipment installed on the motorcade vehicles. Perhaps the only real option would be to change up the location of the protectee within the car as well as within the motorcade (for this to

213

work effectively would require dark tinted windows, which has its own issues). However, with surveillance, the attackers could overcome this.

Offensive Point of View
This is an extremely effective technique if you can find the right triggerman. With the size of the explosive, the fact that the target vehicles are armored becomes moot. With cars parked on both sides of the street, you can perfectly camouflage yourself with the surroundings. The main hurdles would be intelligence on routes taken and the location of the protectee within the motorcade. With patience, though, these are fairly easily acquired intelligence.

JOSE LOMBARDERO: OCTOBER 30, 2000, MONDAY, 0915, MADRID, SPAIN

The ETA (Euskadi ta Askatasuna) detonated a roadside car bomb killing Supreme Court Judge Jose Lombardero as well as his police bodyguard, Garcia Escudero, and his chauffeur, Arming Medina. The day of the attack, as was Lombardero's routine, he was picked up by Medina, accompanied by Officer Escudero, at the front of his home (possibly located at 65 Calle de Torrelaguna). The three drove a short distance, where they stopped to pick up a newspaper at a local stand close to his residence (allegedly another habit). They then proceeded to the courthouse traveling along the same route they always took.

Unbeknownst to any of the three men, the evening before, an unknown individual(s) had arrived in the area and parked a red Renault car on Avenida de Badajoz, approximately one car length from the intersection with an unknown side street that, through ETA surveillance, they knew Lombardero's vehicle would be traveling on. Inside of the Renault had been cached an improvised explosive device consisting of 25 kilograms (55 pounds) of explosive material (type unknown).

The location of the bomb had been perfectly planned, as Lombardero's vehicle was forced to slow down first for the pedestrian crossing, and then to make a right turn onto Avenida de Badajoz. Additionally, the area where the attack was triggered is a busy district with numerous high-rise apartment buildings. These buildings provided the attackers with several advantages. First, they allowed the terrorists to conduct their preattack surveillance of their target's routines, as well as to recon the possible attack sites, all in an inconspicuous manner. Second, the presence of the tall apartment buildings could and should have contributed to the amplification of the force of the blast by means of reflected pressure. Third, Avenida de Badajoz is approximately thirty-eight feet wide (11.64 meters), consisting of a single lane in each direction with cars parked along both curb ways. This prevented the protective detail from putting distance between themselves and parked vehicles, as well as assuring the terrorists that their target vehicle would be within less than a few feet of the device. Last, approximately 60 meters away was a subway station entrance, which may have been the selected escape route of the terrorist(s).

On the day of the assassination, the ETA terrorist, who was standing nearby, was able to detonate the device when he saw his target enter the kill zone. When the bomb was triggered, the force of the blast hurled Judge Lombardero's vehicle approximately 20 meters into the air, landing on the other side of a bus that was passing by. Over seventy people were injured in the attack, including the bus driver.

Unknowns

1. The existence of any recent threats to the judge
2. Reports of possible surveillance or suspicious individuals along the route
3. Prior attacks or indications of targeting of the judge
4. Level of protective services offered to the judge

Analysis

As is so often said in the field of protective operations, routine can get you killed. This is unfortunately another probable case of just such a mistake. However, given the proximity to the judge's residence, there are only so many ways a person can generally depart from his or her community, and if the terrorist is patient, eventually the target will come to him or her. In this case, ETA appeared to have taken its time and selected a perfect site in which to spring an ambush. A traffic intersection, which has been used worldwide with horrifically successful results, was the ideal location. The foot traffic, coupled with the judge's car having to slow to make a right-hand turn, allowed the trigger man to be certain he detonated the device at precisely the right time to gain maximum effect.

The use of a car bomb by ETA also worked greatly in its favor, as it allowed for the device to be constructed at a safe location, then simply driven and parked at the precise spot. However, given the parking problems within most major cities, it is very likely that another involved car was parked in the selected area prior to the arrival of the vehicle bomb, thus allowing for the proper placement as well as for the terrorists to quickly depart the area. During the subsequent investigation into the attack, it was found that the vehicle used to cache the explosive device had been stolen several months prior to the attack in Madrid.

As with any attack, a similar pattern of events is followed to reach the final outcome, in this case a successful assassination of a Supreme Court judge. ETA has proven to be quite proficient at killing its targeted victims by a variety of methods, but the organization tends to prefer the VBIED (when using explosives to strike a target). While this method provides perhaps the most operational concealment, ETA increased its likelihood of success by keeping the weight of the device low enough so that the exterior of the car appeared normal. However, by using a relatively low amount of explosive material, the risks of not completing the mission increase. Given ETA's experience with explosive devices, it would not be a stretch to assume that the ambush location was selected in order to provide the greatest reflected pressure, thereby increasing the damage potential of the device.

The problem this type of attack illustrates is the difficulty in defense on the part of the protective detail. Generally, distance and shielding are the greatest allies to protective professionals when dealing with explosive devices. In this case, the Avenida de Badajoz not only provided zero room for distance between the VBIED and the target vehicle, but also added to the concealment factor by allowing the VBEID to be one car parked among the many.

Another of the trademarks, if you will, of ETA, and demonstrated here, is placing the device out of the immediate area of the residence but close enough to lessen the likelihood of the target taking a different route. This is an effective technique, as most in the field of protective security know to be alert to unknown vehicles in the immediate area of the protectee. By pushing the ambush site out a bit, one succeeds in drastically decreasing the protective detail's ability to identify potential threats.

One of the most difficult parts of assassinating a moving target through the use of explosives is timing. Too early or late in triggering the device, and the force of the blast is not concentrated upon the target. ETA has a history of dealing with this issue by setting the attacks at intersections where the target is known to make a right- or left-hand turn. During the normal nonevasive movement of a principal during the daily course of business, the driver will have to slow the vehicle down to approximately 17 to 22 mph, depending on the angle, to perform a comfortable and smooth turn. This makes timing the triggering of an explosive device nearly foolproof.

In conclusion this case graphically illustrates the need to vary one's route, not just in the immediate area of the residence and office, but along the entire route. In this instance, as in many in the past, surveillance detection was probably the missed indicator. However, those of us in this work should always look at our areas of operation with the eye of an aggressor. Locate the ideal sites of an attack, those that provide your adversary everything it would want, such as concealment, perhaps force multipliers, and of course potential avenues of escape. Obviously this will depend upon your likely opponent, but if suicide attacks have generally been ruled out, and they are not part of ETA's repertoire, then escape routes will have been identified. In this attack, the proximity of the subway station makes for an ideal escape. Given the natural chaos surrounding a bombing attack, it is far easier for an individual(s) to depart on foot by way of a subway a mere 60 meters away. Not having to depart in a vehicle decreases the likelihood of a vehicle description or license plate being obtained by law enforcement, thereby adding to the overall operational security.

STEPHEN SAUNDERS: JUNE 8, 2000, THURSDAY, 0715 (APPROX.), ATHENS, GREECE

British military attaché Brigadier Stephen Saunders was shot four times in the chest and stomach with a .45 caliber pistol. The attack was perpetrated by two gunmen wearing helmets and riding a white off-road-style motorcycle, which they pulled alongside the passenger side of his white Rover car as he was driving to work. Saunders, driving an unmarked car (advice he had followed from security personnel to not be in a vehicle with diplomatic plates), had left his home in the northern suburb of Nea Erithrea at 0700 en route to the British Embassy (located at 1 Ploutarchou Street, in Athens), a distance of approximately 12 miles. He became stuck in morning traffic on Leoforos Kifisias, a large thoroughfare approximately 2 miles away from the embassy when the attack occurred.

After the killing, the motorcycle threaded its way through traffic and escaped through the side streets of the Filothei residential district. Saunders was rushed to a nearby hospital, but died from multiple injuries shortly after the attack. The Greek terrorist group November 17 later claimed responsibility for the killing, stating, "We chose the senior English officer not only because England took part actively in the bombardments as it does with the United States during the periodic bombardment of Iraq, but because the English policy . . . even surpassed the Americans in provocation, cynicism and aggression." Police said that ballistic analysis of four spent cartridges found at the scene of the shooting confirmed that the bullets had been fired from the same .45-caliber pistol used by November 17 in seven previous killings.

Unknowns

1. Whether threats had been received prior to the attack
2. Whether the presence of surveillance had been noted by anyone
3. Whether Saunders had the ability to be armed, or have a protective detail available

Analysis

From a review of the layout of the city streets of Athens, it is readily apparent that on the day of the attack Saunders was traveling on the most direct path (truly only one of two possible routes, the other being a highway of some type) between his residence in the north part of the city and his embassy in central Athens, a distance of some 12 to 15 miles, give or take. This main thoroughfare, consisting of three lanes (each about nine feet in width) in each direction, is marked with perhaps a hundred or more major and minor intersections. Additionally, the area traveled through consists of hotels and multistory buildings that come right up to the street, all of which provide an adversary a plethora of locations in which to position for an ambush, as well as conduct the surveillance that had to have occurred prior to the attack.

In this case, we have a military officer (with prior experience in areas such as Northern Ireland and Cyprus) following the recommendation of security officials to make use of an unmarked vehicle, thereby employing a more covert method of protection. At the time of this killing, the November 17 terrorist organization was very active. It had successfully killed a number of Greek citizens as well as a few American military and intelligence members. While it had not targeted any British citizens or establishments, it was not a stretch that such a targeting would occur (as in my opinion, the rest of the world links our two nations together). Further, that Saunders took to traveling in a nondescript vehicle is evidence that at least a few were thinking along the same lines.

From the review of photographs of the scene, it appears as though Saunders was traveling in the number one lane (if intentional, then he was thinking). The assassins came up along the passenger side, which could have taken advantage of a blind side. Had Saunders been armed, he might have been able to engage the assassins. Regardless, with the traffic situation as it was, the options were extremely limited and required him to take immediate action. Given the scene of the killing, and taking as fact that Saunders was most likely not armed, there were really only two options remaining. Either drive the car over the center median into oncoming traffic or, and perhaps the best option, rapidly exit the vehicle.

Getting out of the car by way of the driver's side door would have allowed Saunders to get out of the confines of his vehicle, which in this type of attack should be considered one big boxed-in kill zone. Once out of the car, Saunders would have instantly had cover between the assassins and himself in the form of his car. His options would have also increased to include running away through the oncoming traffic, either across the street or up the direction he had just traveled, hiding behind other cars, or if armed, engaging the attackers. Once out of the car, Saunders would have then presented a large problem for the terrorists requiring immediate and perhaps difficult action on their part.

This method of attack, as has been seen before, provides the assassins with a number of benefits when conducting an urban ambush. First, both assassins were fully geared up, including the wearing of helmets, which assisted in protecting their identities, nationalities, and even their sex. The second rider, armed with his .45-caliber pistol, could easily conceal such a weapon until needed, perhaps a second or two prior to arrival. The motorcycle, by its nature, can split the traffic lanes when the ambush site has been located and pull right up to the driver's window and open fire. At extremely close range with a .45-caliber pistol, there is little chance for survival, short of immediate action on the part of the target.

While the motorcycle is an ideal mode of transport into and out of an urban ambush scene, it still has some limitations, especially in heavy morning traffic, in that it cannot just immediately turn 90 to 180 degrees on the spot (plus given the gunfire, people in their cars will be panicking, causing other issues for the attackers). In this case had Saunders exited his car, the assassins are now faced with a moving target who can take cover and move quickly in and out of the traffic, and is perhaps (not known to them with absolute certainty) armed himself. Also, the longer they remain at the scene, the more chances there are for them to be identified or captured. Unfortunately none of this occurred.

NEELAN TIRUCHELVAM: JULY 29, 1999, THURSDAY, 0915, COLOMBO, SRI LANKA

Dr. Neelan Tiruchelvam, a prominent member of Sri Lanka's Tamil minority, was assassinated when a male suicide bomber walked out onto the street and threw himself on Tiruchelvam's car while it sat stuck in traffic at the intersection of Rosemead Place (the street of his residence) and Kynsey Place. Dr. Tiruchelvam and the attacker died instantly and five others were injured in the blast. Dr. Tiruchelvam's chauffeur-driven car (with security officer Farouk Moulana seated in the front passenger seat) had just arrived in the area of the office of Tiruchelvam Associates on Kynsey Terrace, an exclusive area of Colombo, not far from the prime minister's office, when the Tamil Tigers (LTTE) bomber attacked. The killer had arrived in the area on a motorcycle, which provided him with the flexibility to cut through the heavy morning traffic. Once close enough, he dismounted and closed with his target on foot.

The bomber had approximately 5 kilograms (11 pounds) of explosives wrapped around his person. He walked between the rear of Tiruchelvam's car and the front of a protective escort vehicle, which was carrying an unknown number of security personnel. The bomber then rounded the rear left side of the Nissan carrying Tiruchelvam, a seat he routinely occupied, and detonated. The blast destroyed the door of the car and threw Tiruchelyam across the rear seat of the car, killing him instantly. The chauffeur and security officer, Farouk, survived the attack.

Farouk later stated that he had been watching the intersection in front of them at the time of the attack and never saw the approach of the bomber. A security officer in the following Jeep stated he spotted the bomber, who at the time was wearing only black pants and a blue checkered shirt, and saw him approach the Nissan only a few seconds before the blast. The security officer stated he was in the process of pulling his weapon at the time of the blast.

Dr. Tiruchelvam was a Tamil lawyer, an academic, and a politician. To many, including himself, he was and never would have been a target of the Tamil Tigers. However, it appears that at some point, for some reason, he crossed a line and became a target of a Tiger suicide squad.

Unknowns

1. The presence of any threats against Dr. Tiruchelvam
2. The availability of different vehicles or ones equipped with tinted windows
3. The availability of an armored vehicle
4. The number of routes available between the residence and office

Analysis

This case is a perfect example of how we may never know when we are being targeted. It also represents one of the relatively rare cases (although not necessarily in this region) where a suicide bomber attacks a single individual. Many, including Dr. Tiruchelvam, never considered himself a target of the LTTE. Further, due to the presence of the prime minister's official residence, this area of Colombo has extremely high security with numerous checkpoints that must be passed to enter, which perhaps added to confidence in his safety. Even so, it appears Dr. Tiruchelvam was security conscious, as he would generally travel only with this driver and chief security officer and would have other members of his family travel in separate vehicles. On those rare occasions he drove himself or with others without a security detail, he was known to have consulted with his chief security officer about which route to take.

At the time of this attack, LTTE members were the foremost users of the suicide bombing tactic for targeted assassinations, and had employed it successfully against previous individual targets of significance. It should therefore have been taken into consideration in determining the level of protection to be afforded. However, given the region in which the attack occurred and the likelihood of tremendous foot traffic moving in and around the area, it is very probable that early detection of the threat would have been difficult at best. Even if the threat is recognized, suicide bombers present a tremendous problem to deal with, as they can detonate themselves whenever they decide. Further, the protective detail needs to almost instantly make a decision on what action to take.

Even if it is known that the attacker is a suicide bomber, the protective detail will most likely not know for certain the location of the explosives and, perhaps more importantly, the type of explosive used. Some of the homemade explosives are highly sensitive to shock or heat, and therefore a bullet strike could cause premature detonation. That leaves only the possibility of a head shot on a moving target at some distance. In this case, the threat was detected, but it was already within striking distance of the target, so even if a shot had been made, the bomber might still have been able to detonate and accomplish his mission.

What is obvious is that some form of preattack surveillance had taken place. The LTTE knew from surveillance and reconnaissance that Dr. Tiruchelvam would be in the area of this intersection in the morning, and that heavy traffic would effectively trap him inside of his car. The employment of the motorcycle allowed the bomber to deal with the traffic in order to make his initial approach. Why the bomber didn't just ride up alongside of the car and detonate is not known; however, as most suicide bombers do not generally act alone, it is quite possible that the motorcycle had been driven by another and dropped the bomber off just prior to the target. If this was the case, then this was a missed opportunity by the protective detail to detect the potential hostile action.

GIOVANNI FALCONE: MAY 23, 1992, SATURDAY, 1800 (APPROX.), PALERMO, SICILY

Giovanni Falcone, an Italian antimafia prosecutor, his wife, Francesca Morvillo (a sitting judge), and three police bodyguards were assassinated in a bomb attack. While the attack was staged outside of Palermo, Sicily, the start actually began much farther away, in Rome. Mr. Falcone had started his morning at his office in Rome. Generally, he would return every Friday evening to his home in Palermo, where his wife remained as she was still working in the city awaiting a transfer to Rome. However, as she had business in Rome that week, they decided to return together that Saturday. He left the Ministry of Justice for the airport (a detail that was picked up by a mafia surveillance team who followed him around Rome).

At about 4:40 p.m., their plane departed the military airport for the approximately one-hour flight to Palermo International Airport (which the mafia surveillance team noted and advised their teammates in Sicily). At the airport the Falcones were met by their seven-man protective detail and motorcade (earlier that morning, a member of the protective detail had picked up Falcone's armored car, which had been witnessed from a nearby shop by a mafia surveillance member, who had subsequently relayed the info). Somewhere at the airport was also a member of the mafia hit team, who advised his teammates of the arrival of the Falcones. Giovanni Falcone decided that he would drive, and his wife sat in the front passenger seat, while the bodyguard sat in the back seat.

The three-car motorcade consisting of three policemen in the front vehicle, followed by the Falcones, and a second car were traveling at approximately 160 kilometers per hour along a four-lane (two lanes in each direction) highway from Palermo International Airport en route to the city of Palermo (along the way passing a two-person mafia surveillance team advising their teammates of the approaching target). At some point they passed over a large-diameter metal drainage pipe that had been packed with approximately 500 kilos of plastic explosives by members of the Italian mafia (a team of five men in construction dress had been working that day at that exact location). As the vehicles crossed, the explosives were command detonated (the trigger men had been hidden in a shack approximately 100 yards away). The force of the explosion threw the first car, carrying the three policemen, approximately 70 yards away into an olive grove, completely destroying the vehicle. The Falcones car, an armored Fiat Croma, was found in the crater; both Falcones were alive but died within hours. The bodyguard sitting in the back seat survived the attack, as did the three men in the follow car.

Analysis

With this case we see that while protective measures were taken, it was the routine nature of these measures that opened the door to attack. Not just one routine but several are evident. Giovanni's weekly travel between Rome and Palermo certainly restricted the steps that could be taken by a protective detail to prevent attack. Even if the mafia hit team didn't know Giovanni's exact schedule, by monitoring his Palermo residence until the protective detail picked up his armored car, they would know he would be soon arriving (which in this case is exactly what they did).

Falcone's weekly travel from the airport to his home in Palermo was obviously observed for a period of time. As there are only two routes that could be taken between these two locations, both on a highway, one direct and the other much longer, this provided the hit team a very good perspective of the routes preferred by the protective detail (if they were changed up at all), the general speed of travel, and the makeup of the protective team and motorcade. Ironically, had the Falcones taken the back seat of their car, they most likely would have survived the ambush.

Offensive Point of View
The use of explosives affords a hit team a great amount of anonymity. By placing an explosive device along the route known to be traversed by the target, the hit team has only the factor of timing to deal with. Placing the explosive in a drainage pipe further reduces the likelihood of it being discovered by chance, or of alerting the protective detail. Additionally, a device hidden under a highway is not a common tactic, and therefore affords the ambushers the element of surprise. Another benefit of the placement of this explosive device is that underground attacks can defeat a lot more armored vehicles (as has been seen in Iraq). Constructing the improvised explosive device (IED) with a command detonator negates any possible electronic or RF jamming equipment (if it is a direct wire trigger) the vehicles may be employing. However, the command trigger device has one major hurdle that the ambushing force must contend with: timing the device correctly.

Defensive Point of View
This type of attack is extremely difficult to defeat, especially when the IED is concealed underground. In the case of IED attacks against moving motorcades, speed of travel is one of the best defensive tools available. Being able to manually trigger the device at the precise time to hit the target becomes increasingly more difficult at higher speeds. In fact, in this case the device was triggered a fraction of a second too early. It was only by luck that the mafia hit team was successful.

ALFRED HERRHAUSEN: NOVEMBER 30, 1989, THURSDAY, 0830, FRANKFURT, WEST GERMANY

Members of the Red Army Faction (RAF) assassinated Alfred Herrhausen, the chairman of the Deutsche Bank. He was killed by a remote-controlled improvised explosive device (IED) near his home in Bad Homburg. He was on his way to his office and within less than 500 yards of his home, traveling in a three-vehicle motorcade consisting of armored limousines along Seedamweg (a route they often traveled) when the attack occurred. The lead vehicle, with two members of the protective detail, passed the attack site, at which point a terrorist hidden on the side of the road activated an infrared beam that, when broken by Herrhausen's Mercedes-Benz 500SE (the second vehicle in the motorcade), triggered the device.

The 20- to 30-kilo IED launched a 5-pound 8-inch-diameter solid copper plate (referred to as an explosively formed projectile) in the direction of Herrhausen's vehicle. The force of the explosion coupled with the projectile, which was concentrated to the right rear side of the car where Herrhausen was seated, lifted the car, which spun in mid-air, landing in the center of the roadway, killing him and severely injuring his driver. The follow car with another two protective detail members was undamaged by the blast. The assassin, after detonating the device, placed a piece of paper containing the RAF symbol with the triggering box on top. The assassin then crossed to the other side of the park in which he had been standing and got into a waiting car.

The device was later determined to have been constructed of TNT and was cached inside a child's backpack, which was attached to the luggage rack of a bicycle parked on the side of the small two-lane roadway (it was later discovered they had parked the bicycle in the same general area for a period of time until it had become routine to the locals). Reportedly, part of the wire was hidden under a nearby sidewalk, and had been found earlier by a city worker and removed. The terrorists came back, dressed as a construction crew, and replaced it. Two men were seen driving away in a vehicle, which was later found to have been rented in early October.

Unknowns

1. Whether there had been any intelligence or detected signs of targeting Herrhausen

Analysis

This attack, the only one known of its kind at the time to employ an infrared trigger, provides a graphic example of the dangers of traveling the same routes. In this case, the attack was within fairly close proximity to the residence and should have fallen just within the area that a protective detail would maintain some sort of monitoring (although it is not known that they didn't). It is also an example of the nature of routines, in this instance of Herrhausen habitually sitting in the right rear passenger seat of the second vehicle. However, it must be noted that while his vehicle had tinted windows, even if he had changed up his position, it was reported that he was a heavy smoker and was known to have kept his window cracked open to allow for the smoke to exit. This would have allowed any adversary with an observation post to alert the attacking force of his exact position.

Obviously the missed opportunity was the placement of the device and the ruse of the construction crew. This portion of roadway consists of two lanes, one in each direction, and is heavily covered with trees and brush on both sides, providing ample concealment, which should have been taken as a potential danger area. Had the detail been more alert to the goings-on in the immediate area, they may have detected a problem. However, given the ruse of the construction, if it was solid, there may have been nothing the detail would have detected. This is even more likely if the hit was actually conducted by government agents, as some have suggested.

While with the device triggering system used it would not have made much difference where in the motorcade Herrhausen sat, changing up where he sat inside of the car could have made a great deal of difference. If all three vehicles in the motorcade had been of the same manufacture and all with tinted windows, it would have given Herrhausen the ability to change up his location within not only the motorcade, but also within each vehicle. Even if the correct car had been targeted, he might have prevented his death by not being seated where he was. However, if the information regarding his smoking habit of cracking a window is correct, it would all be for naught.

MAURICE GIBSON: APRIL 25, 1987, SATURDAY, 0830 (APPROX.), KILLEN, COUNTY ARMAGH, IRELAND

Lord Justice Maurice Gibson and his wife, Lady Cecily Gibson, were assassinated by a 500-pound remote-detonated IED cached inside a parked Ford Cortina. He was the senior judge in Ireland and was returning to their home in Dumbo, County Down. The escort provided by the Gardai Siochana had followed the Gibsons from Dublin to just past the border with Northern Ireland. The Gibsons had just driven away from their escort and were traveling the short distance to the border where they were to meet their Royal Ulster Constabulary (RUC) escort (who were a short distance away and traveling toward the Gibsons, who may have been early in their arrival) when the device was triggered.

Along that short portion of main road between Dublin and Belfast, approximately 100 meters north of Kinney Mills Road and 400 meters north of the border crossing at Dromad, the Irish Republican Army (IRA) had hidden the device, which was later found to have been constructed of a fertilizer-based explosive and parked not 15 minutes prior to the arrival of the Gibsons. The explosion left a crater that measured 10 feet by 20 feet by 6 feet deep in the road. The force of the blast threw the Gibsons' car across the road, killing both instantly.

The device had been placed inside of a Ford Cortina that had been stolen previously in March. The device, which was estimated to have been constructed of between 450 and 500 pounds of homemade fertilizer-based explosive, was command detonated by remote trigger. It was later determined that the VBIED had been driven and parked at the location at approximately 0815.

An IRA spokesman later told the *Sunday Tribune* that the IRA had been aware of Gibson's movements and had known in advance that he would be returning home via Dublin for some time. The spokesman stated that preparations had been made at least a week in advance, adding that that amount of time was required for the preparation of explosives, which in this case were fertilizer based. Time was also required to study the attack site, prep the car to be used to hide the device, and prepare the remote detonator.

Analysis

Lord Justice Maurice Gibson was known to have been on a Provisional Irish Republican Army (PIRA) hit list as early as 1984, after he had sentenced a PIRA member to a long prison sentence. In fact, in July of that year his home in Donegal was destroyed by an arson fire. No suspicious subjects were noted in the area by the officers or witnesses, even though the triggerman had to have been able to see the approach of the victims in order to trigger the device at the correct time.

What is clear in this case, as in all attacks, is that the Gibsons had been under surveillance for a considerable period of time, in this instance, possibly even over three years. It would not have taken much effort to realize that the Gibsons were not at their residence, and were traveling in Ireland, or even England. Given that, and knowing how the travel was to be conducted, in this case by car, it was just a matter of being in a position to strike. The approximate time of travel between Dublin and the Dromad border crossing is just over 2 hours and 20 minutes, covering a distance of roughly 111 miles.

In this attack, continuous surveillance would not have been required and, in fact, would have been an added risk on the part of the adversary. Simply placing a few static surveillance positions along the route would have provided the approximate speed of travel, allowing for the correct timing of the device placement. Either that or conducting a few practice runs of the route. Once the target was confirmed to be taking a particular route, it was just a matter of driving the VBIED to the correct location and parking. In this attack the odds were stacked against Chiesa with little change of survivability.

LEAMON HUNT: FEBRUARY 15, 1984, WEDNESDAY, 1845, ROME, ITALY

Leamon Hunt, the U.S. foreign service officer who was director general in charge of the Multinational Force and Observers in Sinai. was assassinated by members of the Red Brigades terror organization. Mr. Hunt had just arrived at his gated home located at 20 via Sud-Africa and was awaiting the opening of the residence security gates. During this delay, three men who had been waiting inside a Fiat 128 parked across the street got out and open fired. Mr. Hunt's car was armored, resulting in no rounds penetrating the exterior. However, one of the terrorists jumped on the trunk of the car and fired into the upper edge of the rear window with an unknown type or caliber of weapon. One of the rounds penetrated the rubber and metal frame holding the window in place and struck Hunt in the head, killing him. The assassins then fled the scene in an unknown direction.

Unknowns

1. Presence of threats or possible detection of hostile surveillance
2. The availability of an advance or even follow car

Analysis

In this attack the victim was mobile and just arriving at his residence, which is a one-way street, approximately 9 meters wide, and lined on both sides by fences and walls approximately 3 meters tall. Cars can only be parked, at least legally, along one side of the street. This means the assassins, not wanting to have Mr. Hunt drive past them and potentially alert to their presence, would have had to position themselves far enough ahead that Hunt would be less likely to notice them, but close enough for a rapid deployment from the car on attack. If the assassins parked illegally up the street, this could have effectively blocked off the forward escape from the area and, as a result, should have immediately alerted Mr. Hunt and his driver.

This was one of the earlier cases in which the adversary took advantage of security measures to delay the victim from a rapid escape. The gate prevented Mr. Hunt from driving into the relative safety of his residence, although whether some type of protective detail was present beyond a driver isn't known. Sitting in his car, he was effectively locked into one big kill zone that ordinarily would have little to no cover. In this case, however, the vehicle was armored and may have caused some level of false confidence. The fact that the assassins went to a specific point on the car and began firing effectively using a known weakness (at least to them) to attack their target strongly indicates either previous knowledge of the vehicle or some type of source with the vehicle's armor manufacturer.

Should Mr. Hunt have contemplated an escape from his car on foot, the design of the street effectively channeled him into a long kill zone. Short of quickly vaulting a stone wall, on top of which were a variety of vertical extensions of various materials, from man-made to foliage, there would be no place to run. The only viable option then would have been to reverse out of the area as rapidly as possible. Driving with speed backwards requires some skill and training to do efficiently, and in this location the street follows a slow curve, which with the presence of the parked vehicles would only increase the level of difficulty. Another factor was the availability of light, given the season and timing of the attack, coupled with the high density of trees, which could have created a relatively dark street (the presence of street lights at the time isn't known; however, in photos of the area as of 2009, there are street lamps approximately 8 meters high spaced with a fair amount of regularity, but their output isn't known).

This case provides graphic evidence of the potential benefits of an advance car. The methodology of this ambush is very simple, but it has been used time and time again with great effectiveness. The use of the advance car (ideally with two trained protective members aboard) sweeping through the streets prior to Mr. Hunt's arrival would have possibly allowed the detail to detect a potential hostile presence within the proximity of the residence. Given the overall percentages of attacks staged at or near the victim's residence, this would be enough to warrant either contact with the suspicious vehicle, the staging of the advance car in a position of tactical advantage between the gate entrance and the suspect vehicle, or even a wave off of Mr. Hunt's vehicle while contacting local law enforcement.

CARLO CHIESA: SEPTEMBER 3, 1982, FRIDAY, 2125 (APPROX.), PALERMO, SICILY

The Prefect for Palermo, Carlo Alberto Dalla Chiesa (a general of the Italian Carabinieri), was assassinated by members of the Sicilian Cosa Nostra. The attack occurred as General

Chiesa and his wife were returning from the Palace of the Prefecture. As they reached via Isidoro Carini in their small Lancia A112 Coupe, an unknown number of motorcycles with Sicilian mafia assassins suddenly appeared. Armed with AK-47 assault rifles, the gunmen open fired upon the small car. At some point in the attack, Chiesa's car crashed into a parked vehicle on via Isidoro Carini, where the gunmen concentrated their fire, killing Chiesa, his wife, and a police officer driver. It was reported that Chiesa was found slumped over his wife in a vain attempt to shield her from the rifle fire. The motorcycle gunmen then fled the scene of the attack in an unknown direction.

After the attack, it was reported that General Chiesa had previously refused an armored car and armed escort, believing he would be more difficult to effectively target by driving a generic car, and choosing his own routes (a tactic he had employed effectively during his years conducting counterterrorism operations). It was also reported that Chiesa had apparently discovered that some of his domestic servants had relatives who were known mafia members.

Analysis

General Carlo Chiesa was obviously a man that was no stranger to danger, having dealt for many years with various terrorist organizations, including the lethal Italian Red Brigades. He was a man of action and confident in his own abilities, a trait common among men such as him. While given his undoubtedly high level of training and experience, it is hard not to fault his decision to not take an armored vehicle or armed escort; having that extra set of eyes or the added level of protection might have made the difference.

Attacks by a motorcycle-based hit team are very dangerous at any time, but when multiple hit teams approach using motorcycles, the danger dramatically increases. The attack of Senor Chiesa occurred in the urban area of Palermo, not far from the Palace of the Prefecture where he worked. This part of Palermo is laid out in a grid pattern with narrow streets, many of which are one-way only, with wide sidewalks and cars parked on at least one side.

While General Chiesa changed up his routes and routines, the use of motorcycles by the mafia assassins, coupled with the layout of the city, effectively nullified the benefit. The reason for this was not only the flexibility of the motorcycles, but given the distance between the attack site and Chiesa's office, there were only so many ways to travel, at least initially. It only required the positioning of one or more people to watch in order to quickly detect the streets traveled.

The car was found off the side of via Isidoro Carini in a downtown area of Palermo, with tall buildings and streets only approximately nine meters wide with wide sidewalks. With his wife and no protective detail, Chiesa had only one option, and that was to attempt to outrun the motorcycles. This is where the versatility of the bikes really shows. Their general stop-to-rapid-speed times would be considerably less than that of a car, allowing for them to close the distance between the two quickly. Any turns made by the car would have had little to no effect in increasing the distance between victim and adversary. While the hour in which the attack went down wasn't able to be determined, the understanding is that it was in the evening hours, when traffic was very light. The presence of traffic is perhaps the greatest counter to a motorcycle attack, as it can act as a severely limiting factor to their movement, in both speed and turning ability.

While it has been widely reported that the car was being driven by a police driver, from analysis of the photos of the car at the attack site, this does not appear to be true. In one report, the police officer was in a follow vehicle at the time of attack. Not knowing the ability of the driver or if Chiesa was armed at the time prevents knowing with certainty the tactics available. Surely he felt much more vulnerable given the presence of his wife, in that possible counter ambush options were effectively closed. If the driver was capable and he was armed, most likely it was only with a handgun, which would have been of limited use against multiple adversaries armed with automatic weapons. It is not known if the car was armored or if he had an option of using one, but regardless, the only option was to exit rapidly. Unfortunately it appears as though the bodyguards did not immediately go on the offensive.

BORIS GOLDMAN: APRIL 12, 2004, MONDAY, 2000, MOSCOW, RUSSIA

Boris Goldman, an executive with the New Found Quality advertising agency, was killed in a bombing attack along with four other individuals, including his chauffeur and a bodyguard. Mr. Goldman was traveling in his armored Volvo C80 when they stopped for a red light at the intersection of Ulitsa Vavilova and Ulitsa Dmitriya Ulyanova. A motorcycle with a single rider approached and placed a suitcase IED on the roof of Goldman's car. At approximately that same moment, the device was detonated, killing all inside of the car as well as the assassin (later identified as an unemployed Moscow resident). The device was powerful enough to shatter the windows of an adjacent building to the fourth floor.

The dead motorcycle assassin was found to have had a two-way radio in his possession. It is also believed that the device was detonated early, with the intention of killing the assassin to help close any loose ends. It was also reported that Mr. Goldman had been attacked in a similar fashion approximately six months earlier and survived, resulting in his switching to an armored vehicle.

Analysis

Perhaps one of the most unusual and interesting targeted attacks recorded from a method of operation perspective, was the hit on Boris Goldman. The use of an IED placed upon the roof of a vehicle allows for the exact placement of the device at the right time. The use of the motorcycle for delivery allowed the bomber to strike when the opportunity was right. The damage to the car and the fact that Mr. Goldman was killed in the blast indicate that the roof of armored cars, at least at the time, was not as well protected. In fact, in forty-eight years, there have only been three other attacks using an IED placed upon the roof of a car known to have occurred worldwide.

The old adage about the best way to keep secrets appears to have been applied here with the detonation of the device right as it was placed. First, it prevents the protective detail from taking evasive action in hopes of causing the device to slide off. Second, in having a person standing by, most likely from an elevated position in order to keep an eye on things, the adversary gets the advantage usually reserved only for the suicide bombing attack, that being no need for an escape route. In the end this simple and flexible method of attack achieved its goal.

227

NIHAT ERIM: JULY 19, 1980, SATURDAY, 1050, ISTANBUL, TURKEY

Nihat Erim, the former prime minister of Turkey, was assassinated by members of the Dev Sol terror organization. The ambush was sprung when two men open fired, killing Erim in his car as well as his chauffeur/bodyguard. In a publication by revolutionaries in 1996, the entire operation was described in detail.

The Dev Sol terror organization first learned early in the summer of 1980 that Nihat Erim was staying in Istanbul. Upon obtaining this information, they immediately began conducting reconnaissance of the area in an effort to confirm. Within a short period of time they were able to identify the location where Erim was residing. Dev Sol then dispatched a surveillance team consisting of one man and one woman.

As Mr. Erim's apartment was located near the beach in a quiet neighborhood of Istanbul, the surveillance team used the ruse of a young couple enjoying a vacation at the beach. Using this ruse, they were able to maintain surveillance on Mr. Erim's apartment for approximately one week. However, due to the placement of the apartment in relation to the beach, the surveillance team was not able to monitor the front of the residence for extended periods of time without the possibility of someone becoming suspicious. This forced the team to periodically walk up and down the sidewalk in front of the apartment in order to maintain a visual.

The surveillance eventually provided the team the knowledge that Mr. Erim shared the apartment with his wife and a female servant. They also discovered that he did not routinely leave his apartment, but when he did, he was always in the company of his chauffeur/bodyguard. The Dev Sol operatives, however, did note that when traveling through Istanbul, the chauffeur always took the same route. This route passed by a small military post consisting of approximately five soldiers, thereby providing a small measure of security. Additionally, the area of Mr. Erim's residence was routinely patrolled by police vehicles.

After the week of surveillance, the Dev Sol operatives learned that Mr. Erim enjoyed a daily swim in the ocean at a nearby beach club. While the club was only 400–500 meters away from the residence, both Mr. Erim and his bodyguard traveled the distance by vehicle. They generally departed the residence between 1045 and 1100. Mr. Erim would enter through a private entrance into the club for the swim (this portion of the ocean and beach was apparently closed off from the general public), then return home in the same manner.

Armed with their surveillance information, the Dev Sol team began to formulate their attack plan. Ultimately, they prepared two plans of attack. The first involved a four-man hit team that would arrive to the area by car. One of the men was assigned as the driver, who would remain in the car, and a second man would act as security for the hit team. The other two men, one being the team leader, would move to kill the bodyguard first, and then they would "punish" Mr. Erim. The team planned on not harming Mrs. Erim should she be present at the time of the attack. The two shooters were armed with Browning 9mm pistols with fourteen-round magazines in addition to two Browning 7.65mm pistols for backup. The ambush was planned to occur when Mr. Erim and his chauffeur arrived at the beach club. A secondary or backup plan was also developed so that if the first failed, or could not be put into action, they were still in a position to carry out the attack. The second plan consisted of the terrorists opening fire on Mr. Erim's car while he traveled, but only if his wife wasn't with him.

The Dev Sol hit team spent four days in the area awaiting the opportunity to carry out the attack. On the first day, two of the team members arrived in the area of the residence around the 1000 hour. Each man was carrying a beach bag with normal beach gear and had arrived from opposite directions. A third man, who was the driver, remained in the car positioned nearby. The last man also walked in on foot from another direction, and was also carrying a beach bag with beach gear as well as three pistols. Additionally, he had the fourth pistol tucked into his pants behind his back. All four team members met together at a location near Mr. Erim's apartment; however, a police unit was patrolling in the area and did not appear to be leaving, which resulted in the attack being called off for the day.

The next day, the team met at the beach and waited for Mr. Erim to leave his apartment. On this occasion, he departed ten minutes later than usual, and he traveled a different route to the club. This forced the team to consider two options: (1) wait at the entrance to the club for Erim to leave (this would be difficult to do without raising suspicion) or (2) abort the attack for the day. They opted to abort and try again the following day.

On the third day, the team decided to carry out the secondary plan. As Mr. Erim left his house in his car, one of the team members crossed the street as a lookout, while the other three sat in the car parked nearby. As Mr. Erim's car approached the kill zone, another car with women and children approached, preventing the plan from being employed without putting them in harm's way. The attack was aborted yet again.

On the fourth day, the team met up at a nearby café. This time the four were disguised as construction workers. While at the café, they had tea and made conversation consistent with that of men in that line of work. They departed the café, and the driver left and parked his vehicle at a predetermined location. The other three men then walked toward the beach area near the club to wait. As the time drew near, the four men (the driver had met up with them at some point) took their weapons and concealed them in their pants behind their backs. They then departed the beach en route to the attack site in groups of two. Two went toward the parked car, while the other two went to a nearby kiosk and ordered some refreshments. This kiosk allowed the two men to have a good view of the front of Erim's home.

At 1050 hours, Mr. Erim left his apartment with his chauffeur as was their routine. The driver for the hit team opened the door of his car as though he were waiting for someone to get in. The second man waited near some tennis players, securing the area. The other assassins began their final approach to the entrance of the beach club. As the two men waited near the club, a member of the club's security approached and inquired as to what they were doing there, telling them they could not loiter in the area. The two men began a discussion with the security guard using a ruse of wanting to go into the club.

At right about that point, Mr. Erim's car arrived at the club entrance. The bodyguard got out of the car and immediately yelled for the two men to leave the area. One of the two assassins challenged the bodyguard, saying they could be there if they wanted. The second gunman approached, at which point the bodyguard reached for his weapon. One of the gunmen drew his weapon and fired two 9mm rounds into the bodyguard, killing him. The two assassins then approached Mr. Erim, who was still inside of the car, and shot and killed him at nearly point blank range. Mrs. Erim was in the car at the time and began screaming, but was not harmed. The two assassins quickly fled the scene, after taking the bodyguard's weapon and getting into the waiting car. They picked up their security man along the way and rapidly fled the scene. They dumped the car not far away, and transferred to another car.

Unknowns

1. The presence of any recent threats to Mr. Erim
2. Whether Mr. Erim's bodyguard had employed any sort of surveillance detection, and if he had even detected or had been suspicious of any surveillance
3. Had any other people/residents of the area reported suspicious activity
4. The level of autonomy the bodyguard had to make last-minute changes to their travel plans

Offensive Point of View

From the view of the aggressor, Mr. Erim, as is often the case, assisted the enemy in targeting. While he did not leave his villa often, he did have a routine, which was practiced almost daily, that of visiting the athletic club. However, the position of the front door of the villa made it difficult to closely monitor any arrivals or departures without being too suspicious. The use of a male-female surveillance team was a wise move, as it almost immediately removes a major portion of any thoughts of malevolence (at least from those without an intelligence, military, or law enforcement background). Further, the apartment's location near an area popular with the general public assisted in providing cover for the operatives in the area.

Defensive Point of View

From this study, it appears that the selection of the villa provided a fair amount of security and should have assisted in surveillance detection. Steps were taken to travel routes along known military outposts, which probably assisted in preventing attacks. However, as we have seen in other parts of the world, the presence of a military post is not always the deterrent some might believe. While the daily routine was obviously an issue that the protective detail had to deal with, the use of a vehicle to travel the short distance between the apartment and the club was an effective means of providing a rapid evacuation of the area as well as some measure of cover and concealment.

Analysis

This attack highlights not only the steps some will take to accomplish their mission, but also their level of patience. It also reveals, as other attacks have, missed opportunities to detect the presence of hostile surveillance. Had the protective detail maintained some sort of database of what was seen, when, and by whom, then perhaps the sudden appearance of a male and female continually wandering down the street could have been detected as suspicious. The presence of four men, first as beachgoers, then as construction workers, might also have been detected.

Regardless of what, if anything, could have been detected, the fatal error was made by the chauffeur/bodyguard when he exited his vehicle and engaged in the verbal challenge of the two assassins. If he had the authorization to make the decision, he should have remained in the car and driven off, either returning to the residence, driving to the nearby military post, or at the very least, looping out of the area and back. Unfortunately, that mistake caused two men to lose their lives.

AIREY NEAVE: MARCH 30, 1979, FRIDAY, LONDON, ENGLAND

Member of Parliament Airey Neave, who was sixty-three years old, was assassinated by an explosive device attached to his car by the Irish National Liberation Army (INLA). The four-man team who carried out the attack had kept Neave under surveillance for several weeks, allowing them to make note of his travel route and routines. At some point, the assassins were able to gain access to his vehicle. Thereupon, they affixed an improvised explosive device (IED) consisting of approximately a half pound of an unknown explosive material equipped with a wrist watch that, at the predetermined time, activated a mercury tilt switch, allowing for the device to detonate. This allowed the bombers to arm the device at their chosen time. In this case, the device was armed when the vehicle was parked under the House of Commons at Westminster. When the timer activated the device, the mercury switch triggered the explosive as Neave drove up the five-story ramp to exit the Old Palace Yard parking structure. The blast caused the roof and hood to buckle outwards, but did not immediately kill Mr. Neave.

After the attack, the INLA made at least two claims of responsibility, during which they detailed how the attack went down as well as the construction of the device. While it is not known when or where the device was attached to Neave's car, the attack occurred within two days of a new moon. It is reasonable to assume that the placement occurred during the hours of darkness, which considering the lack of moonlight, would have been an ideal time. However, through the investigation it was determined that the device was attached to Mr. Neave's vehicle, a blue Vauxhall Cavalier, through the use of magnets, which would have allowed for a very quick install. The device was placed in the front portion of the car, near the driver's seat.

Unknowns

1. Known recent threats or suspicions of possible surveillance of Mr. Neave
2. The location of Mr. Neave's residence and where his vehicle was kept during hours of darkness

Analysis

Attacks by way of the booby-trap device are a relatively rare occurrence, but are an extremely effective method. In this attack, the use of a mercury switch added a level of complexity that hadn't been seen before. Mr. Neave, who was one of then-Prime Minister Thatcher's close advisors, was also a man that could be considered a hard target, even at his age. This may have been part of the decision by the INLA to employ such a device. Mr. Neave was a former member of Britain's MI9, a group during WWII that was responsible for organizing POW escapes. In fact, it was reported that he was so effective that

231

Adolf Hitler had personally added Mr. Neave to a hit list. Afterwards, he maintained his links to some degree with MI5, Britain's domestic intelligence organization, and MI6, the foreign intelligence organization. Prior to his death, Mr. Neave had been a vocal critic of the various Irish rebel groups.

After revelations by the INLA, it is very obvious that there were missed opportunities to detect the coming hostile action. By their own admission, they had kept Mr. Neave under surveillance for a considerable amount of time as they mapped his routes and routines. While their methods of surveillance in this case aren't known, the Irish groups were by no means amateurs, but then, neither was Mr. Neave. However, in a dense urban environment such as London, surveillance, when being conducted by an experienced crew, can be difficult to detect even by the best trained individual.

This case also provides bitter proof that no one person can remain "on" indefinitely, and it only requires that one missed opportunity for the situation to turn 180 degrees against you.

Interestingly enough, these attacks can be easily detected if a person spends the time to visually inspect his or her vehicle (and therein lies the problem). However, most people, even those that know they may be the target of an attack, do not spend the time to do this. The likelihood of this type of attack can be greatly lessened by parking the vehicle in secured areas, such as garages, while at home and at the office. In many parts of the world, especially the urban city environments, this is often not an option, resulting in people parking their cars out on the street.

Given an extended period of time, a bomber can place the device anywhere on the car with a variety of triggering mechanisms; however, it is important to remember that the target of the attack is generally going to be seated in the driver's seat. A bomber therefore is going to want to focus the device within that general area, and wants to be able to quickly install the bomb and walk away, reducing the chances of detection by the target or a third party. This therefore decreases the number of areas needed to be visually searched prior to driving away in a vehicle, making quick checks of a vehicle after leaving it unattended for a period of time easier.

Today, with many of the modern cars made of carbon fiber or composite material, coupled with the undercarriage being encapsulated, the level of difficulty from a bomber's point of view is increased. This may result in a decrease in the type of devices that are simply slapped on, such as that used in this attack.

FRANCISCO JOSE GUERRERO: NOVEMBER 28, 1989, TUESDAY, 0940, SAN SALVADOR, EL SALVADOR

Francisco Jose Guerrero, the former president of the Supreme Court of El Salvador, was assassinated. The attack occurred as he was driving his daughter-in-law, who sat in the front passenger seat, to her office at the San Salvador judicial center. Also in car was Senor Guerrero's only protective member, seated in the back seat (the second bodyguard never showed up the morning of the attack). As his vehicle came to a stop at the intersection of Boulevard de Los Héroes and Alameda Juan Pablo II, in front of the "Biggest" restaurant, a yellow Volkswagen pulled up behind. As the cars came to a stop, three men quickly exited the VW; one positioned himself behind Guerrero's car, and one ran up to the left side, with another on the right. All three men open fired just as the bodyguard in the back seat, Rivera Monterrosa, began to react.

Monterrosa immediately began firing with his M-16, followed by his .357-caliber revolver, continuing the counterattack even after being wounded, and successfully killed one of the attackers. Mr. Guerrero was struck by five .45-caliber rounds believed to have been fired from a revolver (as the weapon was recovered later by police and apparently matched ballistics). Two of the men fled the scene, one whose body was later recovered with M-16 wounds. The third was never identified.

Mr. Guerrero's daughter-in-law survived the attack, as did Rivera Monterrosa. At the time of the attack, Mr. Guerrero was investigating the massacre of Jesuit priests.

Unknowns

1. Whether he traveled the same route everyday or often
2. If there was cross traffic or vehicles stopped in front of Guerrero preventing him from driving off

Analysis

The adversaries made dramatic use of the traffic intersection to effectively trap their quarry. Attacks employing firearms against unarmored vehicles stuck in an area of traffic are an extremely effective tactic on the part of the adversary. It creates exactly what every ambush site seeks: an area in which the target cannot escape, while at the same time providing an area to concentrate hostile fire. While the principal was ultimately killed in the attack, this graphically demonstrates just how effective a well-armed protective member can be when placed in the rear seat. Having the entire rear seat of a vehicle in which to work from, an armed protective member has the largest field of fire available from inside of a car (especially since he or she would no longer be concerned with the rear window).

While this type of ambush provides the adversary a level of flexibility in that the attack can be initiated at any point along the route, it still requires the assassins to conduct some type of preattack operational surveillance to determine the routes traveled by the target, as well as potential attack sites along the way. While hostiles could stage this attack at any location, the more time they spend tracking the target along their route waiting for the right opportunity, the more chances of their being detected. For this reason, they would want to have identified points along the traveled routes that are ideal for their purposes. While limiting their need to be within close proximity to their target for extended periods of time, this increases their chances of success in that they only have to close the distance as they approach the ambush site.

SIEGFRIED BUBACK: APRIL 7, 1977, THURSDAY, 0900 (APPROX.), KARLSRUHE, GERMANY

West German chief federal prosecutor Dr. Siegfried Buback was assassinated by members of the Red Army Faction (RAF). Buback was traveling from his residence to his office in his Mercedes, driven by his chauffeur, Wolfgang Göbel, along with Georg Wurster, a judicial official. As his vehicle passed a gas station on the side of Linkenheimer Highway, a motorcycle with two riders pulled out.

After traveling a distance of not more than 100 meters, Buback's vehicle came to a stop for a red light at the intersection of Moltkestrasse. The motorcycle with the two riders approached from behind and pulled up alongside of the Mercedes. As it did, the second rider on the motorcycle fired at least fifteen rounds using a large-caliber automatic weapon (possibly an H&K 53A3 assault rifle with either a collapsible or removed stock in 5.56 caliber) into the car, killing all three men. With the driver dead, the Mercedes drifted across the intersection onto the sidewalk. The motorcycle made a quick right turn and fled the scene, later dumping the bike under an overpass nearby. The two riders apparently escaped into a waiting car, where they were driven to another nearby town, and that car was dumped.

The RAF claimed responsibility for the attack. Buback had previously publicly vowed to eradicate the Red Army Faction; however, this was the first instance of the RAF targeting a senior member of the government. Four members of the RAF were ultimately convicted of the killing; however, the identity of the shooter was never officially discovered.

Unknowns

1. If the times and the routes taken by Buback's driver were habitual
2. If any threats had been received prior to the attack
3. If an armored car or protective detail was available

Analysis

Herr Buback has the dubious honor of being the first victim, at least in my research, of a motorcycle-bound hit team. Since that time, it has been used around the world by organized crime families, terrorist organizations, and possibly even government agents with considerable lethal effectiveness. The motorcycle provides a hit team with several benefits. First, motorcycles are numerous, and are often difficult to see in side- and rear-view mirrors. They offer a rapid means of approach to and escape from an ambush site. Armed with a compact submachine gun, the passenger can easily conceal the weapon between his body and that of the driver without looking suspicious. Wearing full leathers (as is common in Europe) coupled with full helmets provides a great degree of concealment of identity, again without being suspicious. Further, in times of heavy traffic, the motorcycle provides the hit team with the ability to move in on their target while the target is essentially "stuck." A static target with no room to maneuver also provides a certain degree of safety for the hit team, as it negates most potential vehicle countermoves a driver might wish to employ.

While this was the first time a senior member of the West German government had been targeted, the RAF had conducted at least three high-profile attacks prior to this. Further, Buback had been vocal about his targeting and goal of eradication of the RAF; therefore, even with a lack of threats, some sort of precautions should have been employed beyond just a driver.

From a defensive point of view, given the overall lack of traffic, evasive maneuvers could have been employed had the threat been detected early enough. Unfortunately, lacking any sort of armed protective detail or armored vehicle, the ultimate outcome would have probably been the same given the inherent flexibility a motorcycle has coupled with the firepower at the team's disposal. This was an easy hit for such an important man.

Of the twenty-nine ambushes using a motorcycle-bound hit team reviewed by this author, twenty-three, or over 79%, came in the form of two people on a bike. The two-person team is logically the best way to employ this method, as it allows one person to focus on the road while the second person can focus on conducting the hit. While it is not uncommon for two people to be riding on the same bike at one time, it is rare enough that any person who is a member of a protective detail, or involved in some manner with counterterrorism, organized crime, or narcotic investigations, take note and should pay slightly more attention to the approach.

LUIS CARRERO BLANCO: DECEMBER 20, 1973, THURSDAY, 0950 (APPROX.), MADRID, SPAIN

Prime Minister Luis Carrero Blanco, his chauffeur, Don Jose Mojeda, and bodyguard, Police Inspector Juan Fernandez, were killed as his Dodge Dart 3700 GT passed over an improvised explosive device. That morning, as was his routine, he departed his home and was driven the 300 yards to the San Francisco de Borja Church on Calle de Serrano for morning mass. Approximately forty-five minutes later, he was again in his car, heading to his office located on Paseo de la Castellana. Leaving the church, his motorcade traveled south on Calle de Serrano (a one-way street) until it made a left on Calle de Juan Bravo (also a one-way street), then an immediate left onto Calle de Claudio Coello.

As Blanco and his detail reached the rear of the San Francisco de Borja Church, at the intersection of Calle de Maldonado the improvised explosive device containing approximately 80 to 100 kilograms of Goma dynamite (attached to some 200 meters of electric det cord along with at least two detonators) was detonated. The device had been cached inside a seven-meter-wide room at the end of a tunnel that had been excavated under Calle de Claudio Coello. In order to assist the triggerman, the ETA terrorists had double-parked a car along Calle de Claudio Coello just past the intersection with Calle de Maldonado, forcing the motorcade to slow down near the device. To further assist the triggerman in correctly timing the device, a vertical line had been painted on a wall. This allowed the triggerman to correctly time triggering the device in correlation to the target's rate of travel. The force of the explosion catapulted the armored Dodge Dart over the five-story

San Francisco de Borga Church, where it landed on the second-floor balcony. A thirty-five-foot hole was left at the blast sight, which rapidly filled with water and sewage.

To trigger the device, the terrorists had run the electric det cord from the explosives back across the street to a room previously rented by ETA. From here it was stretched along the entire distance of Calle de Claudio Coello alongside of the existing exterior telephone lines, where it ended at a trigger box concealed inside of a briefcase.

The investigation into the matter found that some eight weeks prior to the attack, two ETA men posing as sculptors had rented a basement room at 104 Calle de Claudio Coello, across the street and within sight of the church. Once inside, ETA began to tunnel under the road that Blanco routinely traveled. It was also discovered that the original operational plan had been to kidnap Blanco; however, through their surveillance they deemed the protective detail to be effective and decided to use a bombing attack to kill Blanco.

Analysis

It would be difficult to find another attack that involved more planning and required more on-site effort by the aggressors than this one. It is one of the few bombings in which the device was literally constructed at the attack site. This attack also reaffirms the dangers involved in becoming a creature of habit. Blanco was known to be a man of habitual patterns, and in the end, it cost him his life and the lives of his protective detail.

As a result of the investigation, it was learned that ETA had conducted surveillance on its target. Given the stature of this target, there is little doubt that this surveillance would have taken a considerable period of time to complete. It would have included time spent watching his residence, his office, his daily route, as well as routinely visited locations. All of this presented opportunities for the detection of the surveillance, which in this case appears to have been missed or, worse, not acted upon.

The problem with this attack, from the perspective of a protective detail, is that it occurred within the "backyard" of the prime minister's residence. Although to be fair, at the time of this attack, ETA was still relatively new and had only conducted a few small-scale attacks, none of which were bombings. That being said, it is evident that even in the early years, ETA already had an understanding of the benefits of striking outside of the immediate area of its target's residence or office.

In this case, the aggressors made the maximum use of concealment as they went about implementing their plan. First, they identified the habit of Blanco that provided them the opportunity to conduct their bombing attack. Then they proceeded to obtain a basement apartment using the ruse of sculptors looking for a place to live and work. By using a "cover for activity" of sculptors, the aggressors successfully removed or reduced the potential of a local citizen reporting their hammering and chiseling as suspicious activity to law enforcement. However, the earth that was excavated would have had to have been moved out of the location and was perhaps hidden inside of the apartment. By selecting an attack site that sits behind the church and out of view of Blanco's official residence, they further enhanced their concealment.

This attack represents the first time that explosives were set under a roadway to be traveled by the target, and the only one in which the attackers tunneled under the roadway. In fact, even today, some three decades later it is an exceedingly rare occurrence (within an urban environment not experiencing a war), having occurred only about four times (and those were buried in a drainpipe or culvert). The most probable reason for this is the simplicity with which a VBIED can be employed. As illustrated in this attack, and more recently with what has occurred in the Iraq war, buried explosives can and are extremely devastating when employed. Even armored cars have difficulty negating or deflecting the blast force from this type of placement.

Another issue for protective details that this case identifies is dealing with one-way streets. The presence of these prevented Blanco's protective team from periodically changing their travel route. In fact, even if the trip to the church was removed from the travel plans, the one-way streets still required the motorcade to travel past the front of the church and prevented the detail from taking more than a couple of routes, thereby causing an "environmental routine" (an issue that remains to this day in that area of Madrid). Given what has been learned over the past three decades, as well as the level of protectee, today the streets would most likely be temporarily shut down for the brief period needed to travel against the flow of traffic. But for those teams and potential targets lacking the needed status to close down one-way streets, this is a critical issue that must be fully realized.

ALDO MORO: MARCH 16, 1978, THURSDAY, 0900 (APPROX.), ROME, ITALY

Former prime minister Aldo Moro was kidnapped and later murdered by members of the Red Brigades. After leaving his home at 79 via del Forte Trionfale, Moro traveled in his chauffeur-driven (by Officer Domenico Ricci) unarmored blue Fiat 130 en route to the Church of Santa Chiara for morning mass, as was his almost daily ritual. From there Moro would travel to his office at the Italian parliament. Accompanying Moro and his chauffeur was his bodyguard, Officer Oreste Leonardi. Additionally, the follow car (an Alfa Romeo Alfretta saloon) sat three other bodyguards, all of whom were police officers.

The two-vehicle motorcade drove down via Mario Fani through the hotel district and approached the intersection with via Stresa (approximately 1.3 kilometers from Maro's residence). Nearby a blonde woman was standing with a man watching the approach of the motorcade. As the cars slowed for the four-way-stop-sign-controlled intersection, one of the two pedestrians signaled the start of the ambush. A Fiat 128 with diplomatic plates pulled ahead of Moro's Fiat and suddenly came to a halt at the intersection. As a result, the chauffeur had to brake suddenly, causing the follow security car to strike the rear end of Moro's car, which rear ended the blocking vehicle. Witnesses also reported a man on a motorcycle, but it is not known what role he played in the attack.

The male driver and female passenger of the blocking vehicle both exited and acted as though they were going to check their car for damage. These two, however, one armed with a submachine gun, quickly shot Moro's chauffeur and first bodyguard, both of whom were still in the front seat of the car, killing them. At approximately the same time, four men dressed in Alitalia uniforms pulled out automatic weapons from their flight bags and fired upon the follow security vehicle. These men had been at the intersection as though awaiting a bus, when the staged accident occurred. Two of the security guards were killed

237

instantly. The third rolled out onto the street and was able to fire three shots before being killed (which in one report came by a sniper positioned on an adjacent roof).

A third car waiting nearby the attack site quickly drove up, and Moro was forced into the car. The woman and man, along with the four airline-pilot-disguised shooters, got into one of the three cars, and all fled the scene (at least ten terrorists involved). The entire attack was estimated to have been completed in approximately thirty seconds. Through the investigation it was found that at least sixty rounds were fired from weapons manufactured in the Soviet Union as well as Czechoslovakia and Italy.

One of the cars used by the terrorists was located approximately 100 meters away on via Lucinio Calvo. The day after the ambush, a second car was recovered on via Lucinio Calvo. Moro's body was recovered in the trunk of a car approximately two months after the ambush. Through the investigation it was discovered that Moro had not been the original target. The Red Brigade terrorist organization had originally targeted another individual. That unknown individual drove in an armored car, with heavily armed bodyguards following in a second armored car. The routes were changed constantly.

During the initial surveillance process conducted by the Red Brigades, they decided that he was too difficult of a target, and therefore selected the weaker Moro. He and his protective detail had five routes used in their travel. Unfortunately, it is believed that Moro may have identified which route was to be taken in advance. On May 9, Moro was executed by eleven rounds from a Czechoslovakian Skorpian submachine gun (7.62mm).

Unknowns

1. Whether there had been any intelligence information suggesting he was being targeted
2. Whether potential hostile surveillance had been detected prior to the attack

Analysis

Perhaps one of the most famous of targeted attacks ever carried out, this also represents one of the most educational for those in protective operations. This attack was extremely well thought out, where the adversary took advantage of a number of factors that were to its benefit. In this ambush, the Red Brigades employed one of the first documented uses of an intercept technique that takes advantage of a tactic employed by motorcades, that of following each other closely. By causing the motorcade vehicles to slam into each other, the adversary in effect obtains its own blocking vehicle by way of the last protective vehicle.

Another problem for the protective detail or target that was revealed in this ambush was that of having only a limited number of routes in which to travel between the residence and office. This problem is further exacerbated by the large percentage of one-way streets found in Rome, as well as Europe as a whole, although the attack occurred on a two-way street, each side of which consisted of a single lane. The adversaries also used to their advantage the momentary confusion following any traffic collision, allowing them to exit their vehicle, deploy their weapons, and open fire upon the protective detail members before they were even out of their vehicle (this can even be more of an issue in the modern era with the advent of air bags, causing more disorientation and delay).

Apparently Moro's protective detail had previously made several requests for armored vehicles, which had gone unanswered. Unfortunately, there was little for a protective detail to do short of immediately deploying from the attack vehicles and attempt to lay down overwhelming fire. The problem with this type of response by police officers, however, is their need to be aware of nearby civilians. This can severely limit the response, which is yet another benefit to the adversary.

8

Case Studies of Attacks on Pedestrians

EDGAR GOMEZ: MAY 8, 2008, THURSDAY, 0230, MEXICO CITY, MEXICO

Edgar Millan Gomez, the third highest-ranking member of Mexico's public safety secretariat, was assassinated. The attack occurred as he arrived home from work and was in the process of entering his residence. When he turned on the interior lights, he was shot eight times by a lone gunman wearing latex gloves and armed with a suppressed pistol (possibly a .38-caliber weapon). Señor Gomez's two bodyguards were also injured in the attack, but were quickly able to subdue the assassin.

In the subsequent investigation it was revealed that the attack had come at the order of the Sinaloa cartel. Just the week before the murder, Señor Gomez had held a news conference announcing the arrest of twelve Sinaloa cartel hitmen. Three men and two women were ultimately arrested for the attack. The believed leader of the five was a serving federal police officer by the name of Jose Antonio Montes Garfias. He had been assigned to a federal police unit in the northern state of Sinaloa since February, but had never reported to work during that period because he was on medical leave. He was also suspected in the killing of another federal officer days before Señor Gomez's death.

Unknowns

1. Any direct threats targeting Señor Gomez
2. Detection of possible surveillance or notice of suspicious activity
3. The security arrangements of Señor Gomez's residence

Analysis

This attack is rare among all of those studied, in that that the assassin selected an ambush site inside of the victim's residence. This can be profoundly risky to adversaries, as they generally have little to no knowledge of the layout of the home, or of the presence of an alarm system, guard dogs, or other family members. In this case, given the lateness of the

241

hour, the limited amount of lunar light (it was only three days past the new moon) may have provided the assassin the cover and time to make a covert entry.

Undoubtedly, the assassin in this attack was very professional. He surreptitiously entered the residence of a man known to have a protective detail and waited patiently inside for the arrival of his target. The type of weapon used in this attack, a small-caliber firearm equipped with a suppressor, could indicate a more highly trained individual, possibly even former military, certainly beyond your average drug cartel thug. What is apparent was that through its surveillance, the cell had determined that Señor Gomez's protective detail did not generally enter the residence, thus making the inside a better location to stage the ambush. All of the factors, from the time of hit, the location, and the weapon, would have made the task of quietly assassinating Señor Gomez and then escaping into the night very feasible.

It is attacks such as these that are the exception to the rule—that one can reduce their alertness once inside the safety of their home. The protective detail should have swept the house prior to Señor Gomez's arrival, if he allowed them to do so (which, given the level of violence being experienced at the time of the attack, should have been automatic). It is not known if an alarm system was present and had been bypassed, or if dogs or other warning methods had somehow been defeated. It also isn't known if this was Señor Gomez's normal time of arrival at home. What is clear is that some form of surveillance and reconnaissance was conducted by the five-person cell prior to the hit. While it isn't clear if any of this preoperational work had been detected by the protection operation, it does reveal opportunities that were either missed altogether or, worse, not acted upon.

LAKSHMAN KADIRGAMAR: AUGUST 12, 2005, FRIDAY, 2300, COLOMBO, SRI LANKA

The Sri Lankan foreign minister Lakshman Kadirgamar was assassinated while swimming at his home by two suspected Tamil Tiger terrorists. Mr. Kadirgamar had just returned to his residence at 36 Bullers Lane and decided to take a swim before retiring for the evening, as was his normal routine. Unbeknownst to Kadirgamar, inside a neighboring home, in the second-floor bathroom, two men were waiting with a sniper rifle. As Kadirgamar exited the pool, the sniper fired three rounds in quick succession from a distance of approximately 35 meters, all of which struck Kadirgamar. One of the five protective detail members who was collecting Kadirgamar's footwear saw him fall, but did not know Kadirgamar had been shot until he rushed over and saw the blood. The five-member detail rushed Mr. Kadirgamar to the hospital, but he was pronounced dead a little after midnight on August 13.

As a result of the subsequent investigation into the assassination, it was determined that the snipers had made use of a bathroom inside of a home right next door to Mr. Kadirgamar's. This home belonged to an elderly couple, who, due to the wife's paralysis, no longer went up to the upper level. Inside of the bathroom that overlooked Mr. Kadirgamar's pool area, the assassins constructed a tripod out of aluminum pipes approximately 7 feet in height that held the weapon as well as a seat for the sniper to sit on. The weapon was then aimed through a small vented window, some of which had apparently been removed to allow a clear line of sight and fire zone.

Police later recovered five 7.62mm shell casings along with the aluminum tripod that the snipers used as a platform to raise them up to the shooting position. Food items, as well as plastic bags containing urine and excreta, preventing the assassins from having to flush the toilet and alerting the elderly couple, were also found inside of the bathroom. Investigators also reported finding several cyanide capsules, a common item for Tamil assassins.

Immediately after the shooting, while the protective team of Mr. Kadirgamar transported him to the hospital, the killers fled the scene with their rifle and were able to make a successful escape. It was later revealed that an unknown Western intelligence agency had warned Mr. Kadirgamar that he was the target of an assassination plot that was to occur in August. Additionally, a request for more security by Mr. Kadirgamar was delayed until the day of his murder. The delay in forces securing the area, the searching of the adjacent home, the unknown intelligence, and the Tamil Tigers' denial of responsibility have led some to believe the killing was actually a government conspiracy.

Analysis

This is an astonishing case given the location of the sniper's nest. The close proximity between the nest and the kill site, and the fact that no shots were heard by any of the protective detail, would indicate the use of a suppressor, but with the weapon taken with the sniper team, this may never be known. The selection of the nest, however, was genius, as it was located deep inside of the area a protective team would be intimately aware of, but in a location that would normally be overlooked. The fact of the next door neighbors being a disabled elderly couple offered more in the way of operational camouflage, as it would not be difficult to imagine the detail lowering their guard somewhat with this residence.

If a suppressor was used, it would be reasonable for the protective team to perhaps overlook the house immediately next door as "too close" for a sniper attack. Not knowing where the shots were fired from could, at least initially, make it difficult for men on the ground to know with any certainty where to begin looking. However, the area surrounding the Kadirgamar residence is made up of two- and three-story buildings with moderate foliage consisting of bushes and trees. The lateness of the hour in which the attack occurred would have further served the assassins' escape while hampering the security response and investigation.

This case also reveals just how dangerous a highly trained sniper team can be. As any current or former snipers, or even those who have participated on extended static surveillance operations, can attest, long boring periods of time in a cramped location without being able to move or make noise takes considerable discipline. The patience and dedication this team displayed can only be described as impressive.

In this attack, the obvious missed opportunities for detection were the initial movement of the sniper team into their hiding place. Given the level of professionalism displayed by this team, the movement most likely came at an extremely late hour when the protective detail's level of alertness was at its lowest. With the pool located on the second level of the residence, the target was effectively placed in an open area inside of a gated and secured area, all of which can give a false sense of security, which the sniper team used to their benefit.

This ambush also highlights the difficulties that can be faced by a protective detail. While the government was quick to name the Tamil Tigers as responsible for the attack, their denial of responsibility only serves to cause confusion. If the Tigers were in fact behind this assassination, it represents the one and only instance of their use of a sniper team to conduct a targeted attack. It the Tigers were responsible, then they took advantage of their lack of employment of specific techniques to circumvent a protective detail's preparations and expectations of the method of attack that might be encountered.

ANDREI KOZLOV: SEPTEMBER 13, 2006, WEDNESDAY, 2100, MOSCOW, RUSSIA

Two unknown individuals assassinated Andrei Kozlov, the first deputy chairman of Russia's Central Bank. The attack came as Kozlov and his driver/bodyguard were leaving the Moscow sports stadium after attending a game between bank employees. As Kozlov and his bodyguard, Alexander Semynov, approached and started to enter their Mercedes, two individuals waiting nearby approached and open fired upon both men with pistols, killing both Kozlov and Semynov. The gunmen quickly fled the scene in a waiting nearby car driven by a third accomplice.

A total of seven men were later arrested in connection to the killing. The man who ordered the killing was found to be a rival banker who had had his bank shut down by Kozlov. For four years leading up to the killing, Kozlov as deputy chairman of the Russian banking system, had been in the process of shutting banks down that were linked to organized crime and money laundering, and was pushing for increased transparency within the Russian banking system.

Unknowns

1. Any previous threats or attempts against Mr. Kozlov's life
2. Detection of any suspicious activity prior to the attack

Analysis

This was just one of the many deadly attacks that were staged as the target was in the process of entering a vehicle. Timing of an attack when this is occurring takes advantage of a temporary weakness for the victim. The reason being is as the target is seated inside, or in the process of entering a vehicle, he or she is by the nature of the movement severely hampered in making an immediate reaction to an ambush. A protective detail could easily be momentarily distracted as the principal is getting seated or even getting themselves seated.

In an ambush such as this, the only real option would be for immediate action on the part of the protective member. As two gunmen are approaching there would be little to no time to try and shield the principal, much less get in the vehicle and drive away. Like the classic military response to an ambush, the protective member would have to go on the offensive, immediately drawing his or her weapon and charging the attacking force while firing. As with any ambush, it is the worst-case scenario. The only goal is to inflict as much damage as possible to the attacking force.

EDWARD LAMPERT: JANUARY 10, 2003, FRIDAY, 1930, GREENWICH, CONNECTICUT

Edward Lampert, the chairman of ESL Investments (200 Greenwich Avenue), was kidnapped from the parking garage of his office by four masked gunmen, at least one of whom had a shotgun. The men had been waiting inside an SUV parked next to Lampert's car until he arrived. He was bound and blindfolded and forced into their SUV, where he was transported to a local motel. At the motel, he was handcuffed in a bathtub and held for approximately thirty hours before being released. On Saturday, the kidnappers made a ransom demand. Lampert, however, made a deal with the kidnappers and they released him. The police were quickly onto the kidnappers after they used one of his credit cards to order a pizza at the Days Inn motel where they were hiding out, over 50 miles from the site of the kidnapping. Investigators later discovered that the kidnappers, and in particular a former Marine, Renaldo Rose, had searched the Internet looking for the wealthiest people when they came across Lampert.

According to the investigation, Rose carefully planned out the kidnapping over a period of months. Using a notebook, he detailed the kidnapping and what would be needed to carry it out. Using the Internet, he was able to obtain pictures of Lampert to assist in identification. He then trained the other two men and one juvenile in how to carry out the operation. Prior to the kidnap, they ran a practice run in which a UPS truck was robbed. Rose purchased radios, body armor, plastic handcuffs, and masks for the job. They rented cars and switched the license plates. They were armed with one shotgun and one air gun. Prior to the kidnapping, Rose had followed Lampert for a period of several weeks. During the ordeal, they apparently told Lampert they had been hired to kill him for $1 million due to a bad business deal.

Unknowns

1. Had there been previous reports of suspicious activity?
2. Had Rose or any of his teammates been contacted by authorities prior to the kidnapping?
3. The level of security and protection provided by the building and its grounds
4. Availability of a protective detail afforded to Lampert
5. Security at the garage

Analysis

This is a classic case in which the target is thoroughly surveilled and researched by the kidnappers. The mastermind of this caper, Rose, surveilled Lampert for a considerable period of time, mapping out his route and routines, as well as in an effort to locate the ideal site for the abduction to occur. It was here, during this surveillance period, that Rose would have been susceptible to detection.

By striking at the time and location they did, Rose and his team were afforded several factors favorable to their operation. First, the location in the garage near Lampert's car allowed Rose to know exactly where Lampert would be at some point in the day. The lateness of the hour ensured that most employees would have left for the day, reducing the potential for witnesses. By staying hidden in their SUV parked near Lambert's vehicle, Rose and his team had the ability to set up their ambush with little chance of being noticed. After the abduction occurred, it would be only a couple of turns that the SUV could disappear into the night, further reducing their chances of being found. The location of the building itself also provided some benefits to Rose and his team. The parking garage is a mere half mile down Greenwich Avenue from a major highway. This allows for a rapid escape out of the area.

Here again, with the benefit of hindsight, we see all the opportunities to have prevented this ambush. While research over the Internet cannot generally be detected, it is important for any security unit to be aware of what is available regarding their executives/protectees. As previously stated, the act of surveillance on Lampert was the time that detection would have most likely succeeded. While most people are not security/surveillance conscious, a company's security unit, had they been so tasked, would/could have most likely picked up on it (especially given this was a one-vehicle follow).

Author's Note: In preparing for this case study I was able to locate a fair amount of information on Lampert, as well as some of his top executives, via the Internet. On one publicly available document I found out not only the names of Lampert's top two executives, but also their home addresses. Clearly the years that have past since the kidnapping have dulled their sense of self-preservation.

ANTONIO ESPOSITO: JUNE 21, 1978, WEDNESDAY, 0834, GENOA, ITALY

Police commissioner and former antiterrorist squad chief Antonio Esposito was assassinated by three members of the Red Brigades. The attack came after Mr. Esposito had boarded a bus, as he did everyday en route to his office. At that same time a woman had also boarded the bus and had taken a seat near the bus driver. The bus continued along its route, during which it made an unknown number of stops to pick up additional passengers. At two separate bus stops, two other men had boarded.

As Mr. Esposito was reading his paper, one of the two men yelled out "Esposito" and, from a distance of approximately 2 feet, fired his Nagant 7.65mm revolver, striking Esposito in the chest and neck. The second man, using a 9mm pistol, fired two rounds, striking Esposito in the abdomen and groin area. As the other passengers began reacting with horror and fear, the woman who had boarded originally with Esposito had moved in and was standing directly behind the driver. She yelled for the driver to stop the bus. When the bus came to a stop, the two men and one woman dashed out, but not before one of them fired two more rounds, both of which struck Esposito. They then fled in a waiting vehicle.

Unknowns

1. If there had been any previous threats to his life
2. If he had previously noted the presence of possible surveillance
3. If he was armed at the time of his murder
4. The availability of a protective detail

Analysis

On the basis of the information obtained on this attack, it is evident that the Red Brigades had conducted surveillance of Commissioner Esposito for some time. However, given the environment of mass transit, it would have been difficult for him to have detected any sort of passive surveillance. This also illustrates some of the dangers that mass transit presents to law enforcement. The combination of relatively tight quarters and large groups of strangers all doing the same thing at the same time and at the same location makes threat/surveillance detection exceedingly difficult.

Additionally, mass transit violates the single most important rule of protective work, that of avoiding routines. While there is no getting around the starting and ending location of one's residence and office, the times and routes taken between those two points can and should differ greatly. By taking the bus, Commissioner Esposito allowed the Red Brigade terrorists to know the exact start and end locations, as well as almost the exact times their target would be there, in addition to points along the route. Unfortunately in this case, Commissioner Esposito compounded his predicament by not practicing any situational awareness as he read his morning newspaper, thereby assisting the assassins.

The bus that Commissioner Esposito traveled in allowed riders to enter from three locations, the traditional front of the bus, the middle, as is common today, and a third entrance at the extreme back. While Esposito's location on the bus was not known, ideally in most situations, as far back in the bus as possible would have provided more opportunity for a threat to be detected. It would also prevent any would-be assassin from taking a position from behind.

In this case, however, it may have been preferable to stand somewhere toward the front at an angle (if allowed). If armed, could Esposito have gotten to his weapon in time? Given the time of day, it is not unreasonable to believe that the bus was packed with people traveling to work. This would have provided ample cover for the assassins to casually reach for their weapons, just prior to calling Esposito's name. This "jump" on the draw would have greatly reduced any effective reaction by Esposito had he not been reading the newspaper and was on his guard. To further complicate any potential response, at least from the point of view of any law enforcement officer, the number of innocent civilians on the bus would have made returning fire against the killers difficult at best.

At the time of this killing, the trial of Red Brigades founder Renato Curcio had been in progress. Commissioner Esposito had arrested Giuliano Naria, who was one of the forty-five defendants in the case and who also had been involved in the prior assassination of Genoa prosecutor Francesco Coco. Even in the event that the police had no information regarding threats to their members, it would have behooved Commissioner Esposito to have practiced a little more forethought in his own safety. Given that there was a high-profile trial going on against a violent terrorist organization in which he had personally been involved in the arrest of one of the subjects, coupled with his being the former antiterror chief, he should have realized that he was a viable target for retribution.

Prior to this, the Red Brigades had kidnapped Aldo Moro in an extremely bold attack and had assassinated a sitting judge, cases which Esposito had investigated. Esposito has the dubious honor of being the first person, at least to this author's knowledge, to be targeted on a form of mass transit in Italy, or anywhere else for that matter. He was also the first law enforcement member to be targeted by the Red Brigades, although they would go on and target at least three other chiefs, two successfully.

While not common, the targeting of law enforcement officers is certainly not a rare event. This case graphically illustrates the need of members of the law enforcement community to be "on" when they step outside of the doors of their office or residence, especially for those involved in counterterrorism, narcotics, gang, or organized crime investigations, past and present.

ZORAN DJINDJIC: MARCH 12, 2003, WEDNESDAY, 1230, BELGRADE, SERBIA

Zoran Djindjic, the prime minister of Serbia, was assassinated just outside a side entrance of the Serbian government building as he was in the process of exiting his vehicle. While surrounded by his protective detail and moving the short distance between his parked vehicle and the door, Mr. Djindjic was hit by two large-caliber rifle bullets, once in the chest and once in the stomach. A member of Mr. Djindjic's protective team was also injured in the attack. All eight members of the protective detail recall hearing three shots from two separate locations, leading many to believe there was another gunman hidden somewhere. As Mr. Djindjic fell, the team immediately moved him into the protection of the building.

During the subsequent investigation it was determined that the sniper fired from a position hidden in one of the rooms of the Institute of Photogrammetry building that was in the process of being renovated. The distance between the sniper's position and the government building is approximately 362.46 feet (at their closest points). If a second shooter was present, his or her location was never discovered.

The sniper was later captured and found to be a former elite police officer. The leader and mastermind of the assassination, a Mr. Legija was also later arrested and found to be a former member of the French Foreign Legion, as well as the commander of the elite Yugoslavian Red Beret Unit. Also involved in the killing were members of the Zemun mafia, a powerful local organized crime ring.

Mr. Djindjic and his protective detail were aware that he was being targeted by at least one criminal organization. In fact, the previous month his motorcade was the victim of an amateurish attack that took the form of a large truck ramming into the motorcade. It is unknown, but seemingly unlikely given the level of professionalism in the successful attack, whether these two attacks were linked.

Unknowns

1. If anything had been reported as suspicious activity at the photogrammetry building
2. If any surveillance had been detected at Djindjic's commonly visited locations (residence, office, etc.)

Analysis

The threat of a sniper is always problematic for a protective detail for a number of reasons. First and foremost, it vastly increases the distance between the assassin and the principal, thereby making detection difficult at best. Given this area of the world being heavily influenced by the former Soviet Union, it isn't a stretch of the imagination that the weapon used in this assassination was a Soviet Draganov sniper rifle. Regardless, whether it is a .308-caliber or 7.62mm weapon, they are effective out to 1,000 meters in trained hands. Second, soft body armor is not capable of preventing rounds of these and similar calibers. The heavy armor that could, would be or is generally refused by the principal given its bulkiness and the fact that it would have to be worn over the clothing, and is generally not practical.

It is common knowledge that most attacks occur in close proximity of a residence or office. Given that fact, it is critical for protective details to be fully aware of the potential threats that each site has. They need to know the area they are operating in like the back of their hand. What are its strengths and its weaknesses? In this case, Djindjic was a known target in an area that had suffered previous sniper assassinations, so therefore, the protective detail should have been prepared for just such a threat (it is not known if the protective detail had taken any steps regarding this type of threat). It is critical that members of a protective detail think like their adversary, identify the potential threat locations, and take steps to deal with those identified threat locations.

Defensive Point of View

The prime minister was making trips to the government building at least several times a week, if not every day. This represents one of the difficulties in protective operations, that of a forced routine. There are only so many routes to and from a location, and only so many ways to enter a specific building.

The detail on the day of the killing arrived at a side entrance on the north side, with an offload point approximately 20 feet away from the doorway, after ascending a small flight of steps. Their only exposure was from the building (Serbian parliament) north of their location (approximately 50 feet away), which shared the side street, as well as a building southeast of their location, and finally, the sniper's building of choice.

On the northeast side of the building, the area is covered by trees between the government building and an unknown building. They would have only been exposed on the northwest and southwest sides. However, it is unknown if this area allowed access to the building or if this was one of the entrances used, just not on the day of the assassination.

Offensive Point of View

This assassination is an excellent example of the use of a sniper. The positioning in the building provided an overlook of the target area, across an open field of grass and walkways.

The fact that the photogrammetry building is only three stories tall, the change in distance given the potential elevation changes would only amount, at most, to approximately 365 feet—well within the abilities of even an average police/military-trained sniper.

While some reports surmised that the sniper was on the roof of the building, given the training this individual likely had, he would have most probably positioned himself inside one of the rooms of the building and fired through an open window. With the remodel in progress, it most likely wouldn't have been unusual for windows to be open, thereby further adding to the camouflage. Further, with the remodel, the enforcement of not permitting individuals not usually granted access would have been considerably relaxed. However, given the now known links to law enforcement, this most likely wouldn't have been an issue.

The two rapid shots fired by the sniper would have made it difficult at best for the protective team to zero in on the sniper's location. Further, armed with only handguns and perhaps a few submachine guns, they would have been well beyond any effective range. The distance between the sniper's nest and the ambush location would have provided the necessary time for the hit team to quickly make their escape, especially given that the building abuts a large street.

If there had been a second sniper team positioned at a secondary location, it would have increased the protective detail's predicament considerably. A second shooter forces the detail to find cover and prevents them from identifying the location the attack is coming from. Additionally, it adds to the confusion if and when the detail begins calling for assistance. Whether used as a ruse or backup, the tactic as used in this circumstance was very effective.

LAWRENCE FOLEY: OCTOBER 28, 2002, MONDAY, 0720, AMMAN, JORDAN

Lawrence Foley, an American diplomat, was assassinated in front of his home in the Jordanian capital. Mr. Foley, who worked for the American Development Agency, was shot eight times from a suppressed 7mm pistol as he was in the process of entering his vehicle, which had been parked in the carport of his home in a residential area of Amman. His body was found adjacent to the driver's side door of his Mercedes by his wife shortly afterwards.

During the subsequent investigation it was discovered that none of the residents heard any shots being fired. It is believed by authorities that the killers in this attack were linked with Al-Zarqawi and were actively hunting for a target when they spotted Foley's diplomatic plates and surveilled him to his residence. The killers then waited until he left his home and conducted the attack. Much of this was confirmed after the arrest of the two assassins, who were still in possession of the murder weapon. Under interrogation, these two men admitted to carrying out the killing as well as being Al Qaida. They stated that they drove to Foley's residence in a rented car on the morning of the attack. One of the men hid behind Foley's car until he approached, at which time he stood and fired his suppressed weapon. The two men also admitted they targeted Mr. Foley in part due to his lack of a protective detail.

Unknowns

1. Reports of suspicious activity in and around Foley and his residence
2. Security details available to Foley
3. Current or recent threat assessments

Analysis

In Foley's case, he had to deal with several factors aligned against him from the beginning. First, he was an American living in a Middle Eastern country at a time when most of the region was extremely anti-American. Further, he was driving a vehicle with diplomatic plates that also happened to be painted red. The positioning of Foley's home in relation to his driveway, as well as the positioning of the landscaping, prevented Foley from observing any suspicious activity until it was too late.

While it is not known how Foley was ultimately identified as a target (i.e., a person in the neighborhood gave him up, the killers just stumbled upon him, etc.), it is reasonable to speculate that the killers were surveilling locations associated with Americans or Westerners. At some point Foley was spotted and surveilled to his residence. Foley's red car would have undoubtedly assisted in the surveillance by allowing the killers to remain back farther than if the car had been a more subtle gray, silver, or the like. It was also during this surveillance that Foley had his best opportunity to detect the follow.

Given the fact that none of the six shots were heard, it is presumed and later confirmed that suppressed weapons were used and that the killers were well trained and experienced. They therefore would have conducted this operation professionally, meaning detailed surveillance and research into their target's routes and routines. This again would have provided Foley and any potential security detail the best opportunity to detect the threat.

These missed opportunities were the best, perhaps even only, chance for Mr. Foley to have survived this attack. Being unarmed, and perhaps even untrained in any form of hand-to-hand combat, once he was in the kill zone around his car, there was little he could have done. Even if he had managed to overcome the initial attacker, the presence of a second gunman would have greatly complicated matters for Mr. Foley, not to mention that both gunmen may have very well been willing to sacrifice themselves to accomplish their goal.

WILHELMUS FORTYUN: MAY 6, 2002, MONDAY, DAYLIGHT HOURS, HILVERSUM, THE NETHERLANDS

Wilhelmus Simon Petrus "Pim" Fortuyn, a radical right-wing Dutch politician, was assassinated. As the fifty-four-year-old Dutch politician walked out of a radio interview to his vehicle in a parking lot, a man approached and shot Fortuyn six times in the neck, head, and chest with a 9mm pistol. The killer fled, but Fortuyn's chauffeur gave chase and assisted the police in capturing the killer.

The killer, later identified as Van der Graaf, explained his planning and methods for carrying out the attack during his interrogation. He said he had conducted searches of the

Internet for information on Fortuyn's appearance schedule. He then located a map and some photos of the area, known as Mediapark, where Fortuyn was going to be giving a radio interview. On the morning of the attack, Van der Graaf went to work as was usual, then took the afternoon off, at which point he traveled to Mediapark. Van der Graaf had a small pack containing the weapon, latex gloves, dark sunglasses, and a baseball cap with him.

Once at Mediapark, Van der Graaf walked in on foot until he found the building where the interview was taking place. More importantly, as he walked through the park, he recognized Fortuyn's Daimler in the parking lot. Van der Graaf waited in some bushes near the location for approximately two hours. During that time he had hidden his weapon in a plastic bag and buried it in a small hole, in case he was seen by someone passing by.

When Fortuyn departed the interview, Van der Graaf saw that he was in the company of several other people. Van der Graaf walked toward Fortuyn and passed by him and the others. Van der Graaf then turned and from a distance of approximately 5 feet fired the Firestar pistol (which was still in the plastic bag) striking Fortuyn in the back and head. A sixth shot missed. At that point Van der Graaf fled the scene.

Unknowns

1. History of threats being received
2. Any recent threats that may have seen unusual
3. Was the chauffeur trained in protective work, or was he just a driver?
4. Van der Graaf's level of, if any, military, tactical, or weapons training
5. Prior physical surveillance of Fortuyn, as Van der Graaf stated he was familiar with Mr. Fortyun's vehicle

Analysis

There were several areas in this attack where the possibility of detection/prevention could have occurred. Ideally, the driver should have been alert while at Mediapark awaiting the return of Mr. Fortuyn. Granted, while a park by its very nature draws people, a person sitting in the same location near or in bushes for almost two hours should have caught someone's attention (given the unknown fact of whether Van der Graaf was visible).

The assassin was obviously close enough to maintain a visual on the exit of the radio station, and positioned in a way to intercept his target. As Van der Graaf approached, it is hard to believe that there were no obviously visual clues that something was amiss with this man. He has a weapon in a bag and is approaching a man he plans to kill. Did he appear nervous, was he staring at his target, was he looking around to check for potential witnesses, police, etc.? This is where the presence of even a single protective detail member could have made the difference. More than likely, as Fortuyn and the six other people were walking and in discussion, they were completely oblivious to their surroundings.

Van der Graaf made an excellent approach and attack, taking advantage of one of the most common protective rule violations: "checking your six." The placing of the weapon into a plastic bag offered a degree of concealment as he approached his target. By walking toward his target from the front, he was able to correctly identify his target's location within the group of people. Van der Graaf then turns after passing the target and, from a distance that allows accurate fire, but also some protection from any immediate action taken by the target or his colleagues, shoots Mr. Fortuyn in the back and then quickly flees.

This attack reiterates the need to be aware of what information is freely available on a protectee. Mr. Fortuyn was a vocal politician on the far right, which should cause one to be even more aware of his or her surroundings than the average person. Additionally, it was just days away from a national election in which Mr. Fortuyn was running for office. Interestingly enough, Van der Graaf later told authorities that he would not have attacked Mr. Fortuyn that day had there been a security detail.

The area of Mediapark is fairly wide open with expansive grassy areas and trees sporadically placed, all of which is accessible via meandering walkways. This assassin displayed considerable resolve and patience in this final stalking of Mr. Fortuyn. It is unknown how many pedestrians were in the area at the time, but regardless, Van der Graaf had the wherewithal to hide the weapon to prevent a chance discovery. Further, either Van der Graaf was able to show remarkable composure as he closed with his intended target, or the visual clues were missed by the intended targets. Either way, he was able to close undetected with his target.

REHAVAM ZE'EVI: OCTOBER 17, 2001, WEDNESDAY, 0630 (APPROX.), JERUSALEM, ISRAEL

Israel's outgoing tourism minister and retired army general, Rehavam Ze'evi, was killed just outside his suite located on the eighth floor of the Jerusalem Hyatt Hotel. His wife, returning to their room approximately a half hour later, discovered him in the hallway just before 0700. He was taken to Hadassah-University Hospital, where he was pronounced dead on arrival. Mr. Ze'evi had suffered three bullet wounds to the head and neck area. The attack was later claimed by the Palestinian Front for the Liberation of Palestine (PFLP). It was later learned that Mr. Ze'evi had refused a previously offered protective detail, in part due to his military background.

Through the subsequent investigation it was learned from Mrs. Ze'evi that on the morning of the attack, her husband had noted during breakfast an Arab-appearing man staring at him, but nothing was followed up. Mr. Ze'evi then later went to his room alone. Per police, Ze'evi did not have any bodyguards, but usually carried a pistol with him. As no shots were heard by any hotel guests staying on the same floor, it was believed the killers used suppressed weapons.

Later, a man by the name of Bassel Asmar was arrested and convicted of the killing. During the hearing he stated that the team consisted of the lead assassin Hamdi Quran and himself, who acted as protection against any protective detail. The two men were each armed with a handgun, and one had an assault rifle, all of which had been smuggled into the hotel earlier. As Ze'evi exited the elevator on his floor and was walking to his room, Quran passed him, and then called his name before shooting him.

Further, it was later learned that it was common knowledge with the hotel staff that when Ze'evi stayed at this particular Hyatt, he would stay in the same room, number 816.

Police also stated that the hotel is located close to two nearby Arab communities, allowing for quick escape.

Unknowns

1. The presence of any accomplices working for the hotel staff that could have assisted in smuggling the weapons in as well as providing information
2. Whether Mr. Ze'evi was armed at the time of the attack

Analysis

Targeted attacks conducted at hotels, while not uncommon, are a unique location for an ambush. This is primarily due to the transient nature of the location. Generally, the advance knowledge that an individual will be at the hotel at a specific time is limited to family and perhaps some friends and colleagues. This can be useful to investigators in their search for suspects during the investigation. In this case, however, the victim was a frequent visitor to the hotel and preferred to stay in a certain room. While this is not a common occurrence, it is certainly isn't unheard of. Unfortunately, there have been some dramatic attacks conducted under similar situations of a target visiting the same room at the same hotel.

As no shots were heard inside of the hotel, it is reasonable to assume that suppressed weapons were used. This gives the assassins a major advantage, as it allows for the attack to occur with relatively little chance of being immediately detected, and thus allowing for an escape from the enclosed area prior to an alert being sounded. The major risk facing the assassins would have been waiting in the area of the attack. Positioned on the floor of their target, waiting for an extended period of time, would have been a major risk for detection, unless of course they were able to wait in a nearby room. Further, the two men would have had to have remained on the floor, and therefore would have had no knowledge of Mr. Ze'evi's movements. This makes it much more likely that a third person was positioned in the restaurant surveilling their target (perhaps the Arab man previously mentioned).

In the end, Mr. Ze'evi was in a precarious position with little chance for survival. Lacking a protective detail, his only option would have been to engage the assassin; if he was in fact armed at the time and could get to the weapon quickly. If not armed and not able to get into a position of cover quickly, the only remaining option would have been to assault his attacker. With the presence of a second man, however, coupled with the age of Mr. Ze'evi, this may have been a futile effort.

FRED CAPPS: JUNE 5, 2000, MONDAY, 0550 (APPROX.), BURKESVILLE, KENTUCKY

Fred Capps, a prosecutor in Louisville, Kentucky, was shot and killed in an attack that occurred inside of his residence. The attack occurred when the assassin, Eddie Vaughn (a longtime criminal known to be violent and unpredictable), armed with an SKS rifle and two thirty-round clips, a sawed-off shotgun, and several knifes, arrived at the Capps' residence. He had been driven by his brother and wife (both who claimed he threatened them into it, as Vaughn didn't know the location of Capps' residence). Vaughn exited the vehicle and approached the front door of the two-story colonial-style home, whereupon he shot his way through the front glass door. The noise of the gunfire awoke the Capps, who were still in bed.

Reacting quickly, Fred Capps grabbed a .357-caliber revolver he kept under his bed and headed toward the trouble. As he did so, a single 7.62mm round penetrated the drywall and struck Fred in the liver. Even though critically injured, he fought on and met Vaughn in the hallway of the first floor outside of the master bedroom, a distance of less than 10 feet apart. Vaughn continued to fire his SKS, in which four rounds struck Fred Capps. Fred returned fire, getting off two rounds, both of which struck Vaughn in the chest. Both men fell and died where they met in the hallway. It was later determined that Vaughn was to be prosecuted by Capps later that day for charges of child molestation.

Analysis

This was one of the more unusual targeted attacks to have taken place and goes against the general rule that you can let your guard down while in the home. It ranks as also one of the bravest defenses to an attack ever recorded, in that although the target died in the attack, he successfully killed the adversary and, more importantly, saved the lives of his family. As with any successful ambush, the use of surprise, speed, and violence of action will generally allow for the adversary to be successful.

Vaughn employed all three well as he blasted through the front door at an early hour in the morning, when dawn's early light was still minimal. Even though Vaughn was probably not familiar with the inside of the home, it wouldn't take much time to figure out as he moved through the house (if he had spent anytime in surveillance, he would have been able to obtain a rough idea of the layout of the house). Once inside, he moved with haste toward his target's approximate location. Fred Capps, awakened by the sudden noise of his front door being shot open by a large-caliber weapon, would have had only seconds to realize what was going on. While his training and background beyond being a prosecutor isn't known, it is apparent that he did not hesitate.

In this situation, Mr. Capps did what needed to be done. Before even obtaining a complete understanding of what was occurring, he grabbed his weapon and headed toward the sound of the violence. Unfortunately, Mr. Capps was struck by a 7.62mm round almost immediately. However, he continued with the only option when faced with an ambush: he charged the aggressor, returning fire. While it ultimately cost him his life, he took care of business and killed his enemy. In the end, he was successful in that he saved the lives of his wife and two children. There can be no greater honor.

RAJIV GHANDI: MAY 21, 1991, TUESDAY, 2220, SRIERUMBUDUR, INDIA

Former prime minister Rajiv Ghandi was assassinated by a Tamil Tiger suicide bomber while campaigning in southern India. The explosive blast also killed seventeen other people that were within close proximity when the device was triggered. The thirty-five-year-old female suicide bomber, who was later described as pretty and innocent looking, used the ruse of placing a flower garland upon Ghandi to allow her to get close. Several other people had already placed garlands around Gandhi's neck.

Wearing a red wig and holding the flowers at the time, the bomber approached Ghandi as he walked through the crowds. After placing her garland, the bomber bowed as though she was going to touch his feet. As she did so, she detonated a waist bomb filled with five sticks of RDX explosives and metal bearings. The device was later found to have had two switches, one to activate the device as she closed with the target, and the second to actually trigger the explosive. Gandhi, the bomber, and seventeen others were killed in the explosion. The Indian government filed a charge sheet a year later against forty-one LTTE members and supporters, of whom only twenty-six were arrested. During the subsequent investigation it was found that five other colleagues of the bomber were located within the crowd, and all but one was killed in the blast.

Analysis

This is truly the nightmare scenario in that a large crowd has gathered around a protectee and former world leader. The custom of the laying of flower garlands, along with the touching of feet, allowed for the bomber to close the distance. The use of a pretty female suicide bomber as part of the ruse served to decrease the level of suspicion that may have been focused upon the bomber. Although the type of energetic material as well as the amount directly relate to the blast effects, in this case five sticks of RDX—the main component of military C-4 explosives—were used. Given that the average size of a suicide bomber device is around 10 pounds, coupled with the detonation velocity of RDX of approximately 26,800 feet per second, the bomber only needed to get within about 10 feet of Ghandi before she reached the lethal air blast range. The addition of improvised shrapnel would effectively decrease the minimum distance she would have needed to be in relation to Ghandi prior to detonation.

Once within close proximity there was little a protective detail could have done short of a head shot on the bomber if they had detected the attack prior to her triggering the device. The use of an attractive bomber could have also been a consideration of the LTTE to cause a moment's hesitation in reaction on the part of the security forces. Therein lies one of the true dangers of the suicide bomber. With the explosives and triggering mechanism hidden from view, it is very difficult for protective personnel to recognize a threat before it is too late. Lacking any intelligence, the protective personnel will be forced to make a decision to end a person's life based almost exclusively on their belief that the man or woman is a suicide bomber. A difficult decision for anyone to make, and in that moment of indecision, the bomber can win.

SIDNEY RESO: APRIL 28, 1992, TUESDAY MORNING, NEW JERSEY

Sidney Reso, the president of Exxon International, was practicing his normal morning routine when he was kidnapped. On the morning of the attack, as was his habit, he was to drive himself into work rather than using a chauffeur, which as one of the most powerful executives in the United States, he certainly would have been entitled to. As was usual, he started his car, and then walked down his 200-foot driveway to retrieve the morning newspaper. As he reached his paper, at some point a man approached him armed with a handgun and attempted to force him into a nearby van. During a brief struggle, Reso was shot in the arm, at which point he was forced into the van.

The kidnappers then transported Reso to a public storage facility, where they had rented a garage two months previously. Inside the garage was a 6-feet-4-inch-long by 3-feet-high by 3½-feet-wide box with holes drilled into it. Reso was placed inside this box, after having his eyes and mouth covered in tape. Inside the box were placed a sleeping bag and blankets for comfort. Twice a day, the terrorists visited Reso, where he was given vitamins and forced to make recorded messages. Unfortunately, Mr. Reso died five days later. The terrorists later transported Reso's body to a secluded area of New Jersey and buried him. His death was not discovered until June 1992, when the terrorists were apprehended and one of them confessed.

The kidnappers were identified as Arthur Seale and his wife. Arthur Seale had been a police officer until he was medically retired. He then turned himself into a security expert and eventually went to work for Exxon, where he assisted in the development of the company's response to executive kidnappings. In 1987, Seale left Exxon to pursue other interests; however, after a series of failed businesses and a huge debt, he came up with the plan to kidnap an Exxon executive for ransom. He may have been motivated by an earlier kidnapping of an Exxon executive in South America, which resulted in a $15 million ransom payment. Regardless, he began his research on which executive would be the easiest, and ultimately settled upon Reso.

Seale finalized his decision to kidnap an Exxon executive around December 1991. He and his wife had researched the homes and routines of several Exxon executives, and decided that Reso offered the best chances of success. He was a creature of habit, and his home offered a good amount of seclusion. Seale ran a surveillance operation on Reso for several months before he and his wife struck. They attempted to carry out their plan several times, but had been thwarted by changes in his schedule.

Unknowns

1. Whether any threat assessments had been conducted by Exxon
2. Whether Reso and or any of his neighbors had noted any unusual activity, such as the presence of strange vehicles or people in the neighborhood
3. If Reso always took the same route to and from work, and if he had ever noted vehicles following him

Analysis

Seale's background as a police officer as well as in protective work with Exxon obviously gave him considerable training and experience in surveillance and the conducting of a tactical operation. Further, his time with Exxon, especially in helping in the development of the company's kidnap response, would have placed him in a position of considerable knowledge on security practices in use by the Exxon security department.

Obviously, as has been seen so often in the past, Reso's routines and habits not only allowed for him to be identified as a good target, but also assisted Seale in determining how to conduct the operation. Given that Reso was then one of the most powerful executives in the world, with an obvious large net worth, he chose not to take part in some of the perks that come with the position, such as a chauffeur and bodyguard.

Offensive Point of View
The routines of Reso's lifestyle allowed for detailed planning to be conducted without apparently alerting anyone. Obviously Seale's background afforded him the ability to discreetly carry out his intelligence gathering undetected.

Defensive Point of View
One of the biggest difficulties in protective work is convincing individuals that they are or could in fact be a target given their position. Understandably, many do not want the inconvenience that comes with chauffeurs and bodyguards. They continue to go about their business in the false belief that no one is watching or targeting them. The protective adage "you never know when you are successful, but you know when you have failed" certainly rings true in these situations.

So perhaps it is incumbent upon those in the protective world to take steps in the form of discreet countersurveillance. While the protectee believes there is no danger, the protective detail can be running proactive operations of hunting for people surveilling or watching the homes of the executives. Nothing says the security department cannot run a protective surveillance upon their protectees, in the chance of an attack, etc.

While proactive work such as this is no guarantee of preventing an attack, in this situation, had Seale's presence been detected in the area of an Exxon executive, it might have triggered some sort of response or inquiry. While it isn't known if Seale's financial difficulties were well known, given his past association with Exxon, there would have been a distinct possibility that Seale could have been recognized and noted. Additionally, had Seale believed he had been detected, it might have been enough of a deterrent to force him to look for another target.

FATHI SHQAQI: OCTOBER 26, 1995, THURSDAY MORNING, SLIEMA, MALTA

Fathi Shqaqi (aka Fathi Shiqaqi), founder of the Palestinian Islamic Jihad (PIJ), and once affiliated with the Muslim Brotherhood, was assassinated outside of his hotel. At the time of the attack, he had been traveling under the alias of Monsieur Ibrahim Dawish, posing as a businessman. The attack occurred as he was walking up to the entrance of the Diplomat Hotel, returning from some morning shopping. At some point within close proximity of the hotel, a motorcycle with two men aboard pulled up and the rider, armed with a suppressed pistol equipped with a device used to catch the ejected shell casings, fired five to six rounds into Monsieur Shqaqi's head. The two killers then drove off a short distance, where they dumped the motorcycle. It is believed that they then quickly got into a waiting car and fled the scene.

Through the subsequent investigation by Malta law enforcement authorities, it was discovered that two days prior to the assassination, two men had arrived from Israel. Each had taken alternate circuitous routes into Malta, one arriving via Rome, and the other via Athens. Both of these men presented British passports to the custom's officials upon their arrival. They then checked in separately to their respective rooms at the Diplomat Hotel, located at 173 Tower Road, Sliema SLM 10, Malta. Later that same evening, one of the men obtained a motorcycle under the guise of wanting to tour the island. Also that evening, a freighter en route to Italy from Haifa called and advised Malta Port authorities that it was having engine problems and needed to anchor offshore to make repairs, for which it was given permission.

The authorities discovered that shortly after the killing, a small boat had departed Valletta Harbor and had stopped at the freighter moored on the coast. Not long thereafter, the freighter advised Malta that the repairs had been made, and that it was returning to Haifa. It was the belief of the investigators that the killers made their escape from the island on that small boat, and were on onboard the ship when it departed Malta waters.

Analysis

This is an attack that appears to have been the work of professional and highly trained individuals, who were in possession of a considerable amount of intelligence prior to the hit. The area where this attack was staged is characterized by wide-open streets and promenades that follow along the coastline. The hotel itself sits on the corner of the street directly across from the coastline promenade, offering very little in the way of cover. This resulted in an ideal location to stage this type of attack. The victim, while on foot, without any protective detail (it isn't known if he was armed at the time), with little to no immediate cover, and being attacked by a motorcycle hit team, has very little chance of survival.

What is interesting in this case is the allegation that the assassins obtained rooms in the same hotel as the target. While this certainly provided the opportunity for close surveillance of the target, it had its risks in that they could have been detected as hostile by the target (who was no doubt a veteran of being alert). However, this can also provide some cover or confusion during the resulting investigation. This stems from the statistic that many killers who have targeted individuals at or near hotels have used other locations for their temporary base of operations. Perhaps using the hiding in plain sight principle was a part of the plan all along.

UMARU DIKKO: JULY 5, 1984, TUESDAY, 1200 (APPROX.), LONDON, UNITED KINGDOM

Umaru Dikko, a Nigerian national and former transport and aviation minister and opponent of the then current Nigerian government, was kidnapped as he was leaving his home to meet a colleague. The attack occurred just before noon as Mr. Dikko departed his

Dorchester Terrance residence en route to a lunch meeting with an associate. As he walked past a parked van on foot, two men jumped out and quickly overpowered Mr. Dikko, forcing him inside of the van. Mr. Dikko's personal secretary by chance witnessed the attack from Mr. Dikko's residence and quickly called police. Within minutes police had arrived, as well as the commander of Scotland Yard's antiterrorist squad. He quickly ordered all ports and airports to be on the alert.

Through the subsequent investigation it was learned that on June 30 a Mossad agent spotted Dikko by chance as he was walking on Queensway, just off of Bayswater Road in West London. The agent, who had reportedly been one of many searching for Dikko, immediately parked his car and began foot surveillance. Eventually, the agent ended up at Mr. Dikko's home in Dorchester Terrace. After contacting his superiors, a second agent arrived, and a full-time surveillance of Mr. Dikko and his home was begun.

Within a day or so, a doctor arrived from Israel and checked into a local hotel. On July 2, another Israeli flew in from Amsterdam and checked into the Russell Square Hotel. This man then contacted the head of the Nigerian team assisting in the operation, and ordered him to obtain a moving van (they ended up with a bright yellow one). On July 3, a Nigerian Airways 707 landed at Stansted Airport, about 30 miles northeast of London. On the aircraft were several security members, who were ordered by Scotland Yard to remain with the plane. The aircraft had arrived empty and the security members stated their purpose was to retrieve some diplomatic bags.

Around 1000 on the morning of July 5, the yellow van pulled out of a Notting Hill Gate parking garage and headed in the direction of Mr. Dikko's home. Inside the van, in addition to the driver, were the doctor and two other men, along with a wooden crate. The van arrived in the area of Mr. Dikko's home shortly before noon and parked. At around the same time, the Nigerian aircraft filed a flight plan for a 1500 departure, stating it would be transporting two diplomatic crates for the Ministry of External Affairs. As Mr. Dikko passed by the yellow van, he was grabbed by two men and forced inside.

At approximately 1500, the yellow van arrived at Stansted Airport. As the crates were in the process of being loaded, one of the customs officers heard something from the crates. Suspicious something wasn't right, coupled with the previous alert sent out by the Special Branch, he ordered the crates to be opened. Despite fierce protests, the crates were opened and inside of one was Mr. Dikko, who was unconscious with a tube down his throat. Sitting beside him was the Israeli doctor with a syringe containing an anesthetic. The other crate was found to contain the other two accomplices. All three men were arrested and Mr. Dikko was freed.

Analysis

Certainly this is one of the more dramatic kidnappings carried out anywhere in the world, let alone on the streets of London. This case is very interesting in that as a result of the investigation, it was discovered that a twenty-four-hour surveillance had been established for a period of five days prior to the snatch. While the operators conducting this surveillance were no doubt very skilled, five days of continuous surveillance provided ample opportunity for the detection of the presence of potential hostiles.

What was apparent was that Mr. Dikko apparently didn't believe he was in any danger, and further did not take any steps to provide for his own protection. While it isn't known if he was ever aware of hostile activity in and around him, once the attack began there was little he could have done. This attack would have gone much differently had a protective detail of some fashion been employed. Assuming they had some degree of training, the protective detail would have been better able to detect the surveillance or, at a minimum, suspicious activity around the residence. Certainly when the attack went down, they would have been better able and prepared to defend Mr. Dikko.

GEORGI MARKOV: SEPTEMBER 7, 1978, THURSDAY, 1330, LONDON, UNITED KINGDOM

Georgi Markov, a Bulgarian defector and dissident, was assassinated by government agents. The attack occurred as Markov waited at a bus stop near the Waterloo Bridge on his way home from his office at the BBC. At some point while standing at the bus stop, he was jabbed in the leg by another man with an umbrella. Markov reportedly felt a sting where he had been struck by the umbrella and looked at the man, who politely apologized and walked away. Several hours later, Markov developed a high fever and was later transported to the hospital were he died four days later.

It was during the autopsy that a pinhead-sized platinum-iridium pellet was found embedded in his calf. The pellet, which toxicology later determined contained the deadly toxin Ricin, had been cross-drilled with 0.016-inch holes that allowed the poison to seep into the body. The amount of Ricin that Markov had received was approximately 425 mg.

Analysis

One of the most sensational targeted attacks ever carried out by any organization, the attack on Markov was also one of the earliest known attacks carried out by a high-tech device that Q of the James Bond films would have been proud of. Regardless of the training and experience of the victim, or the presence of protective personnel, everything about this targeted attack made it nearly impossible to detect, let alone deter.

However, as with any attack, and certainly in the case of highly trained intelligence operatives, surveillance and reconnaissance had to have been conducted for a period of time. As with any targeted attack, this is the best, and in some cases the only, opportunity to detect hostile activity before it is too late. Ultimately, the assassins were able to determine Markov' routines and general routes of travel to the point they had a man armed with a high-tech weapon waiting for their target's arrival. Once the attack had been made, the assassins blended into the masses and disappeared. Given that it took four days before Markov died, let alone time involved to detect the cause of death, there was ample time for the assassins to quietly make their escape.

MARGARET THATCHER: OCTOBER 12, 1984, FRIDAY, 0254, BRIGHTON, UNITED KINGDOM

IRA terrorists attempted to assassinate Prime Minister Margaret Thatcher while she was staying at the Grand Hotel by detonating an IED. She and most of her cabinet had been at the hotel for a conference at which she was to give a speech. The attack came when an explosive device with approximately 60 kilos of Semtex plastique detonated in the bathroom that adjoined Prime Minister Thatcher's. She and her husband survived the blast; however, five others were killed, including Member of Parliament Sir Anthony George Berry (an uncle of Princess Diana), and another thirty-four people were injured, including two police officers. The blast ripped a large hole in the hotel façade and brought large amounts of rubble tumbling down seven floors.

IRA member Patrick Magee was later arrested and convicted of the attack in September 1986. It was found through the investigation that three and half weeks prior to the attack, he stayed at the hotel in room 629 from September 14 to 17 under the name Roy Walsh. During that time he hid the device, with a long delay timer set for twenty-nine days ahead, in the wall that separated his room from that which would be occupied by Minister Thatcher. It was believed that Magee learned his bombing skills at a Libyan terrorist camp.

Prior to the attack, intelligence had been developed in both the United Kingdom and the United States that revealed an IRA assassination cell had been activated and was planning on hitting an unknown target. As a result, Scotland Yard's Special Branch security for Prime Minister Thatcher had been increased. It was after this attack that the now infamous statement was read by the IRA: "Today we were unlucky, but remember, we only have to be lucky once; you will have to be lucky always."

Analysis

Fortunately, attacks such as these are exceedingly rare; in fact, of all of the attacks researched, only one other could be found to have been employed in such a manner. As with any explosive-based attack, they can be very difficult to detect and are extremely dangerous. What is clear with this case was the amount of intelligence information the IRA was able to develop that allowed for the attack to occur. While it is not uncommon for events such as these to be well publicized, the revelation of the room that Mrs. Thatcher was to be staying in would have generally been kept strictly confidential.

The only real way to detect an attack such as this would be to have prior intelligence of it. Lacking such information, if explosives are known to be used in the area of operations, and the protectee is within a category that would be targeted by the local groups, then a thorough search of the room prior to his or her arrival would be necessary. While room searches such as these are generally only by sight, an explosives-sniffing dog should be used as well as some of the electronic explosives-sniffing equipment that is becoming increasingly available.

BARNETT SLEPIAN: OCTOBER 23, 1998, FRIDAY, 2200, EAST AMHERST, NEW YORK

Barnett Slepian, a physician who also provided abortions as a part of his practice, was shot and killed while inside of his residence (187 Roxbury Park) by James Charles Kopp (a former University of California, Santa Cruz graduate). The attack occurred while Slepian was working in his kitchen. Kopp had positioned himself within a fairly dense area of foliage, which lay approximately 25 meters behind the backyard fence of the Slepian residence. Armed with a scoped 7.62mm-caliber SKS rifle, Kopp took careful aim and fired a single round. The round traveled the approximate 30 meters through the kitchen window, striking Slepain. After firing the fatal shot, Kopp fled the scene.

Through the subsequent investigation, it was discovered that Kopp had been conducting reconnaissance of the Slepian residence and neighborhood over a four-day period. He had been in the area of the residence on at least six occasions prior to the attack. He had purchased the Russian-made rifle at a pawn shop using an alias, and had switched the license plates on his vehicle. After the attack, he abandoned the car at Newark International Airport in New Jersey (a distance of 386 miles, or roughly a 6½-hour drive) and caught a flight to Mexico. From there he took a flight to Ireland and then traveled into Scotland. Eventually, he made it into France, where he remained until his capture.

Unknowns

1. The presence of any current/active threats of violence
2. Any reports to the authorities of suspicious activity prior to the attack

Analysis

Kopp took advantage of a number of factors that were in his favor and selected an extremely effective location to conduct his ambush. The location, part of an open-space area moderately forested, is approximately 80 meters wide between the fences of the opposing residences. The nearest street access point is approximately 80 meters away and is also heavy with foliage. By conducting at least some of the surveillance as well as the attack from the rear of the residence, Kopp took advantage of the lack of coverings over the windows facing the backyard. This is a common feature, at least in the United States, which at night, with interior lights on, would have allowed Kopp to see into the house with little to no chance of detection, especially given the time of year and hour.

Hidden inside the trees and foliage that runs behind the residence at 2200 on a night just three days past the new moon, he was perfectly positioned. Given the hour of the night, coupled with the effects that occur when lights are on inside of a residence, even if it had been a full moon, it is doubtful that anyone would have seen Kopp. Looking through the scope, he was patient waiting for his opportunity. By firing a single round, he lessened the likelihood that anyone would notify authorities immediately, possibly passing it off as a vehicle backfire, kids playing with fireworks, etc.

In this kind of targeted attack, there was really little that Slepain could have done to prevent it, short of having his windows armored. This represents one of the problems or fears when dealing with an adversary that might employ a sniper tactic.

CONCLUSION

The use of targeted violence against specific individuals continues at an ever-increasing rate. Every region on the planet has witnessed the violence, no class of victim has been spared, and almost every attack methodology has been employed. Regionally, North America has seen the greatest total number, largely due to the continuing violence being experienced in Mexico. Russia and its republics follow closely behind, with the majority of those attacks taking place inside of Russia proper. Mexico documented the most targeted attacks occurring in 2009 for a single country followed by Pakistan and the United States.

Pedestrian-based targets continue to be the preferred point of attack, accounting for 57% of the total. Law enforcement officials are the most targeted victims of the attacks, accounting for 17% of all victims followed by activists/dissidents at 14% of the victims. Business executives, military officials, and underworld figures are tied for third each at 7% of victims.

Firearms or explosives are the most used weapons. However, documented attacks also include kidnapping and stabbing. Only the use of poison is not being used. Firearms continue to be employed the most often, documented in 78% of the targeted attacks. In the majority of the attacks, we don't know how many shooters there have been, but in those we did know about, a lone shooter accounted for 36%. Teams of two shooters were used the next most often accounting for 24%. The remaining attacks, in order of occurrence include teams of three to five shooters, drive-bys, motorcycle based hit teams and sniper attacks. When explosives are used, usually it is by a suicide bomber. The remaining explosive attacks included booby-trap devices, IEDs, and VBIEDs.

As the old adage goes, "Variety is the spice of life," but in the case of targeted violence, variety just might be the only thing that keeps one alive. For those readers finding themselves within one of the most often targeted classes of individuals, the importance of changing up your routes and routines can not be overemphasized. For those involved in providing protection for another, this work should serve only as a start of your continuing study. Make no mistake; the ambush is a tactic that has been employed throughout history by men and women in every corner of the world—a practice that to this day and age continues to have enormous success.

To kill for the sole reason that a person's beliefs are not in alignment with another's, or for the reason of keeping a corrupt and illegal enterprise going, or for the purpose of making a political statement, is very difficult to predict. While for some of those being targeted, it could be taken as a sign that the work being done is having its desired effect, it is of small comfort. Many of the men and women performing these jobs need the protection they deserve, in order for them to continue their work. It is up to those in the protective services to provide that service in the most effective means possible.

To achieve this effectiveness, it is important to study targeted attacks in order to increase the knowledge of the strategy and tactics employed by would-be assassins and kidnappers. This work should serve only as a beginning. Training and experience are invaluable and are the most important part of the learning process. However, it is just as important to understand one's adversary and the nature of the urban ambush.

One of the best ways to obtain a more thorough perspective is to visit the sites of past attacks. This is preferably done in person, but with the current Internet mapping systems, it is possible to visit these sites through photographs, both at street level and by overhead satellite. Regardless of how the site is visited, ask yourself the questions: Why was this site selected over the others? What advantages did it provide the adversary over the target? What was the most likely avenue of approach or escape? Was this route of travel the most logical or expeditious one from a residence to the workplace? Only through this analysis will one be able to truly see the potential attack site the way your adversary does.

For those of you who by choice or circumstance find yourself in situations in which you may be the target of a violent attack, never fall into a rut. Always vary your routine, from the car traveled in, to the position within the car, to the time and route traveled. When leaving a protected area, make every effort to remain "on," to remain alert to your immediate surroundings. For as one protection expert once said, "You may never know when you have successfully thwarted an attack, but you will always know when you have failed."

Be safe,
Glenn McGovern

BIBLIOGRAPHY

Alexander, Yonah, and Dennis Pluchinsky, *Europe's Red Terrorists: The Fighting Communist Organizations* (Frank Cass and Co., Oxon, U.K., 1992).

"Ambush in a Civil War" *TIME*, September 19, 1977, www.time.com/time/magazine/print-out/0,8816,915477,00.html (accessed February 10, 2007).

"Apartheid-Era Minister Pleads Guilty," *USA Today*, August 17, 2007, www.usatoday.com/news/world/2007-08-17-apartheid-trial_N.htm?csp=34 (accessed August 23, 2007).

"Attacks Against Israelis Embassies and Representatives Abroad," www.mfa.gov.il/MFA/Terrorism (accessed March 29, 2004).

"An Attempt Made on the Life of Ingush President Murat Zyazikov," www.kommersant.com/p251/r_500/An_Attempt_Made_on_the_Life_of_Ingush_President_Murat_Zyazikov/ (accessed December 15, 2006).

Ayoob, Massad, "Drama at Blair House: The Attempted Assassination of Harry Truman," *American Handgunner*, March/April 2006.

Baker, Susan P., *Murdered Judges of the Twentieth Century and Other Mysterious Deaths* (Austin, TX: Sunbelt Eakin, 2004).

Barbash, Fred, "Violent Basque Group Has Been Losing Ground," (*Washington Post*) *San Jose Mercury News*, March 12, 2004.

Bar-Zohar, Michael, and Eitan Haber, *The Quest for the Red Prince* (Guilford, CT: Lyons Press, 1983, 2002).

Belden, Anne Chappell, "A Dramatic Kidnapping Revisited," *Los Altos Town Crier*, October 13, 1997, latc.com/1997/10/13/special_sect/exclusive1.print.html (accessed December 31, 2006).

Ben-David, Alon, "Jordanian Indictment Reveals Operations of Jund al-Shams Terror Network," *Jane's*, June 16, 2003, http://www.janes.com/security/international_security/news/jtic/jtic030616_1_n.shtml (accessed December 26, 2006).

Bishop, Patrick, "Corsican Nationalist Who Had Renounced Violence Is Shot Dead," *Telegraph UK*, www.telegraph.co.uk/news/main.jhtml?xml=/news/2000/08/08/wcors08.xml (accessed January 7, 2007).

Blanford, Nicholas, *Killing Mr. Lebanon* (London: I. B. Tauris, 2006).

"Blast Rocks Sri Lankan Rallies," BBC News, December 18, 1999, news.bbc.co.uk/2/hi/south_asia/571192.stm (accessed January 14, 2007).

"Bomb Attack on Campolat, Governor of Hakkari–Deniz, Driver of Campolat Who was Seriously Injured in the Attack, Dies," Anadolu Agency: News in English, www.hri.org/news/turkey/anadolu/1999/99-04-09.anadolu.html#01 (accessed January 13, 2007).

"Bombings Kill Four; Police Blame Rebels," *San Jose Mercury News*, August 27, 2004.

"Bomb in Van Defused outside US Consulate." *San Jose Mercury News*, March 15, 2004.

CACI Analyst, "South Ossetian Official Killed by Bomb," Central Asia-Caucasus Institute, July 10, 2006, www.cacianalyst.org/?q=node/4070 (accessed May 16, 2008).

"Car Bombs—Favorite Weapon of Terrorist Group ETA," *Praesidia Defence*, www.praesidia.de/Welcome/Press_and_publications_on_terr/car_bomb_executive_protection_/hauptteil_car_bomb_executive_protection_.html (accessed December 29, 2006).

Carlo, Philip, *The Iceman: Confessions of a Mafia Contract Killer* (New York: St. Martin's Press, 2006).

Chu, Henry, "When Revolt Hit Rio: Leftists Who Abducted a US Ambassador in '69 Now Are Part of Brazil's Mainstream. They See Their Action as a Key Step Towards Democracy," *Los Angeles Times*, September 23, 2004, www.grossmont.edu/carlos.contreras/History115/articles/When%20Revolt%20Hit%20Rio%20-%2069%20kidnapping.pdf (accessed December 17, 2006).

"Clashes Erupt after Slaying of Spanish Politician," CNN World News, July 13, 1997, www.cnn.com/ WORLD/9707/13/spain.clash (accessed May 5, 2007).

Cockburn, Patrick, "Russian Politician Killed by Car Bomb," *Independent* (London), October 21, 1999, http://findarticles.com/p/articles/mi_qn4158/is_19991021/ai_n14281499 (accessed September 27, 2007).

"Colombian Lawmaker Assassinated in Bogota," Associated Press, *Miami Herald*, October 8, 2001, www.latinamericanstudies.org/auc/colmenares.htm (accessed April 28, 2007).

"A Conspiracy to Murder," *Royal Gazette*, June 23, 2006, www.theroyalgazette.com/apps/pbcs.dll/ article?AID=/20060623/MIDOCEAN/106230158&SearchID=73251353660905.stm (accessed February 10, 2007).

Cowell, Alan S., *The Terminal Spy: A True Story of Espionage, Betrayal and Murder* (New York: Doubleday, 2008).

De Becker, Gavin, Tom Taylor, and Jeff Marquart, *Just 2 Seconds: Using Time and Space to Defeat Assassins* (Studio City, CA: The Gavin de Becker Center for the Study and Reduction of Violence, 2008).

"Deputy Director of Russia's Central Bank Dies after Assassination Attempt in Moscow," *Prada*, September 14, 2006, http://english.pravda.ru/hotspots/crimes/14-09-2006/84436-assassination-0 (accessed February 4, 2007).

"ETA Blamed for Double Killings," edition.cnn.com/2001/WORLD/europe/07/14/spain.blast/ index.html (accessed December 29, 2006).

"Ex-Chechen President Dies in Blast," Associated Press, February 13, 2004, www.msnbc.msn.com/ id/4261459 (accessed January 13, 2007).

Freed, Donald, and Fred Landis, *Death in Washington: The Murder of Orlando Letelier* (Westport, CT: Lawrence Hill & Company, 1980).

"From the Revolutionary Left: Action Teaches, Part 2," 1996, www.dhkc.org/www/en/news.php?h_ newsid=422 (accessed June 25, 2007). (A 28-part series titled "Action Teaches" was published in Turkey with the goal to educate revolutionaries about armed struggle. Part 2 dealt with the assassination of Nihat Erim.)

Ghazal, Rym, and Hani M. Bathish, "March 14 MP Walid Eido Assassinated in Beirut Bombing," *Daily Star*, June 14, 2007.

Gilson, George, "Relatives of November 17 Victims Speak Out," Athens News, http://www.helleniccomserve.com/archivedgreeknews27.html (accessed December 25, 2006).

Gottschalk, Keith, "The Rise and Fall of Apartheid's Death Squads, 1969–93," in *Death Squads in Global Perspective: Murder with Deniability* (New York: Palgrave Macmillan, 2000, 225–259).

Grady, Alan, *When Good Men Do Nothing: The Assassination of Albert Patterson* (Tuscaloosa: University of Alabama Press, 2003).

"Greek Terrorists Blab Everything Snitching Brings Them Tumbling off Pedestal," www.sfgate. com/cgibin/article.cgi?file=/c/a/2002/08/11/MN144962.DTL&type=printable (accessed December 17, 2006).

Hatoun, Leila, "Investigations into Gemayel Murder Focus on Fingerprints, Surveillance Footage," *Daily Star*, Lebanon, www.dailystar.com (accessed November 28, 2006).

Heakes, Greg, "Body in Woods Probably Kidnap Victim," *The Standard*, October 20, 1996, www.thestandard.com.hk/archive_news_detail.asp?pp_cat=&art_id=19562&sid=&con_ type=1&archive_d_str=19961020 (accessed January 1, 2007).

"Historical Fact: The Assassination of Bashir Gemayel," www.lebaneseforces.com/hobeika.asp (accessed January 6, 2007).

"Historical Fact: The Assassination of Rene Moawad," www.lebaneseforces.com/hobeika.asp (accessed January 6, 2007).

Hoffman, Paul, "Abduction Raises Tension in Italy," *New York Times*, April 22, 1974.

Hollington, Kris, *How to Kill: The Definitive History of the Assassin* (London: Century, 2007).

Howard, Russell D., and Reid L. Sawyer, *Terrorism and Counterterrorism: Understanding the New Security Environment* (New York: McGraw Hill, 2002).

Hunter, Stephen, and John Bainbridge, Jr., *American Gunfight: The Plot to Kill President Truman and the Shoot-out That Stopped It* (New York: Simon & Schuster Paperbacks, 2005).

"In Austria, a Bomb Explodes at the Home of Nazi Hunter," *New York Times*, June 12, 1982, http://query.nytimes.com/gst/fullpage.html?res=9406E3DA163BF931A25755C0A964948260 (accessed May 26, 2007).

"In Cold Blood," *Royal Gazette*, June 16, 2006, www.theroyalgazette.com/apps/pbcs.dll/article?AID=/20060616/MIDOCEAN/106160126&SearchID=73251353909636stm (accessed February 10, 2007).

"Ingush President Survives Suicide Attack," www.mosnews.com/news/2004/04/06/ingush.shtml (accessed December 15, 2006).

Jaber, Hala, *Hezbollah: Born with a Vengeance* (New York: Columbia University Press, 1997), p. 240.

Jdeideh, Mohamad Bazzi, "Minister's Killing Could Unleash Sectarian Feuds," *Sidney Morning Herald*, November 23, 2006, www.smh.com.au/news/world (accessed February 23, 2006).

Jonas, George, *Vengeance: The True Story of an Israeli Counter-terrorist Team* (New York: Simon & Schuster Paperbacks, 1984).

Katz, Samuel M., *The Hunt for the Engineer* (Guilford, CT: Lyons Press, 1999).

Katz, Samuel M., *Relentless Pursuit: The DSS and the Manhunt for the Al-Qaeda Terrorists* (New York: Forge, 2002).

Khan, Kamran, "Pakistan Official Survives Attack," (*Washington Post*) *San Jose Mercury News*, July 31, 2004.

Khan, Zarar, "10 Slain in Pakistan, but Top General, the Target, Survives," (Associated Press) *San Jose Mercury News*, June 11, 2004.

Korn, David A., *Assassination in Khartoum* (Bloomington, IN: Indiana University Press, 1993).

Lancaster, John, and Kamran Khan, "Pakistani Radicals Tied to Foreign Al-Qaida Forces," (*Washington Post*) *San Jose Mercury News*, August 29, 2004.

Landau, Saul, and Ralph Stavins, "This Is How It Was Done," *Nation*, March 26, 1977, http://www.tni.org/letelier/index.htm (accessed December 2, 2006).

"Lebanese Christian Leader Killed," news.bbc.co.uk/2/hi/middle_east/6169606.stm (accessed November 23, 2006).

Lefkovits, Etgar, "Rehavam Ze'evi Assassinated. PFLP Claims Responsibility for Jerusalem Hotel Shooting," *Casualties of War*, October 18, 2001, info.jpost.com/C002/Supplements/CasualtiesOfWar/2001_10_17.html (accessed December 31, 2006).

"Major Terror Attacks Against Israeli Embassies and Representatives Abroad," www.jewishvirtual-library.org/jsource/Terrorism/embattacks.html (accessed December 17, 2006).

"Marco Biagi, Government Labour Law Consultant, Murdered," European Industrial Relations Observatory online, www.eiro.eurofound.eu.int/2002/03/inbrief/it0203108n.html (accessed December 30, 2006).

Markey, Patrick, "Mayor Escapes Assassination," *IOL World*, http://www.int.iol.co.za/index.php?from=rss_World&set_id=1&click_id=3&art_id=nw20070301203941378C277610 (accessed March 6, 2007).

Markham, James M., "Senior Bonn Official Is Slain by Masked Gunman," *New York Times*, October 11, 1986).

Masood, Salman, "Pakistani Leader Escapes Attempt at Assassination," *New York Times*, December 26, 2003, http://query.nytimes.com/gst/fullpage.html?sec=health&res=9807E6DD173EF935A15751C1A9659C8B63 (accessed December 26, 2006).

McGraw, Seamus, "Envy: The Kidnapping and Murder of Sidney Reso," www.crimelibrary.com/gangsters_outlaws/outlaws/sidney_reso_kidnap/index.html (accessed December 10, 2006).

McFadden, Robert D., "Kidnapped Executive Is Freed in Bronx," *New York Times*, February 13, 1998, http://select.nytimes.com/search/restricted/article?res=F5091FF638580C708DDDAB0894D0494D81 (accessed January 21, 2007).

"Minister Murdered in Western Samoa," World Socialist website, August 3, 1999, www.wsws.org/articles/1999/aug1999/sam-a03.shtml (accessed April 21, 2007).

Montgomery, Paul L., "Belgian Politician Is Freed by His Kidnappers," *New York Times*, February 15, 1989.

Morris, Christopher, "Tigers Blamed for Murder of Security Hawk," *Guardian*, March 4, 1991, http://www.guardian.co.uk/fromthearchive/story/0,,1428590,00.html (accessed July 22, 2007).

Mroue, Bassem, and Joseph Panossian, "Bomb Kills Former Lebanese Prime Minister," Associated Press, news.yahoo.com/news (accessed February 14, 2005).

"Murdered Sheriff's Family Wins $776 Million," *Brown v. Dorsey*, Lawyers USA, www.lawyersweeklyusa.com/usa/3topten2004.cfm (accessed January 13, 2007).

"Murder in Paris," *TIME*, May 24, 1976, www.time.com/time/magazine/article/0,9171,879721,00.html (accessed June 23, 2007).

"Musharraf Assassination Bid Carried out by Experts," Radio Singapore International, http://www.rsi.sg/english/newsline/view/20031216220825/1/.html (accessed December 26, 2006).

Napoleoni, Loretta. *Modern Jihad: Tracing the Dollars behind the Terror Networks* (London: Pluto Press, 2003).

Nelan, Bruce W., "Bombs in the Name of Allah," *Times Magazine*, August 30, 1993, www.time.com/time/magazine/article/0,9171,979103-1,00.html (accessed January 28, 2007).

"1979: IRA Bomb Kills Lord Mountbatten," BBC News: On This Day, news.bbc.co.uk/onthisday/hi/dates/stories/august/27/newsid_2511000/2511545.stm (accessed December 25, 2006).

"On This Day 22 March: British Ambassador Assassinated in Holland," BBC, http://news.bbc.co.uk/onthisday/hi/dates/stories/march/22/newsid_2543000/2543867.stm (accessed July 14, 2007).

"On This Day 28 October: Minister's Wife Survives Bomb Attack," BBC, http://news.bbc.co.uk/onthisday/hi/dates/stories/october/28/newsid_2477000/2477645.stm (accessed July 14, 2007).

"Paraguay TV Reports Details of Argana's Assassination," BBC News World Media Watch, http://news.bbc.co.uk/2/hi/world/monitoring/301911.stm (accessed June 3, 2007).

Pepper, Curtis Bill, "The Possessed: The Murder of Antonio Esposito by the Red Brigades," *New York Times Magazine*, February 18, 1979.

Popov, Julian, "Bulgaria's Second Richest Man Shot Dead," Scotsman.com news, October 24, 2005, http://news.scotsman.com/topics.cfm?tid=1164&id=2150562005 (accessed February 25, 2007).

"RAF Attack on Hans Tietmeyer," http://www.germanguerilla.com/red-army-faction/documents/88_09_20.html (accessed March 3, 2007).

"Recent Terrorist Attacks in Israel," Anti-Deflamation League website, www.adl.org/Israel/israel_attacks.asp (accessed March 29, 2004).

Reeve, Simon, *The New Jackals: Ramzi Yousef, Osama Bin Laden and the Future of Terrorism* (Boston: Northeastern University Press, 1999).

Rempel, William C., "Tale of Deadly Iranian Network Woven in Paris: Terrorism: An Assassination Trial's Threads Lead as Far as California, Uncovering a Wealth of Spy Data along the Way" *Los Angeles Times*, November 3, 1994.

"Ricin and the Umbrella Murder," CNN.com World, October 23, 2003, www.cnn.com/2003/WORLD/europe/01/07/terror.poison.bulgarian (accessed February 10, 2007).

Rohonczy, Imre, "Lessons Learned: The Kidnapping of Hans Martin Schleyer," *The Tactical Edge*, Spring 2002.

"Salvatore Lima," Reference.com, www.reference.com/browse/wiki/Salvatore_Lima (accessed Decembe 29, 2006).

Sambandan, V.S., "Assassination and After," www.frontlineonnet.com/f12218/stories/20050909006100400.htm (accessed August 3, 2007).

Sambandan, V.S., "Peace-Maker as Terrorist Target," FRONTLINE Sri Lanka, www.hinduonnet.com/fline/fl1617/16170970.htm (accessed January 15, 2007).

Shay, Shaul, *The Shahids: Islam and Suicide Attacks* (New Brunswick, NJ: Transaction Publishers, 2004).

Sneider, Daniel, "The Lessons of Chechnya," *San Jose Mercury News*, May 13, 2004.

"Spanish Politician Shot Dead," BBC News, news.bbc.co.uk/2/hi/europe/857310.stm (accessed January 7, 2007).

Stille, Alexander, *Excellent Cadavers: The Mafia and the Death of the First Italian Republic* (New York: Vintage Books, 1995).

Stubblefield, Gary, and Mark Monday, *Killing Zone: A Professional's Guide to Preparing or Preventing Ambushes* (Boulder, CO: Paladin Press, 1994).

Tanveer, Khalid, "Roadside Bomb Kills 2 in Pakistan," Associated Press, "A Tempting Target," *TIME*, May 31, 1971, www.time.com/time/magazine/article/0,9171,944414,00.html?promoid =googlep (accessed September 14, 2007).

Tetley, Prof. William, *The October Crisis, 1970: An Insider's View* (Montreal: McGill-Queen's University Press, 2006), www.mcgill.ca/files/maritimelaw/D.doc (accessed February 11, 2007).

"Three Charged in Millionaire's Abduction," CNN.com/U.S. edition.cnn.com/2003/US/ Northeast/01/13/kidnapped.millionaire/ (accessed December 31, 2006).

Thomas, Gordon, *Gideon's Spies: The Secret History of the Mossad* (New York: St. Martin's Press, 1999).

Thomas, Gordon, "William Buckley: The Spy Who Never Came in from the Cold," Canada Free Press, October 26, 2006, http://www.canadafreepress.com/2006/thomas102506.htm (accessed August 3, 2007).

"Two Gunmen Kill Basque Region Judge," Associated Press, www.washingtonpost.com/wp-srv/ aponline/20011107/aponline053321_000.htm (accessed December 29, 2006).

"$2 Million Ransom Frees Japanese Executive," CNN World News, August 20, 1996, http://edition. cnn.com/WORLD/9608/20/executive.kidnap (accessed March 2, 2007).

U.S. Department of State, *Patterns of Global Terrorism 1986* (Washington, DC: U.S. Department of State, 1987).

U.S. Department of State, *Patterns of Global Terrorism 1991* (Washington, DC: U.S. Department of State, 1992).

U.S. Department of State, *Patterns of Global Terrorism 1999* (Washington, DC: U.S. Department of State, 2000).

U.S. Department of State, *Significant Incidents of Political Violence against Americans: 1988* (Washington, DC: U.S. Department of State, 1989), www.state.gov/documents/organization/20305.pdf (accessed December 16, 2006).

Whitlock, Craig, "Saudi Fighters in Iraq Pose Threat at Home," (*Washington Post*) *San Jose Mercury News*, July 11, 2004, p. 15A.

Wingett, Yvonne, and Chris Hawley, "Agua Prieta Police Chief Assassinated," *The Arizona Republic*, February 27, 2007, www.azcentral.com/news/articles/0227MexShooting27-ON.html (accessed March 6, 2007).

INDEX

303